WHAT LIES BENEATH

TEXAS

PIONEER CEMETERIES AND GRAVEYARDS

CYNTHIA LEAL MASSEY

TWODOT®

GUILFORD, CONNECTICUT
HELENA, MONTANA

*Dedicated to the Unknowns buried in Texas cemeteries and
in forgotten graveyards.
Time takes all but memories.*

A · TWODOT® · BOOK
An imprint and registered trademark of Globe Pequot, the trade division of
The Rowman & Littlefield Publishing Group, Inc.
4501 Forbes Blvd., Ste. 200
Lanham, MD 20706
www.rowman.com

Distributed by NATIONAL BOOK NETWORK

Map by Melissa Baker

British Library Cataloguing in Publication Information available

Library of Congress Cataloging-in-Publication Data available

ISBN 978-1-4930-4860-1 (paper : alk. paper)
ISBN 978-1-4930-4861-8 (electronic)

∞™ The paper used in this publication meets the minimum requirements of American
National Standard for Information Sciences—Permanence of Paper for Printed Library
Materials, ANSI/NISO Z39.48-1992.

CONTENTS

CONTENTS

CONTENTS

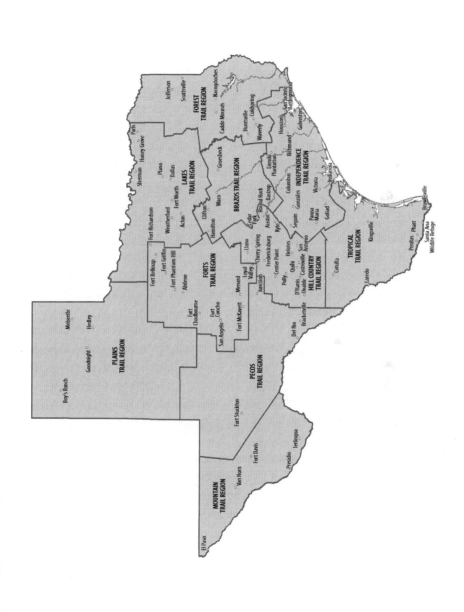

The *camposanto* in front of Mission San José in San Antonio has two marked graves.

INTRODUCTION

We generally think about cemeteries and graveyards only at funerals and during Halloween. For the past year, I've not only spent a lot of time thinking about cemeteries and graveyards but also visited more than a hundred throughout Texas in preparation for this book, traveling thousands of miles. From large and stately to small and obscure, from well-maintained to abandoned and overgrown, pioneer cemeteries tell a surprising and fascinating story about the deceased and also about us—humanity—how we cope, how and why we memorialize, and why it is so important to do so.

On my journey through Texas's cemeteries, I encountered a sobering number of graves of infants and children. The mortality rate for children in the nineteenth century was about 30 percent. For every ten children born, three died. The incidence of mothers dying in childbirth was also much higher. The gravesites of these mothers and their children tell a story of hardship, pain, and love.

The myriad emotions elicited when visiting a cemetery are vast. The Texas State Cemetery in Austin filled me with awe. I opened the doors of the reception building and was greeted with a view of a crescent pond lined with limestone boulders, manicured grounds, and rolling hillocks. It is a stunning cemetery with magnificent monuments, more than 2,000 of them dedicated to Texas's Confederate dead.

The Opp-Bihl Cemetery in Menard County, a small family graveyard on private property that overlooks a bluff on the San Saba River, is the quintessential pioneer cemetery symbolizing what Texas was in the nineteenth century: beautiful, beckoning, and dangerous. Among the twelve grave markers is a plethora of yucca cactus called Spanish dagger, along with thorny bushes. A Texas Ranger is buried there, along with some of his family members—one, a cowboy upon whose tablet tombstone is carved a hand with a cigarette lodged between a forefinger and middle finger pointing to heaven. The message? That he was a smoker seems too simple.

My cemetery trips were mostly uneventful, except when they weren't. At an inner-city cemetery in Houston, I encountered a man raving about the travesty of slavery. In a couple of coastal towns, one at dusk and another in the early morning, I was swarmed by mosquitoes with no repellant in sight. On another occasion in the piney woods of East Texas, my SUV got stuck in sand on a dark country road in search of a cemetery I never found. During a cemetery search in the Forts Trail region, I encountered a rattlesnake on a path at one of the fort parks and hightailed it back to the ranger station before calamity struck.

For the most part, however, my cemetery tours were as quiet and peaceful as you'd expect, and what I saw and learned about how we commemorate our dead will be forever seared in my memory.

Texas, the second-largest state, in both land mass and population, has more than 50,000 cemeteries, graveyards, and burial grounds. As the final resting places of those whose earthly journey has ended, they are also repositories of valuable cultural history. The pioneer cemeteries—those from the nineteenth century—provide a wealth of information on the people who settled in Texas during its years as a Republic (1836–1845), and after it became the twenty-eighth state in 1845.

But it was not only the people that interested me. The grave markers and statuary—ornate, simple, crumbling—also told a story. I learned some interesting accounts of individuals buried within a cemetery whose markers were lost to history, but whose stories begged to be told. Many nineteenth-century tombstones contain engravings that symbolize occupations, secret and fraternal societies, and/or religious beliefs. Engraved words of solace adorn many tombstones, providing poignant reminders of the affection felt by those still living or a reflection of the individuals buried within. Statues of ethereal women, obelisks with shrouds, treestone monuments, draped cinerary urns, Celtic crosses, and other symbols and funerary objects adorn these graves.

The most touching statues in pioneer gravesites depict angels and cherubs, often erected upon the grave of a child or young person. The Angel of Grief or Weeping Angel statue presides over at least five gravesites in various Texas cemeteries. The first Grief statue, ten feet tall and carved from Carrera marble, was commissioned in 1904 for the East Texas Scottsville Cemetery grave of William Scott Youree, an only son, who was killed in Mexico in January of that year at age thirty-one. Frank Teich, who crafted the statue, is among several renowned sculptors in Texas who created funerary monuments. The statue is based on the 1894 monument designed by American sculptor William Wetmore Story for his wife Emelyn, erected in Rome, Italy, at the *Cimitero acattolico* (Non-Catholic cemetery), also referred to as The Protestant Cemetery of Rome. Teich advertised in his catalog that he received $40,000 worth of orders "in Shreveport alone," because of the Scottsville monument.

With so many cemeteries, how does one choose which to include in a book like this? The Texas Historical Commission (THC) has designated several cemeteries in the state as Historic Texas Cemeteries. I selected many for inclusion. I combed the Internet and books to find others of significance or intrigue. The website findagrave.com played an important role in my initial selections, but it was not the ultimate arbiter. The Facebook group "Texas Cemeteries" also helped me in my quest for pioneer cemeteries. While the Internet provides much vital information, there is nothing as meaningful as field research. I often came away from the cemeteries with new individuals to feature, primarily because of intriguing gravesites and tombstones.

My objective was to tell the story of the founding of Texas through those buried in pioneer cemeteries and to illuminate the importance, beauty, and meaning of funerary symbols and objects from the nineteenth century. I included a representative sampling of cemeteries and individuals—those who may not have been famous or infamous—but who nevertheless were vital to the settlement of our state. I included stories that were indicative of nineteenth-century mores, but that had a universality that we could all relate to—tales of conflict, drama, and poignancy.

The book is organized using the Texas Heritage Trail Regions (THTRs) designated by the THC, a program initiated in 1967 as ten scenic driving trails in Texas. Anyone who has driven across Texas comes away knowing two things—it's a long drive (268,601 square miles) and the terrain changes from one region to the next. Acknowledging the immensity of our state, THC historians and geographers selected and refined the ten regions as a way to help delineate Texas's vast history.

The THC put some towns in two regions. San Antonio, for example, is not only in the Independence Trail Region but also in the Hill Country Region. The towns I selected that are within two regions will be featured in this book within one, with a mention of their dual placement.

Within these regions, listed in alphabetical order—Brazos Trail, Forest Trail, Forts Trail, Hill Country Trail, Independence Trail, Lakes Trail, Mountain Trail, Pecos Trail, Plains Trail, and Tropical Trail—are ancient burial mounds, battlefields, beaches, caverns, deserts, forts, missions, mountains, remnants of old towns, vestiges of cotton plantations, and so much more. Each region differs in terrain, culture, and historical context. The cemeteries within each tell the story of Texas.

A statue of a guardian angel cradling an infant stands over the graves of forgotten babies at Fairview Cemetery in Bastrop.

CHAPTER 1

BRAZOS TRAIL REGION

The Brazos River, with its many tributaries, flows southeast across West Texas, draining into the Gulf of Mexico two miles south of Freeport. Named *Brazos de Dios* (Arms of God) by early Spanish explorers, it is the longest river in Texas. Many of the state's early Anglo settlements are located along its basin. Stephen F. Austin, an American impresario known as "The Father of Texas," founded the first successful Anglo-American settlement in the lower river valley of the Brazos in 1825, bringing 300 families from the United States to settle in what was then the Tejas province of Mexico. The fertile soil around the river was ideal for growing cotton, and after the Civil War, this area became one of the most productive cotton-growing regions in the nation.

BASTROP

The city of Bastrop (pop. 9,500), named in honor of the Baron de Bastrop, an impresario who assisted Stephen F. Austin in his quest to establish a new colony in Texas, was founded in 1832, although people had been living in the area since 1804. It is in both the Brazos and Independence THTRs.

Fairview Cemetery, at 1409 Highway 95 North, is significant as a Republic of Texas cemetery. Twelve acres were originally set aside for burials; today the cemetery, with more than 3,500 graves, consists of thirty-six acres on a wooded hill northeast of the city's historic district with a view of downtown Bastrop and the Colorado River Valley. Fairview Cemetery has numerous unique monuments and statuary, including one honoring an "Unknown Stage-Coach Driver."

Crescentia Augusta Fischer née Borg (1807–1841) is buried on a hill in the oldest known marked grave in Fairview, in what was then called the City Cemetery. Crescentia was a teacher, daughter of a public official in Munich, and mother of a young son when she married the Evangelical Protestant minister Dr. Josef Anton Fischer in 1834. The couple had two more children, Augusta and Laurie. A year after Crescentia's eldest son died, Dr. Fischer received a new assignment in the Republic of Texas. The family arrived at the port of

Wrought-iron fences, such as the one surrounding Crescentia Fischer's gravesite, were commonly used to protect family plots and single graves from vandalism or destruction by wildlife.

New Orleans in 1840. A yellow fever epidemic was raging and their two children became ill. Augusta seemed to recover, but Laurie died in late 1840. The family left the city in June 1841 on a journey to Austin. When they reached Bastrop, about thirty miles from Austin, the city was also in the midst of a yellow fever epidemic. Both Crescentia and seven-year-old daughter Augusta, still weakened from her first bout, contracted the disease. While Augusta survived, Crescentia did not. She passed away on June 26, 1841, at age thirty-four. Fischer wrote, "Up to the last ten minutes, she was conscious, prayed and ended with the words, 'I'm going insane,' and died in my arms." Her husband left the city with their daughter, never to return.

An iron cross attached to the fence serves as Crescentia's marker. Now rusted and almost illegible, her German epitaph is translated: "Here rests Dr. J. A. Fischer's wife, Crescentia Augusta Fischer, born boos von Munchen in Bavaria, died here the 28 of June 1841, 34 years old. Dedicated by her brother-in-law Carl U. Ulrich Fisher." Crescentia's life and death (and that of her young son) illustrate the dangers awaiting so many nineteenth-century immigrants to Texas: the threat of infections and diseases for which there was no known cause and therefore no remedy.

NINETEENTH-CENTURY MORTALITY

A large number of infants' and children's graves populate pioneer cemeteries, with some sections designated "Babyland." In the nineteenth century, the death of a child was not uncommon nor was the death of a mother during childbirth. Most women who married had an average of six to eight children, but families with many more were common. By 1900, about 30 percent of children died before they turned five—in some US cities, 30 percent of infants died before reaching the age of one, according to the *Morbidity and Mortality Weekly Report*, Centers for Disease Control and Prevention. The leading causes of death were pneumonia, influenza, tuberculosis, and enteritis with diarrhea. Children under five accounted for 40 percent of all deaths from these infections. Because of sanitation improvements, vaccines, and antibiotics, today children, who would have died from childhood infections then, live long and healthy lives. By 1999, less than 1.4 percent of children died by their fifth birthday. In the nineteenth century, six to nine women in the United States died from pregnancy-related complications for every 1,000 births. By 1999, the maternal mortality rate also went down, to less than 0.1 deaths per 1,000 live births.

Among numerous notable Bastrop citizens buried at Fairview Cemetery is the politician **Robert A. Kerr** (1833–1913). Born in Louisiana, Kerr was the offspring of a mixed marriage. His father was white and his mother was black. In 1855, he and his father moved to Port Lavaca, where they opened a shipping business. The Texas Republicans named him an alternate delegate to their National

Convention, an unusual honor for a man of mixed race at that time, and in 1872, he moved to Victoria. By 1880, he'd moved to Bastrop, where he was elected to the Texas House of Representatives, becoming the area's first black legislator. Kerr served on the Bastrop County School Board and helped establish a high school for black students. The following appeared in the *Galveston Daily News* after his death: "R. A. Kerr, an old negro of this place, died some time [*sic*] last night. For years, he had been engaged in the business of barber and was well-liked by both races. He at one time represented this county (Bastrop), in the legislature." He is buried under a simple tombstone, scalloped on the top, upon which is inscribed: "It is hard, indeed, to part with thee, But Christ's strong arm supported me."

WAR BABIES GUARDIAN ANGEL

Although not a nineteenth-century-era memorial, the war babies guardian angel statue that stands over the area in Fairview where at least sixteen infants were buried during World War II is one of the most poignant gravesites in Texas. The wives of many Camp Swift soldiers—more than 300,000 troops trained there over the course of the war—had traveled to Bastrop to be near their husbands. Many women became pregnant and some lost their babies during childbirth. Too poor to arrange a funeral and burial or to ship them back home, the mothers were left in a quandary. A benevolent soul donated burial ground at Fairview and a local funeral home provided shrouds, tiny coffins, and free burial.

After the mothers returned to their hometowns, the graves were abandoned. The Bastrop County Historical Society placed small crosses where they believed the babies were buried.

CEDAR PARK

In the mid-nineteenth century, this community was known as Running Brushy, named after a spring that formed the headwaters of a creek of the same name. In 1873, George and Harriet Cluck bought 329 acres that included the Running Brushy spring. Their ranch formed the core of the community that would one day become Cedar Park (pop. 84,500). Considered a suburb of Austin, this town is in both the Brazos and Hill Country THTRs.

George Washington Cluck (1839–1920) and his wife **Harriett "Hattie" Louisa Standefer Cluck** (1846–1938) are buried in the historic **Cedar Park Cemetery**, 110 S. Bell Street, today a three-acre burial ground with about 120 graves. Encased oval photographs of the couple are inset on their double tombstone. The first burial in this family cemetery took place in January 1901, when George and Hattie's infant grandson died. In 1907, the family deeded the property for a community cemetery.

Hattie was one of the first white woman to travel the Chisholm Trail to cattle markets in Abilene, Kansas. Hattie's story has been sensationalized over the years, but the following appears factual: in April of 1871, a pregnant Hattie and her three children, the oldest seven and the youngest two, joined George's trail ride to Abilene despite his protestations. George found his family sitting in a wagon in line with several others. Rather than argue with his diminutive but feisty wife, he allowed them to join the trail drive. Along the way, cattle rustlers attempted to steal some of the herd and Hattie either picked up a shotgun in defense or helped the cowboys load their weapons. Her main role on the 1,247-mile round-trip trail drive was to care for her children.

The Cluck family reached Kansas in the fall, and their son, Euell, was born there on October 17, 1871. The Clucks spent the winter of 1871–1872 in Kansas, and the following spring, they returned to Williamson County and settled in Running Brushy, where Hattie served as postmistress from 1874 to 1880. She had six more children and was forty-three when the last was born.

An eight-foot-high bronze statue called "The Pioneer Woman," depicting Hattie "boldly striding" with a walking stick, carrying a canvas grub bag, is one of several nineteenth-century iconic images erected in the Chisholm Trail Commemorative Park in Round Rock.

CLIFTON

Twenty-seven miles west of Waco, Clifton (pop. 3,400) is known for being the largest Norwegian settlement west of the Mississippi and "The Norwegian Capital of Texas." Thousands of Norwegian immigrants, some from Norway and others from northern states, settled between Clifton and Cranfills Gap by the early 1900s, induced by liberal land offers, and social and economic betterment. Most had been farmers in rural Norway and were attracted to the similar landscape of Texas's Bosque River area.

Cleng Peerson (1782–1865), "The Father of Norwegian Immigration to America," led the early Norwegian pioneers to the area in 1854 and is buried in the historic **Our Savior's Lutheran "Old Norse" Church Cemetery**, 152 County Road 4145, eight miles west of Clifton, in the old community of Norse, now a historic district. The 111-acre graveyard purchased in 1871 overlooks the Bosque valley and has more than 1,500 graves, many with historic and unique tombstones, and is partially fenced within a handmade rock wall. A pavilion to the left of the cemetery contains a map of the graves. At the central gated entrance is a monument recognizing the seventeen Norwegian settlers who founded the town.

On the base of Cleng Peerson's grave marker—one side in Norwegian and on the other English—is inscribed: "The Pioneer of Norse Emigration to America; Born in Norway Europe, May 17, 1782; Landed in America in 1821; Died in Texas, December 16, 1865. Grateful Countrymen Erected This To His Memory." A plaque commemorating the 1982 trip of King Olav V of Norway was placed in front of Peerson's pillar monument in the center of the church graveyard. The Norwegian king visited the graveyard to lay a wreath and dedicate the monument on the 200th anniversary of Peerson's birth. That event brought 2,000 people to the cemetery.

The King of Norway dedicated Cleng Peerson's pillar monument in 1982, the 200th anniversary of Peerson's birth.

CEMETERY VERSUS GRAVEYARD

With the mention of a cemetery associated with a church, it should be pointed out that although used interchangeably, the correct term for a burial ground associated with a church is "graveyard," while the word "cemetery" implies that the land is specifically designated as a burial ground. "Grave" comes from the Proto-Germanic *graban*, meaning "to dig," while the term "cemetery" originated from the ancient Greek *koimeterion*, meaning sleeping place.

GROESBECK

Groesbeck (pop. 4,300), named after Abram Groesbeeck, a railroad director, became a township in 1869, with a city government beginning in 1871. Four miles northwest of this town and thirty-nine miles east of Waco is the historic Old Fort Parker Historic Site, preserved to tell the story of Cynthia Ann Parker, who was captured by Indians and became the mother of Quanah Parker, the last Comanche chief.

The **Fort Parker Memorial Cemetery**, on FM 1245, is two miles northwest of Groesbeck, and one-and-a-half miles from the fort. This historic cemetery, with more than 1,800 graves, is still an active burial site. The oldest part of the cemetery, started in 1836, contains the graves of settlers who died in the attack on Fort Parker that year. A group of Comanche and Kiowa Indians attacked the fort, killing **Elder John Parker, Benjamin F. Parker, Silas M. Parker, Samuel M. Frost**, and **Robert Frost**. They are buried under a large oak tree in a mass grave, over which lies a large granite slab engraved with their names and the words, "Here rest the martyrs of Fort Parker, Killed by Comanche Indians May 19, 1836. . . . In memory of those who laid foundations others have built upon." The attack on Fort Parker also left two wounded and five taken captive.

The mass grave, surrounded by a bar fence, is to the left of what is the centerpiece of the cemetery—a twenty-foot-high monument of Italian marble and Texas granite, erected in 1922 to memorialize the Fort Parker settlers. There are several inscriptions on the base. One of them reads, "Fort Parker, established by Illinois colonists in 1833— Three years later, at 8 o-clock a.m., as the dew drops glistened in the sun rays, it fell by the hand of the Comanches."

The Fort Parker Memorial features a life-size statue of Silas and Lucy Parker and their daughter Cynthia Ann, added to the monument in 1932.

The cemetery was originally known as Union Burial Ground (named perhaps for a church that once stood nearby). On the northern part of the cemetery are rows of old tombstones etched with the word, "Unknown." There are hundreds. According to William

Reagan, chairman of the Limestone County Historical Commission, these are older graves that were not marked or may have been marked with rocks. Some may have had wooden markers that rotted away over the years. At some point, the cemetery placed markers inscribed "Unknown." Reagan's fifth great-grandmother died around 1848 and is buried in the cemetery in an unknown location. The rows of tombstones are a poignant reminder of lost and forgotten pioneers.

HAMILTON

Hamilton (pop. 3,000) was named after James Hamilton Jr., an American lawyer and politician who served as the fifty-third governor of South Carolina. He lent $216,000 to the Republic of Texas, making him a person of great importance in the new Republic. In 1858, the town was named the county seat.

School teacher **Elizabeth Ann Whitney** (1835–1867), who gave her life to protect her students, is buried in the **Hamilton Cemetery**. This small burial site is in the back of a cluster of small cemeteries—100F (Odd Fellows Cemetery), Old 100F, Graves-Gentry, and Hamilton—at the corner of East Francis Marion and West Rice Streets. Although settlements in Texas were expanding, Indian threats continued into the 1870s. One Comanche raid in Hamilton led to the harrowing death of this brave school teacher. According to local tradition, Ann was repeatedly struck by arrows fired through cracks in the schoolhouse walls. Fatally injured, she aided the escape of all but one of her students.

Whitney's obelisk monument reads: "In Memory of Ann Whitney—frontier school teacher—Born in Massachusetts about

1835. Killed by Comanche Indians July 9, 1867. Resting in hope of a glorious resurrection. Erected by the schoolchildren of Hamilton County." Her gravesite is a Recorded Texas Historic Landmark. A memorial monument dedicated to her stands in the southwest corner of the Hamilton Courthouse lawn.

DEATH BY COMANCHE

The Comanches were a serious threat to the settlement of Texas well into the nineteenth century. When the Spanish tried to settle in Texas in the 1700s, the Comanches kept them in the southern part of Texas. In 1867, after years of relentless skirmishes, raids, and battles, a treaty was established for a reservation for the Comanches, Kiowas, and Kiowa Apaches in what is now Oklahoma. In 1874, a Comanche band attempted one last ditch effort for a victory over the whites—the attack at Adobe Walls. They lost. This uprising was the impetus for the Red River War, implemented to once and for all force the Comanches to enter the reservation and stay there. The strategy was to destroy the tribe's horse herd and supplies during a very cold winter in the Panhandle. It worked and the Comanches, knowing they could not survive the winter, surrendered. According to an 1875 reservation census, the Comanche population, once estimated to number in the thousands, had been reduced to 1,597.

A renowned Norwegian writer, teacher, artist, and community activist, **Elise Waerenskjold** (1815–1895), is buried in **Howard Cemetery**, between North Lemmons and North Howard Streets in Hamilton. This cemetery of more than 400 graves may have started as a family cemetery with the unmarked grave of Shadrack Howard, a notorious rancher who escaped the consequences of one murder in the 1850s only to be hung for cattle theft in the early 1860s. His daughter, Amanda, was instrumental in sounding the alarm during the Comanche attack of the Hamilton schoolhouse that ended in Elizabeth Ann Whitney's death. Many of the early graves have no markers and those that remain—old tombstones and broken stone sarcophagi shaded beneath oaks and other canopied trees—give the cemetery an eerie atmosphere. A marble pillar tombstone and a Texas Historical plaque mark Waerenskjold's burial site in a family plot under a copse of trees that includes her daughter-in-law and five grandchildren, one of them an infant granddaughter who died in 1880. Waerenskjold's marker reads: "Gifted pioneer whose 1846–1895 writings brought many settlers to Texas from her native Norway. Countrymen also found her home open to newcomers. She is now called 'Lady with the Pen.' She and her husband had 3 sons, many descendants. Recorded – 1968."

Waerenskjold was an abolitionist and involved in the temperance movement. Her stories—personal letters written to friends and family in Norway—were compiled into a book published in 1961 titled *The Lady with the Pen*. Her stories document her life in the harsh landscape of Texas, and yet what she wrote was instrumental in encouraging many Norwegians to settle in Texas. In 1865, referencing

Seated portrait of Elise Waerenskjold.
CREDIT: WISCONSIN HISTORICAL SOCIETY, WHS 7235.

the Civil War, she wrote: "Union men were those who did not favor secession of the Southern states from the union with the North. Practically all the Norwegians were Union men." A year later, on November 17, 1866, her second husband, Wilhelm, was murdered. Stabbed by a "scoundrel of a Methodist minister," named N. T. Dickerson, according to Elise, it was claimed that Wilhelm was killed because of his Union sympathies, although the motive for the murder was never formally established. He is buried in Four Mile Lutheran Church Cemetery in Van Zandt County, where the couple lived with their sons. Almost thirty years later, and a year before her death, Elise moved to Hamilton to live with her son Otto and his wife. She died on January 22, 1895, at age eighty.

ROUND ROCK

Round Rock (pop. 119,500), twenty miles north of Austin, straddles both sides of the Balcones Escarpment. On one side, the fault line stretches east of Interstate 35, where the land is flat, with the fertile soil of the Blackland Prairie. To the west lies the hilly terrain associated with the Texas Hill Country. For this reason, Round Rock is in both the Brazos and Hill Country THTRs. The community was formed in 1851 on the banks of Brushy Creek near a large, oval rock in the middle of the creek. The rock marked a low-water crossing for stagecoaches, wagons, horses, and cattle traveling along the Chisholm Trail. By 1854, the settlement was called Round Rock and the town was incorporated in 1913.

Round Rock Cemetery, 1100–1400 blocks of Sam Bass Road (Country Road 175), was established in the early 1850s in what is now known as Old Round Rock. One-half acre in the northwest part of the almost five-acre cemetery was used as a burial ground for slaves and freedmen during the nineteenth century. There are more than 2,000 gravesites.

One of the most famous, or rather infamous, gravesites is that of outlaw **Sam Bass** (1851–1878). Born in Indiana, he arrived in Texas in 1870 and began robbing stagecoaches in 1876. He quickly moved on to holding up trains, a lucrative, if more dangerous, occupation. His money and gregarious personality gained him many acquaintances, several of whom he recruited into what would become known as the Sam Bass Gang. They staged four train robberies in two months in north Texas, starting in February 1878. By April, residents had had enough, imploring the governor to do something. He called in the Texas Rangers. Exemplifying the old adage, "There is no honor among thieves," one of the gang members, in exchange for impunity and collection of the reward money, betrayed the gang. He slipped away and sent a letter to the leader of the Texas Rangers, saying that Bass was on his way to Round Rock to rob a bank.

On July 19, 1878, Bass and two of his partners in crime (one of them **Seaborn Barnes**, who is buried next to Sam) went into town to survey the bank. Two sheriff's deputies, one of them **Alijah W. Grimes** (1850–1878), saw the men. Having been notified that the Sam Bass Gang was plotting a heist in Round Rock, Grimes observed these three strangers and decided to investigate. When he confronted Bass, he was met with a barrage of gunfire, killing him instantly. Grimes, his body riddled with bullets, never even had the opportunity to draw his gun.

A gun battle ensued in which Bass was seriously wounded. He was found later in a pasture leaning against a tree. They took him back to town, where he died two days later on his twenty-seventh birthday. A few years after his death, Sam's sister had a tombstone erected on which was engraved the following epitaph: "A brave man reposes in death here. Why was he not true?" The monument was chipped away by souvenir hunters. Years later, it was replaced with a granite tombstone erected by the Sam Bass Centennial Commission. Seaborn Barnes's tombstone inscription gives a long description of who he was and what he did, including being "shot through the head." The last sentence reads, "He was right bower (sea anchor) to Sam Bass."

Alijah W. Grimes was born in Bastrop on July 5, 1850. Married to Charlotte Lyman in 1874, he worked as a printer before enlisting in Ranger Company A, Frontier Battalion in September 1877, serving for almost three months. After leaving the company, he moved his family to Round Rock, where he took on the job of Williamson County Deputy Sheriff and was killed in the line of duty just seven months later. At the time of his death—also, like Bass, at the age of twenty-seven—he had three small children, one of them just a few months old. The townspeople raised almost $200 for Grimes's family, and gave his wife one of the outlaws' horses for compensation.

On Grimes's headstone are the words, "Gone But Not Forgotten." Ironic, of course. Everyone remembers the outlaw Sam Bass, but virtually no one recalls Deputy A. W. Grimes. The street in front of the cemetery is called Sam Bass, along with many businesses along the road. Seeking to rectify this emphasis on the outlaw, the city passed a resolution in 2000 to change the name of a street called "Arterial B" to A. W. Grimes Boulevard. In 2016, the Williamson County

The Williamson County Sheriff's Department dedicated a new grave marker and memorial to honor A. W. Grimes in 2016.

Sheriff's Department dedicated a new tombstone and memorial to Grimes. His original marble tombstone that had been broken in half was donated to the Williamson County Museum.

FRATERNAL SOCIETIES—FREEMASONS

The greatest popularity of fraternal organizations in the United States was in the mid-nineteenth century and after the Civil War. Many of these societies provided a death benefit as part of membership perks, ranging from a tombstone to a plot in the organization's cemetery. The most represented fraternal society in a cemetery is the Freemasons and the symbol most associated with this group is the Compass and Square as depicted on the tombstone of A. W. Grimes. Members of the Freemasons or Masons, as they're also known, use the customs and tools of stonemasons as allegorical guides to indicate their constructive role in society.

The **Old Round Rock Slave Burial Ground**, a Texas State Historic Cemetery, is on half an acre of Old Round Rock Cemetery. This burial ground was enclosed at one time by cedar posts and barbed wire. The gravesites are marked head and foot with large limestone rocks, some hand-grooved with names and dates that are no longer legible. Only thirteen graves—the oldest dated 1880—have been confirmed, although there are believed to be forty to fifty graves of freedmen. In an interview conducted not long before he passed away, **Joe Lee Johnson** (1883–1977), told interviewers that his father Simon, born in 1850, and his grandfather were both slaves. They were buried in the cemetery in an unknown location. A grave marker for a child, **Melchoria Harris** (1881–1882), is one of a few remaining tombstones in the slave cemetery.

WACO

Founded in 1849 on the site of a Hueco Indian village along the Brazos River near where a Texas Ranger fort was established in 1837, Waco (pop. 142,000)—the phonetic spelling of the Indian word—was a farming and plantation area in the nineteenth century, with an economy almost exclusively based on cotton. Waco village was incorporated as the town of Waco in 1856. Waco's economy grew after 1870, when the Waco Bridge Company opened a suspension bridge spanning the Brazos. After its completion, Waco was reincorporated as the "City of Waco." In 1871, with the arrival of the Waco and Northwestern Railroad, Waco became an important debarkation point for thousands of prospective settlers headed west and the primary shipping point for a broad area. At one time, Waco was called "Six Shooter Junction."

MAMMOTH BURIAL GROUND

Waco is the location of the "the nation's first and only recorded discovery of a nursery herd of Pleistocene mammoths," according to the National Park Service. Their burial site is now within the five-acre Waco Mammoth National Monument, 6220 Steinbeck Bend. The mammoth bones were discovered in 1978 near the Bosque River, a tributary of the Brazos. Archeologists determined that approximately 65,000 years ago, water rose quickly and flooded the site. At least nineteen mammoths from a nursery herd were trapped in the steep-sided channel and drowned.

First Street Cemetery, IH-35 at University Parks Drive, is the historic designation for three contiguous cemeteries on the south bank of the Brazos River. Two of these cemeteries were established in 1852: City Cemetery, Waco's first public cemetery, which originally covered five acres and a two-acre Masonic cemetery. The third cemetery, an almost three-acre plot, was acquired by the Order of Odd Fellows between 1868 and 1869. Within three decades of its opening, the City Cemetery reached capacity.

By 1881, the cemeteries contained some 7,000 graves, according to a newspaper article published that year in the *Waco Examiner*. In 1882, the City of Waco obtained additional land to expand the cemetery to more than twice its original size. However, cemetery boundaries were never clearly defined and records on burials were not accurately or completely kept. The remains of about 200 people from unmarked graves in one of the First Street cemeteries were discovered in the excavation of a construction project behind the Texas Ranger Hall of Fame and Museum, which is adjacent to the old cemeteries. They were reburied in another Waco cemetery.

INDEPENDENT ORDER OF ODD FELLOWS

Several cemeteries in Texas are designated as IOOF or **Independent Order of Odd Fellows**. The symbol associated with this group is a three-chain link, referring to their motto of friendship, love, and truth. This benevolent society was formed to protect widows and orphans, bury the dead, and help each other in want at a time when there was no system in place to ensure one's welfare, health, or job protection. During the nineteenth century, life insurance was available only to the wealthy. Sickness or death of the breadwinner meant poverty for a family with no means. According to the manual on Odd Fellowship, published in 1888, Odd Fellows differed from Masonry by being composed almost exclusively of "the great middle industrial classes," while Masons were almost exclusively composed of the "titled and proud." The meaning for the term "Odd Fellows" has never been fully established; however, a likely explanation is that its members were engaged in various "odd" trades and didn't have the numbers to form a trade union or guild like the Masons.

First Street Cemetery is a Texas Historic Cemetery and State Antiquities Landmark. Among many prominent Confederates buried in this cemetery is **Brigadier General James Edward Harrison** (1815–1875). Born in South Carolina, he moved to Texas in 1857, after having served two terms in the Mississippi Senate. As a commissioner for the state of Texas in negotiations with Indians, he worked to persuade the "Five Civilized Tribes"—Cherokee, Chickasaw, Choctaw, Creek (Muscogee), and Seminole—to join the Confederacy in the case of war, which, for the most part, they did. After the war started, Harrison rose to be commander of the Seventeenth Texas Infantry and the Twenty-Second and Thirty-First Texas dismounted cavalry regiments. He was a prominent member of Waco and served as a trustee of Baylor University.

One of the most striking tombstones in the **First Street City Cemetery** is that of **Irene Davis Kellum** (1854–1886) in the Davis family plot, surrounded by a low brick wall. Calla lilies, which symbolize marriage and fidelity, are carved onto the top portion of her marble pillar monument. Next to her grave is that of her baby daughter, with a diminutive tombstone also carved with flowers, in her case, Lily of the Valley, the symbol for innocence and purity, and forget-me-nots. The inscription on Irene's monument reads: "Oh, the loneliness and sorrow/In Our hearts and in our home./When we know on no tomorrow,/Will our absent darling come./Why this cross? we grieving question./God, who took our idol knew./If our treasure were in heaven./We would long to follow too."

Irene was from a family of prominence and scandal. Twelve years after her death, her brother, **Thomas Davis** (1856–1898), shot **William Brann** (1855–1898), the vitriolic editor of *The Iconoclast*, a magazine in which Brann used to criticize many organizations and entities, especially what he considered the hypocrisy of the Baptist clergy who ran Baylor University. Davis was a Baptist and an ardent supporter of Baylor University. That fateful day, they had an altercation and Davis shot Brann, who, though mortally wounded, returned fire. Both men died the next day. Although Thomas is buried in the family plot, his grave marker is missing.

William Brann is buried in Waco's **Oakwood Cemetery** at 2124 South 5th Street at La Salle Avenue. Today, all that's left of his original marker is the bottom block foundation, his initials inscribed on one side and a cameo silhouette of a man's face on the other. His original marker included a large marble "lamp of truth" on a pedestal with a scroll upon which was inscribed the word, "Truth." Just before Christmas in 2009, vandals stole the top portion of the grave marker and hauled it away. As one Waco writer pointed out, "The 'Wicked Wizard of Words,' is still despised today in some quarters." A Texas Historical Marker for the Brann-Davis shooting is located in the 100 block of South 4th Street.

Oakwood Cemetery, next to Holy Cross Cemetery where one of the five weeping angel statues in Texas is located, was established in 1878 on a 157-acre tract that was once fairgrounds and a race track. Among the more than 36,000 graves, are those of early pioneers reinterred from First Street Cemetery. A Texas State Historic Cemetery, Oakwood Cemetery is stately, well-laid-out, and well-maintained, with many old monuments and statuary canopied with mature oaks. Throughout the cemetery are large and impressive statues and monuments of angels marking family plots and graves.

Three Texas governors are buried in Oakwood: Richard Coke, L. S. "Sul" Ross, and Pat M. Neff. A Volunteer Firemen's Monument, erected between 1883 and 1893, is the centerpiece of an area dedicated to firefighters. The towering pillar monument, etched with dozens of names of early volunteers, includes a life-size marble and granite statue, the figure of a fireman holding a hose. In this cemetery is also what is purported to be the oldest memorial marker in Texas honoring Confederate veterans of the Civil War. The seventeen-foot-tall gray obelisk marker is surrounded by some forty-five graves, some with tombstones upon which is inscribed "Unknown."

The memorial monuments made by sculptor Frank Teich and erected in the 1920s for Governor **Richard Coke** (1829–1897) and

Dr. David Wallace (1825–1911) attest to their great friendship. Marble figures of the two men standing upon towering granite pillars face each other from their family plots. Born in Virginia, Coke moved to Waco in the 1850s. After the Civil War, he was elected to the Texas Supreme Court. In 1873, he defeated the despised Reconstruction governor and former Union officer E. J. Davis. His election marked the end of Reconstruction in Texas. He resigned as governor in 1876, upon being elected to the US Senate, a position he held for three terms, until 1895. Wallace, born in North Carolina, moved to Waco in 1861. He'd served as a surgeon in the Confederate Army. After the war, he focused on the treatment of people with mental disorders. Because of this, he is considered the father of modern psychiatry in Texas.

Governor Coke called Dr. Wallace, "his friend through eternity." Coke's monument is on the left.

GOLDEN AGE OF AMERICAN MEMORIALS

After the Civil War, the monument industry took off, due to the desire to commemorate war heroes. The period after the Civil War up to World War I is considered the golden age of American memorials. Monuments were larger and could be less expensive depending on the material used. Many were mass-produced in stock patterns and sizes, and by 1900, the Sears catalog was advertising marble monuments, ranging from small markers at a cost of $5 to large three-piece pillars that cost $27. The price for inscriptions was two to six cents per carved letter. Marble and granite continued to be in high demand, but the addition of zinc changed the playing field, at least until metal became too valuable during World War I. Additionally, in some parts of the country, the powerful stone industry convinced some cemeteries to ban monuments not made from stone.

Angel of Grief in Scottsville Cemetery.

CHAPTER 2

FOREST TRAIL REGION

East Texas's strong Southern heritage is apparent throughout its towns and cemeteries. A region of big thickets, timberlands, and natural lakes, this part of Texas was a Confederate stronghold; the northeastern town of Marshall was the capital of the Confederacy west of the Mississippi River after the fall of Vicksburg. But the region also has a strong Native American heritage as home of the Caddo Indian Tribes that inhabited the piney forests beginning around 800 AD. Spanish explorers called this tribe *Tejas*, meaning "friends." Another tribe that settled in this region is the Alabama-Coushatta, who migrated from the east in the late eighteenth century. A trade route called El Camino Real de los Tejas, also known as the King's Highway and Old San Antonio Road, was established across this region into Mexico. Today, East Texas is home to four national and five state forests and the largest cypress grove in the world.

HUNTSVILLE

Huntsville (pop. 42,000), seventy miles north of Houston, was founded in 1835 as an Indian trading post by brothers Pleasant and

Ephraim Gray from Huntsville, Alabama. By the 1840s, farmers and well-to-do families from Alabama, the Carolinas, Mississippi, and Tennessee, enticed by the timber industry and fertile soil, began to settle the town, incorporated in 1845. In 1849, with a population close to 600, the town built Texas's first penitentiary after receiving a contract from the state. Today, the Texas Department of Criminal Justice (TDCJ) is the largest employer in Huntsville, with more than 6,000 people working in the prison system. However, the city's claim to fame is its association with **General Sam Houston**, who had a family home in Huntsville and is buried in Huntsville's historic **Oakwood Cemetery**.

Old Oakwood Cemetery on Ninth Street between Sam Houston Memorial Drive and Ryan's Ferry Road, is a three-acre graveyard, part of a much larger cemetery complex collectively called **Oakwood Cemetery**, with the earliest marked burial from 1842. It is the final resting place for many historical figures, including seven Union soldiers who were victims of the scourge of the nineteenth century—yellow fever. In early August of 1867, a stagecoach passenger arrived sick from a coastal city. He stayed at a Huntsville tavern, got progressively worse, and died on August 9. Those in contact with him fell ill and the disease spread throughout Huntsville. Many residents fled town, but many also stayed to tend to the sick. Between August 9 and October 18, 1867, some 150 people—approximately 10 percent of the 1,500 residents of Huntsville—had died from yellow fever.

Yellow Fever

From 1800 to 1879, the United States had an annual yellow fever epidemic every year except two. The disease appeared in the spring and ended in the fall. A scourge of the nineteenth century, yellow fever, a viral disease transmitted by mosquitoes, inflicted a miserable death and took the lives of up to 50 percent of the people who contracted it. Mild cases cause flu-like symptoms; more severe forms are characterized by internal bleeding and liver and kidney damage. Jaundice is a common feature, thus the name yellow fever. One of its most horrid manifestations indicating the approach of death was vomiting copious dark blood clots. Mexicans called it the *vomito negro*. Because people didn't understand the cause of the illness, they suspected it might be caused by lack of good hygiene and sanitation. They burned barrels of tar and whiskey outside their homes in hopes that the smoke would clear the air of toxins. Bloodletting, purging, and administration of mercury were the standard treatments. As early as 1848, a doctor proposed that yellow fever was likely spread by moths or mosquitoes. In 1881, a Cuban doctor concurred that it was likely that mosquitoes caused yellow fever. Army doctors, led by Dr. Walter Reed, began to test the hypothesis and successfully proved that it was indeed caused by mosquitoes. The first efforts to eradicate the disease included removing stagnant water where mosquitoes bred and spraying insecticide, which began to control the large-scale epidemics. In 1927, scientists isolated the yellow fever virus, and in the 1930s, two vaccines were developed.

The town's entrance sign, "Welcome to Huntsville, Home of Sam Houston," says it all. Texans were raised on the stories and exploits of **General Sam Houston** (1793–1863), a key figure in the battle for Texas Independence, the first president of the Republic of Texas, and one of the state's early governors. Born in Virginia, he came to Texas in 1832. The thrice-married Houston led a tumultuous and controversial life as an adopted member of the Cherokee tribe in Tennessee, a military leader, and a political figure. Because he opposed secession and refused to sign a loyalty oath to the Confederacy, he was ousted as governor in 1861.

A year later, he retired to Huntsville, where he died from pneumonia at his home on July 26, 1863. Because he did not support the Confederacy, few mourners other than his family and close friends attended his funeral. Although his last residence in Huntsville was brief, he's been buried in the town's historic Oakwood Cemetery for almost 160 years.

In 1911, a twelve-by-twelve-foot monument dedicated to General Sam Houston was sculpted by renowned artist Pompeo Coppini and placed at the entrance of Huntsville's Oakwood Cemetery. The high-relief sculpture of Houston on a horse riding to victory is flanked on either side by the allegorical figures of History and Victory.

The city of Houston and Fort Sam Houston Army Post in San Antonio, among many other entities and institutions in Texas and other states, are named after Sam Houston. His wife, **Margaret Lea**, with whom he had eight children, died of yellow fever on December 3, 1867, in Independence, Texas. Because of fear of contagion, her body was not moved to Oakwood. She was buried in Independence beside her mother.

Houston selected the spot of his burial near his friend **Henderson King Yoakum** (1810–1856), a prominent lawyer, statesman, and historian. Born in Tennessee, Yoakum graduated from the US Military Academy in 1832 and served on the frontier and in the Mexican War. He practiced law and served in the Tennessee Senate before

This monument honoring General Sam Houston stands at the entrance of Old Oakwood Cemetery.

moving to Texas in 1845. In Huntsville, he became a civic leader, helping in establishing Austin College and becoming its first librarian and a teacher of law. In 1855, he published a comprehensive two-volume history of Texas, *History of Texas from Its First Settlement under La Salle in 1685 to Its Annexation to the United States in 1845*.

Yoakum died unexpectedly on a trip to Houston where he delivered a Masonic address and attended to some courtroom duties. While at court, he suffered a severe tubercular attack. He was treated but did not recover, dying on November 30, 1856. A Texas Historical Marker was erected next to his obelisk tombstone, upon which an interesting image of the Grim Reaper pulling on the hair of a woman is carved. Yoakum and his wife **Eveline Cannon Yoakum** had nine children. Eveline's grave is marked by a small rectangular marble stone next to her husband's monument. She died on October 1, 1867, at age fifty-four, during the yellow fever epidemic.

Joshua Houston (1822–1902), a slave for the family of Sam Houston's wife Margaret Lea in Alabama, is buried in the Negro section of Old Oakwood. He joined Houston's household upon his marriage to Margaret in 1840. Joshua traveled with Houston, becoming his body servant. During the 1840s, Joshua learned to read and write, becoming a skilled wheelwright and blacksmith. Although it was illegal to do so, Houston freed Joshua and all his slaves in 1862, after reading Abraham Lincoln's "Emancipation Proclamation."

A successful businessman, church leader, deacon, and supporter of education, Houston served as the first African American alderman in Huntsville and was active in the Republic Party on the local level.

After the Civil War, Joshua Houston became one of the county's leading African American leaders, c. 1898.
FROM THE COLLECTION OF THE SAM HOUSTON MEMORIAL MUSEUM, HUNTSVILLE, TEXAS.

He worked to stamp out discriminatory laws and was a Texas delegate to the Republican National Convention in 1888 in Chicago, Illinois. Father of eight children, he is buried next to his third wife, **Sylvester**

Baker Houston (1823–1898). As indicated on the granite pillar tombstone she shares with her husband, Sylvester was a member of the Household of Ruth, the female counterpart of the **Grand United Order of Odd Fellows.** Founded in 1843 as a benevolent organization providing assistance with burial costs and other necessities, its membership, not to be confused with the **IOOF** as described in Chapter 1, principally included African Americans.

The **TDCJ Captain Joe Byrd Prison Cemetery**, 398 Bowers Boulevard, east of Sycamore Drive, a Texas Historic Cemetery, is the final resting place of more than 3,000 inmates who died while incarcerated within the Texas prison system. The twenty-two-acre cemetery near the grounds of Sam Houston State University and a mile southeast of the Walls Unit is called "Peckerwood Hill" by inmates. The term "peckerwood" is a pejorative referring to poor inmates. With its neat rows of uniform markers and crosses, the cemetery is a sobering glimpse into what awaits prisoners whose bodies are unclaimed. Many of the concrete crosses include only prison numbers and dates of death. If the inmate was executed, the headstone has an "X" or "EX," or a prison number beginning "999," the designation for death row.

Although the Huntsville prison cemetery was established in the early 1850s with a few burials, it officially began in 1855 after the land was donated to the state. According to prison historian Jim Willett, former warden of the Walls Unit at Huntsville, there were no written records of who was buried at the cemetery until 1974. When Captain Joe Byrd, an assistant warden after whom the cemetery is named, began a cleanup of the cemetery in 1962, he and his crew of "offenders" located more than 900 graves. At least 300 had no identifying information. The crew marked them with white concrete crosses. Some of the graves have tablet-style tombstones that were discontinued in the 1940s. About 100 deceased inmates are buried there each year, coming from the state's 109 prison units, the TDCJ hospital at Galveston, or the prison system's hospice facility near Palestine.

INDIAN CHIEF SATANTA

Kiowa Indian Chief Satanta (1820–1878) was buried in the Huntsville prison cemetery (today called **Captain Joe Byrd Prison Cemetery**) for eighty-five years, from 1878 to 1963, when, at the request of his grandson, the Indian chief's remains were removed and reburied at Fort Sill Cemetery in Lawton, Oklahoma, following traditional Kiowa burial rites.

Satanta was imprisoned twice at the Huntsville penitentiary. The first time was in 1871 for leading a raid that resulted in the gruesome murders of seven teamsters. Found guilty and sentenced to death, his punishment was commuted to life in prison due to fear of Kiowa retribution. He was paroled in August 1873 and began raiding again. In the fall of 1874, he was again arrested and sent back to prison. Four years later, he died after jumping out of the second story of the prison hospital. He was unceremoniously buried in a pine coffin in the prison graveyard.

A memorial to Satanta remains at the top of the hill underneath a large pine tree in the center of the prison cemetery. It consists of a small monument and a pillar upon which stands a carved wooden bust of an Indian head. The memorial is surrounded by a white pole fence. The chief's death leap from the second story prison cell was the inspiration for Blue Duck's demise in Larry McMurtry's *Lonesome Dove*.

NACOGDOCHES

This city (pop. 33,000), claimed to be the "Oldest Town in Texas" based on its origins as a Caddo Indian village, was founded around 800 AD. When Spanish explorers arrived in East Texas in the late seventeenth century, they encountered a Caddo tribe called the Nacogdoche. Until 1716, the settlement remained a Caddo Indian village, but when the Spanish began to build missions to claim the land, the demise of the village was all but certain. Don Antonio Gil Y'Barbo is credited with founding the town of Nacogdoches in 1779. The town has been the site of many battles for ownership, with the 1832 Battle of Nacogdoches being the first clash of the Texas Revolution. A group of Texas revolutionaries forced the Mexican garrison out of the town and freed East Texas from military rule. Today, the entire downtown district is listed on the National Register of Historic Places.

Nacogdoches's historic **Oak Grove Cemetery**, 200 North Lanana Street, is the final resting place of many legendary

Revolutionary-era Texans. On tree-studded land once owned by Empresario **Haden Edwards**, leader of the Fredonian Rebellion, the earliest marked burial is that of **Franklin J. Starr**, who died in 1837. Many graves from the early Spanish cemetery were relocated to this site after the county courthouse was erected on the original cemetery grounds in 1912. The earliest grave from that burial ground was marked, "Father Mendoza" 1718. There are several "false crypts" in this cemetery. Common in East Texas and Louisiana, such above-ground domed or rectangular sarcophagi primarily serve as grave markers with below-ground burials. This cemetery also has several granite Texas Centennial markers affixed with a bronze Texas star.

TEXAS CENTENNIAL MARKERS

In 1936, the State of Texas held a Centennial celebration, with expositions in Dallas and Fort Worth. To celebrate the 100-year anniversary of the founding of the Republic of Texas, the state authorized the construction of memorial museums, community centers, restoration of historical structures, park improvements, statues of important Texans, and more than 1,000 historical markers, grave markers, and highway markers throughout the state. The Texas Centennial markers, primarily fashioned from pink granite, in this and many other Texas cemeteries, were erected near and sometimes replaced broken tombstones as a way to honor those who played significant roles in the founding of Texas.

Haden Edwards (1771–1849) was born in Virginia. In 1823, Edwards joined Stephen F. Austin and others to persuade the Mexican government to allow American settlement in Texas. A lawyer known for his quick temper and abrasive personality, he made his money from land speculation and was often called upon to help finance Austin's endeavors. Because of their efforts, in 1824, Mexico authorized *empresarios* to introduce settlers to Texas, and Haden received a grant near Nacogdoches for 800 families.

His leadership was fraught with problems, and by 1826, his grant was revoked. This led to the "Fredonian Rebellion" of 1826–1827, which Haden led, along with his brother Benjamin. Haden called for a separation from Mexico in the name of an independent republic he called Fredonia, a re-representation of the word "Freedom." Stephen F. Austin, siding with the Mexican government, helped to quell this rebellion and Haden and his revolutionaries fled to Louisiana. Haden returned to Texas during the Texas Revolution, participated in the Battle of Nacogdoches, and continued to live there until his death. He died four months after his wife **Susannah Beall Edwards** (1774–1849), with whom he had thirteen children. A Texas Centennial monument marks their graves; their original markers lay flat, broken, and mostly illegible.

Thomas Jefferson Rusk (1803–1857) was the first secretary of war of the Republic of Texas and a general at the Battle of San Jacinto. Born in South Carolina, Rusk was practicing law in Georgia in 1834, when he learned that the managers of a gold mining company in which he had invested had embezzled a large sum of money and fled to Texas, then a part of Mexico. Rusk pursued them to Nacogdoches, but never recovered the money. Seeing opportunity, he stayed and became a citizen of Mexico in 1835. However, he was quick to support the move for Texas Independence, and he organized troops. He signed the Texas Declaration of Independence and chaired a committee to revise the Constitution for the Republic of Texas. In December of 1838, the Texas Congress elected Rusk to be chief justice of the Republic's Supreme Court.

A supporter of Texas's annexation, he was appointed by the Texas Legislature to the US Senate, serving from 1846 to 1857. While Rusk was in Washington D.C., his wife **Mary Frances Cleveland Rusk** (1809–1856) died of tuberculosis on April 26, 1856. Despondent over his wife's death and ill from a tumor at the base of his neck, on July 29, 1857, Rusk shot himself in the head with a rifle in his backyard, where one of his slaves found him.

The Texas Legislature appropriated $1,000 for the granite obelisk memorial marking the grave of Thomas Jefferson Rusk at Oak Grove. When it was unveiled on September 27, 1894, thirty-seven years after his death, all the businesses and schools in Nacogdoches were closed. At ten o'clock that morning, the Stone Fort Rifles, a brass band, and a school band led a procession from the town square to the cemetery, with many dignitaries and family members in attendance.

SLAVE BURIALS IN EAST TEXAS

Near the Rusk family plot is the grave of **Eliza Walker** (1817–1915), a former slave. A simple tablet stone marks her grave. Her inscription reads: "Our Mother, Sweetly Sleeps in Jesus." Walker is representative of the slaves residing in East Texas at the onset of the Civil War. Anglo settlers brought their slaves with them from the United States. Although the Mexican government had issued an order abolishing slavery throughout Mexico, Texas slaveholders resisted the edict and the Mexican government rescinded the ban. But on April 6, 1830, the ban was reinstated. Texans skirted the law by claiming their slaves were contracted workers. The state census of 1847 showed that Nacogdoches County had a population of 4,172 individuals, of whom 1,228 were enslaved. For the most part, former slaves were buried in the "Negro" sections of cemeteries, but in some cases, they were buried near the families that once owned them.

While the inscriptions on most tombstones are fairly simple—Name, Date of Birth, Date of Death—some are more elaborate, even explaining how the individual died. Take, for instance, the obelisk monument at Oak Grove Cemetery of **James Condy Raguet** (1822–1868), his sister **Mary Helen** (1833–1868), and their brother **Major Henry W. Raguet** (1825–1862). Their monument, which stands on a four-sided pedestal, gives tribute to each of them, describing how they died. The inscriptions on James's and Mary's slabs read, "Lost on Steamboat America on Ohio River, December 5, 1868." James and Mary died after the steamship they were on collided with the steamship *United States*. The night of December 4, the ships met at a dangerous bend on the Ohio River where other ships had met their demise. The *United States* was transporting barrels of petroleum oil, which caught fire and quickly spread to the *America*. James and Mary were among the seventy-four people who lost their lives either from burns or drowning.

Their brother Henry's slab reads, "He fell at the Battle of Glorietta, New Mexico." A defining battle of the Civil War, Glorietta Pass was where Union forces stopped the Confederate invasion of New Mexico Territory, an attempt to take the "West" for the South.

The Angel Marker in the center of the cemetery near the **Raguet** monument memorializes several members of the Clark family. The angel stands regally with an arm in the air, finger pointing up, and wings outstretched. **William Clark** (1798–1871), born in North Carolina, was a merchant, a signer of the Texas Declaration of Independence, and a legislator in the Republic of Texas. His namesake son **William Clark Jr.** (1828–1884), with whom he is often confused, was also a Texas state legislator. In the family plot, a Texas Centennial marker also commemorates Clark's contribution to Texas.

Caddo Burial Mound

A **Caddo Burial Mound** is one of the three mounds at the **Caddo Mounds State Historic Site** at 1649 State Hwy 21 West, twenty-five miles west of Nacogdoches. Temples and houses for community leaders were built on the largest mound. A lower platform mound was used for ceremonies. The third mound was the burial place of religious or political leaders.

From 800 AD until around 1300 AD, a Caddo group called the Hasinai inhabited this site. At the height of their mound-building culture, they were 250,000-people strong. The Caddo were farmers and enjoyed good growing conditions until the Great Drought from 1276 to 1299 AD, which affected an area extending to present-day California and disrupted many Native American cultures.

When the village was abandoned, the **burial mound** was about twenty feet tall and ninety feet in diameter. Archeological excavations beginning in 1939 determined that the burial site was built in successive stages and contained around ninety bodies in about thirty burial pits. Because of the type of objects found buried with the dead, archeologists believe that the mound was reserved for community leaders. Evidence also suggests family members or servants may have been sacrificed and interred along with them. Some graves were covered with a framework of poles and long grass, to make a roof-like covering over the bodies, and basket loads of soil were dumped on top of a mound to start a fresh surface. Layers of fresh earth were brought in to cover the tomb and make a new surface on the mound, and the cycle continued.

After abandoning this site, the Hasinai Caddo continued to live in their East Texas homeland in the Neches and Angelina River valleys through the 1830s, but ten years later, they moved to the Brazos River area because of Anglo-American colonization efforts. The US government placed them on the Brazos Indian Reservation in 1855, and then in 1859, they (about 1,050 people) were again displaced, this time to the Washita River in Indian Territory, now western Oklahoma, where a remnant of this once mighty tribe lives today.

COLDSPRING

Coldspring (pop. 900), the county seat of San Jacinto County, at the junction of State Highway 150 and Farm Roads 1514, 946, and 2025, is sixty-five miles north of Houston and adjacent to the Sam Houston National Forest. The land upon which Coldspring was founded was part of a 640-acre land grant deeded to Robert Rankin, an American Revolutionary officer. The name for the town, an agricultural and lumbering community in the nineteenth century, came from cold spring water found there. Its first post office opened in 1847 and was called Coonskin, named after a trading post, but within a year it was renamed Fireman's Hill. By 1850, the name was changed to Cold Spring, officially respelled Coldspring in 1894.

Laurel Hill Cemetery at 410 FM 1514 (Byrd Avenue) in Coldspring is named after the laurel trees that grew around the baptismal pool of Laurel Hill Baptist Church. An active cemetery, Laurel Hill has more than 600 gravesites, with the earliest marked grave dated 1850. **General James B. Davis** (1790–1859), adjutant-general of the Republic of Texas Army, donated the land for the cemetery in 1848. A historical marker details his service to the Republic of Texas above his slab crypt. Born in Virginia, Davis was also a US Army officer in the War of 1812.

A set of tombstones for a father, son, and daughter within an iron fence enclosure tell the sad and cryptic story of the Smith family. The Smiths were among many Southern families who came to the Republic of Texas attracted by inexpensive land acquisition. Patriarch **Robert Smith** (1812–1869) from South Carolina acquired 3,000 acres on the west side of the Trinity River in 1845 at a sheriff's sale. The chain of untimely deaths started with that of Smith's namesake son on January 21, 1869.

The gunshot-riddled body of Smith Jr. was found lying by the front gate of his family's plantation near the Trinity River, his head resting on his saddle. Because of where and how he was found, many believed he died at the hands of someone who knew him well. Nevertheless, his murder was never solved. His father

The tombstone of Robert E. Smith, who died at age twenty-two, is inscribed: "Assassinated in Cold Blood."

was so grief-stricken that he succumbed just five months later. Part of his tombstone inscription reads: "He never smiled again. Died of grief and broken spirits." A third grave marker is for daughter **Edith Smith** (1854–1872), aged seventeen. Upon her tombstone is carved a lamb sitting underneath a willow tree. Her inscription reads: "Died a victim to an experiment of surgery by Dr. Warren Stone Sr. of New Orleans." The type of surgery done on Edith was not given and is not known. Interestingly, Dr. Stone himself died seven months after his patient, on December 9, 1872, of Bright's disease, a kidney malfunction (see Victoria, Evergreen Cemetery, Alexander Borland, for another of Stone's cases). The grave marker (a slab crypt) for matriarch **Sarah Carson Smith** (1825–1891) is the only one that does not give the cause of death but is inscribed: "The Lord is my shepherd, I shall not want."

An impressive marble obelisk marker in this cemetery tells the sad story of the premature deaths of members of the Snow family. The first death memorialized on the monument is that of **Frances California Snow**, who died in 1854, "Aged 5 years, 10 mo. & 1 day." Her brother, **Samuel**, died in 1857, "age 5 Mos, 13 days." Eight months later, in June of 1858, their father, **Thomas**, died, "aged 43 years, 3 Mos, & 12 days." Carved on the Snow obelisk is a lyre with a broken string, entwined with a twig of leaves symbolizing the end of mortal life. According to his last will and testament, **Thomas H. Snow**, a planter with considerable property in Polk County, left the management of his plantation to his wife, Elvira Moorer, and divided the property equally among his surviving children. Another stipulation in his will was that his "body be decently buried," a request that his wife, who survived him by several years, took to heart.

JEFFERSON

Jefferson (pop. 2,000), founded in the 1840s, was named after Thomas Jefferson and conceived as a port city for its prime location on the Big Cypress Bayou. A major shipping hub for agricultural products, especially cotton, this port town became a destination for traders from cities as far away as Dallas, 167 miles west of Jefferson. After traveling by ox wagon with loads of cotton, they sold it to merchants for markets in New Orleans and St. Louis.

In 1845, after obstructions were removed from Big Cypress Bayou, steamboats were able to reach Jefferson from New Orleans. With the arrival of the first steamboat, Jefferson became a boom town where many early pioneers first set foot on Texas soil. From 1845 to 1875, a time considered Jefferson's "Golden Era" as a steamboat port, the town had a confluence of cultures and businesses, much like that of New Orleans. In 1873, the water level decreased after the Army Corps of Engineers removed a log jam known as the "Great Raft," a phenomenon unique to the Red River area in northwest Louisiana and northeast Texas in which an enormous log jam extending for more than 100 miles clogged the lower part of the river. Steamboat navigation was threatened, and after railroad service was extended, the town ceased to be a prominent port city and commercial center.

Oakwood Cemetery, East Webster and North Main, is a Texas Historic Cemetery in Jefferson with many noteworthy graves and monuments. Allen Urguhart donated the land, part of a Republic of Texas land grant, in 1846. The earliest marked grave is that of the **Reverend Benjamin Foscue**, who died of cholera on January 1, 1850. There are several "sections" within this cemetery of more than 15,000 interments, including Jewish, Catholic, and "Free Ground." National and state officials, merchants, bankers, railroad builders, religious and cultural figures, outlaws, a sensational murder victim, and even a Confederate spy, **John Burke** (1832–1871), whose old broken tombstone lies obscurely on the ground, are buried here.

The US soldiers sent during Reconstruction who died from suicide, drowning, and other mishaps, and various illnesses of the era—diarrhea, dysentery, venereal diseases, and pneumonia—are also buried here. Today, thanks to an effort by citizens of Jefferson, twenty-five headstones identify these "occupation" soldiers as the locals called them. The original graves were marked with wooden markers that did not last long. Recalling the bitterness of the war and Union occupation, no one was willing to replace them until the 1990s, when citizens obtained markers from the Department of Veteran Affairs.

The cemetery has several above-ground burial sites similar to those found in southern Louisiana, along with elaborately ornamental monuments, statues, and wrought-iron fencing. Many locally famous and infamous people are buried at historic Oakwood. One of them, **"Diamond Bessie,"** is buried within a small fenced enclosure with a fading tablet monument. Her story lives on because of her tragic death in 1877 and the subsequent murder trial that became known as "The Trial of the 19th Century."

Diamond Bessie was born Annie Stone in Syracuse, New York, in 1854. She became a mistress at age fifteen to a man whose last name was Moore and she began calling herself **Bessie Moore.** Her relationship with Moore was of short duration, but she kept his name. She later met a man named Abraham Rothschild, a traveling salesman for his father's jewelry business.

According to newspaper accounts, on January 17, 1877, they arrived in Marshall, seventeen miles south of Jefferson, and checked into a hotel there as husband and wife. Two days later, they took a train to Jefferson and checked into a hotel under the name Monroe. Last seen in Jefferson on Sunday, January 21 on the way to a picnic with her "husband," Bessie, aged twenty-three, was wearing a diamond

Diamond Bessie's grave is one of the most visited in Jefferson's Oakwood Cemetery.

necklace. Two days later, Rothschild left town alone. After a week or two of snow and bad weather, a young woman out looking for firewood found the body of a well-dressed woman sans jewelry near the remnants of a picnic lunch by a tree, a gunshot wound to her head. It didn't take long to identify the victim or the suspect.

Abraham Rothschild's trial was notorious in Texas. His family poured a lot of money into the defense, which attracted many prominent attorneys, while the Texas governor appealed for aid to the prosecution and allowed for two Texas assistant attorney generals to be involved. Rothschild was found guilty of murder in the first degree and was sentenced to death by hanging. In December 1878, a mistrial was declared and the sentence was vacated. A second trial, riddled with rumors of bribes and threats to the jurors, ended in a verdict of not guilty on December 20, 1880.

The citizens of Jefferson took up a collection to bury Bessie in Oakwood, but it was not until the 1930s that a benevolent citizen purchased her headstone, albeit inscribed with the wrong death date—December 31, 1876. The day of the picnic and date of her death would have been January 21, 1877. A garden club in Jefferson later financed a wrought-iron fence around Bessie's grave and put a bench next to it. A plaque with the incorrect death date is attached to the fence.

A notorious burial spot is that of **Jessie Robinson** (?–1871) and **William E. "Billy" Rose** (1834–1871). Robinson had killed the town cobbler and was rumored to have bribed his freedom out of jail. Rose was a town blacksmith who enjoyed his liquor and who'd killed a town marshal. On April 4, 1871, the two men killed each other in a gunfight in Jefferson. "Our community breathes more freely, being rid of two men that were a terror to all who knew them" was published in a Jefferson newspaper after their deaths. Boozers and murderers, they were buried together in a cheap wooden coffin in a single grave marked only by two short poles linked by a chain to symbolize their associated life of crime and violence. There is no tombstone and no inscription. Just two rusted poles and a thick rusted chain.

The **Russell-Bagby** family plot at the corner of Line and Magnolia Street within Oakwood Cemetery is noticeable for its beautiful wrought-iron fence, its poles fashioned to look like oak branches topped with acorns, its zinc and marble monuments, and the sad and intriguing inscriptions on some of the tombstones. A marble obelisk memorializes **James W. Russell** (1828–1871), his wife, **Lucy J.** (1833–1871), and their son **James D.** (1864–1871), who all died in a steamboat accident on the Mississippi River. The boilers of their steamer *W. R. Arthur*, from New Orleans to Louisville, exploded, tearing away the forward part of the cabin and decks. The boat caught fire and burned until the bow sank in the early morning hours of January 28, 1971. The Russells were among at least sixty who perished, according to a *New York Times* article published the next day. The inscription on their monument reads: "Father, Mother, and only surviving child lost on the Steamer *Arthur* near Memphis. God moves in mysterious ways, his wonders to perform." According to the 1870 census, James Sr. was a grocer in Jefferson.

A prime example of how well zinc monuments stand up over time is this 1880 grave marker in the Russell-Bagby family plot at Jefferson's Oakwood.

ZINC MONUMENTS

Zinc monuments seen in Texas cemeteries have stood up well over time, with inscriptions in relief easily readable, unlike those on early granite and marble monuments. They also came with easily removable panels. The Monumental Bronze Company in Bridgeport, Connecticut, made many zinc monuments seen in

> Texas cemeteries, such as the one for **T. M. Bagby Jr.** (1839–1880) in the Russell-Bagby family plot in Oakwood. According to Carol A. Grissom, Smithsonian Museum Conservation Institute, such white-bronze monuments, which were meant to remain unpainted, have survived remarkably well, likely because the cast metal was relatively pure (more than 99 percent zinc) and the joining metal was also composed of zinc.

The **Grigsby** monument is one of the largest and most impressive in Oakwood. **George Marshall Dallas Grigsby** (1852–1906), who was born in Kentucky and became a railroad magnate in Jefferson, commissioned the memorial for his wife, **Mattie Lee Rowell Grigsby** (1864–1904), who died during an operation in Portland, Oregon. George died two years after his wife. Having no children, Grisby left his entire estate of $5 million and some life insurance policies to his sister, who, according to an *Investor* magazine, was the wife of a "poor mechanic."

The more than twenty-foot-high Grisby monument is fashioned from marble and topped by an angel. On the four corners of the center pedestal are female figures dressed in Grecian robes. They represent four of the seven virtues sculpted in human form and commonly seen in cemeteries. The three theological virtues are Faith, Hope, and Charity and are the most prevalent. The four cardinal, or moral virtues are Fortitude, Justice, Prudence, and Temperance and are not as often depicted. Considering Mattie's epitaph, "She was pure in thought, sincere in purpose, sweet in spirit, noble and simple in life, consecrated unselfish in nature, and grandly beautiful," and how each of the figures is depicted, it is likely that the Grecian figures on the monument represent the virtues of Faith, Hope, and Charity, and perhaps, Fortitude.

SCOTTSVILLE

Named after **William Thomas Scott** (1811–1887), who moved to Texas from Louisiana in the 1830s, Scottsville (pop. 350), is twenty-one miles southeast of Jefferson, via Marshall, a major Confederate town during the Civil War. Scott, known as Colonel "Buck" Scott, established five plantations and owned 500 slaves, more than anyone else in Texas at the time. The Scott plantation home, built by slaves in 1840, was patterned after Jefferson Davis's Biloxi, Mississippi mansion. During the Civil War, the plantations provided provisions for Confederate troops. A post office was established in 1869. Today, Scottsville has a few businesses and a city government—the town was incorporated in 1962—but is known primarily for its cemetery, one of the most picturesque in Texas.

The **Scottsville Cemetery** on Farm Road 1998 near its juncture with Farm Road 2199 is a six-acre family cemetery founded in the 1840s with splendid monuments, crypts, and statues—more than 300 of 850 graves mark the extended family of the Scotts, Roses, and Yourees. In 1982, during an interview about the cemetery, a nursery saleswoman quipped, "We got more dead people here than live ones." The names upon the markers and the grandeur of the monuments demonstrate the relationships between pioneer families in the early development of East Texas and the wealth of a once prominent nineteenth-century plantation family.

At the entrance of this cemetery, an impressive twenty-five-foot-tall monument topped by a statue of a life-size Confederate private was erected in 1915 in memory of Scottville's Confederate soldiers whose names are etched upon the base and who are buried in the Scottsville cemetery.

The graves markers for town founder **William Thomas Scott** and his wife **Mary Rose Scott**—marble pillars topped with cloth-draped urns—are impressive, but simple, compared to the monuments of the much wealthier Youree family, into which their daughter, **Mary Elizabeth** married. William, born in Mississippi in 1811, lost most of his assets due to the war, recouping some funds after his disfranchisement was lifted by President Andrew Johnson and he returned to political life as a Texas Senator from 1879 to 1882. He died at his plantation in 1887 and was buried in the cemetery next to his wife, a formidable woman in her own right.

Mary Rose was born in Louisiana in 1819 and graduated from a boarding school in Copiah County, Mississippi. One of the nine children, she married William Scott in 1834, and they had twelve children. She and William moved to East Texas, and in 1839, her parents, **William Pinckney Rose** (1787–1851) and **Mary Vardaman Smith Rose** (1794–1863) joined them, bringing a large group, including their other children, several married, with their spouses and children, and many in-laws. While her husband was away from home, Mrs. Scott was the "Colonel." She managed her household and children, and the four other plantations in addition to the one on which she lived. She died in 1883, four years before her husband, while in New York.

Captain Peter Youree (1843–1914) and his wife **Mary Elizabeth Scott Youree** (1851–1934), who financed the Confederate monument, also paid for the beautiful rock chapel and the Weeping Angel monument for their son **William Scott Youree** (1872–1904), for which the cemetery is most famous, as mentioned in this book's introduction. William was the general manager for a wire nail factory in Monterrey, Mexico, at the time of his death and is said to have perished in an accident.

A magnificent open mausoleum with Roman columns covers the crypt of **Peter Youree**, a Shreveport businessman, banker, and politician, upon which is inscribed: "The shadow of his loss moved like an eclipse, darkening the world for me." His wife **Mary Elizabeth**, who died twenty years after her husband, is buried next to him. Her slab reads: "She was the Soul of her home."

The monument for Peter Youree's brother, **Henry Hudson Youree** (1856–1910), features a female figure in mourning, her chin resting on her hand. She holds a wreath, symbolizing the victory of the Redemption. Henry was a prominent businessman and philanthropist in Shreveport, Louisiana. He moved to Scottsville in 1876, working in the mercantile business, later becoming a railroad contractor and builder. After his marriage in 1887 to **Mary Rose Austin** (1866–1919), granddaughter of William and Mary Rose Scott, he and his wife moved back to Shreveport. After a long illness, he died

The Youree family plot includes many fine monuments and statues, including the famous Weeping Angel, seen here on the right.

and was taken by train back to Scottsville where he was buried in the family cemetery. The back of his large marble monument, upon which stands an urn, is no less impressive. Two palm fronds entwined through a wreath, signifying triumph over death, are carved into the stone. The accompanying inscription is most poignant: "All my heart is buried with you/All my thoughts go onward with you/Come not back again to labor/come not back again to suffer/soon your footsteps I shall follow/to the land of the hereafter!"

And yet, **Mary Rose**, demonstrating resilience, remarried a year later. In 1911, she married Edward Hughes Randolph (1858–1934), a prominent Shreveport attorney. Eight years later, Mary Rose died from ptomaine poisoning. Her body was conveyed by train to Scottsville.

WAVERLY

Known as Old Waverly, and no longer a town, all that remains of this once thriving nineteenth-century community is a cemetery, a Presbyterian church, and a rural subdivision of about fifty people. In 1852, 300 people from Alabama, including slaves, moved into the Waverly area and established a slave-plantation system. Locals believe the town was named after the Waverley novels of Sir Walter Scott, a place of "moonlight, magnolias, and landed gentry." The town, twenty-four miles southeast of Huntsville, was surveyed and incorporated in 1858. What killed the town was the refusal by Waverly leaders to give the Houston and Great Northern Railroad right-of-way, believing that it would bring "tramps and ignorance to the town and kill cattle." The town of New Waverly was established ten miles west of Waverly in 1870 to take advantage of the railroad. Today, that town has a population of about 1,000.

Old Waverly Cemetery, off Jim Browder Road and on Old Waverly Cemetery Road, is a Texas Historic Cemetery established on land originally purchased in 1853 by the Lewis and Scott families. In 1857, the Waverly Institute, an academy for both male and female students, purchased 200 acres, including the burial ground. Through the efforts of **Colonel Henry Marshall Elmore** (1816–1879), president of Waverly Institute Board of Trustees, twelve acres were officially set aside for the cemetery in 1873. An active cemetery with more than 900 gravesites, the old section is marked by several large trees draped in moss.

Elmore's wife **Elizabeth** (1816–1859) died twenty years before he did. The monument he chose for her grave includes a bas-relief carving of several people prostrate in grief over a tombstone. Another touching tombstone is that of their son **Hamlin Lewis**. Just one year old when he died in 1854, his tombstone has a bas-relief carving of an angel in flight carrying a child to heaven.

Three gravestones dated 1852 for **Hamlin F. Lewis, John Elliot Scott**, and **Robert Lindsey Scott** were reinterments rather than earlier burials. The three men were on their way to Texas from Alabama, contracted cholera, and died. They were buried along the way. Relatives of the men retrieved their remains and brought them back to Waverly for burial in 1859.

A pedestal tombstone topped by a marble column with a ragged edge, signifying untimely death, marks the grave of **Robert Lindsey Scott**, who died at age thirty-two. His inscription reads: "In the language of a brother on the occasion of his death. He was the impersonation [*sic*] of honesty, modesty, and kindness of heart. And this just estimate of his character it is proper to add that he died trusting in his Savior, and with the hope of a glorious immortality."

On the monument of **John Elliott Scott**, who died at age seventeen, is inscribed, among other text: "died while on the way from Alabama to his home in Texas. He was energetic, affable, generous, dutiful, and affectionate. Our first born and dearly beloved. This tablet is consecrated in his memory."

The Scott family, apparently eager to memorialize in words the life of their family members, engraved long epitaphs on their tombstones, including the fact that they were "in communion with the Methodist Episcopal Church South."

CONSORT AND RELICT

From the seventeenth through the nineteenth centuries, the terms "consort" and "relict" were used on tombstones. The term "consort" means that the woman was married and passed away prior to her husband, while a tombstone that says "wife" means the woman died after her husband. "Relict" is an archaic word that means "widow" and is rarely seen. An interesting family tombstone collection in the Old Waverly Cemetery that depicts this is that of **Mary Elizabeth Thompson** (1811–1860), "consort" of **Andrew J. Thompson** (1816–1887). Her marble pillar tombstone upon which stands an urn is substantial, especially when compared to the modest tombstone of **Mary Anna Thompson** (1844–1908), "wife" of A. J. Thompson. Mary Elizabeth was married to Andrew at the time of her death, while Andrew's second wife Mary Anna lived several years after his death. Interestingly, Mary Anna was not referred to as "relict," but rather as "wife," although she was a widow. The fact that his first wife's tombstone is so much more elaborate than that of his second may simply be because he was not there to select and pay for the memorial for her.

A Texas Ranger grave at Belknap Cemetery.

CHAPTER 3

FORTS TRAIL REGION

Lonely outposts on the western border, frontier forts were established primarily in Central West Texas to protect new settlers from Indians determined to protect their traditional hunting grounds. During the eighteenth-century Spanish era, *presidios* built to protect missions were unable to ward off Indian attacks and were abandoned by the dawn of the nineteenth century. The government of the Republic of Texas and private citizens erected some fortifications along the frontier from 1836 to 1845, but the major fort system occurred from 1848 to 1900, when the US Army built forty-four major posts and set up more than 100 temporary camps in Texas, the nation's largest military district.

The Forts Trail Region, which includes a Spanish presidio and eight historic frontier forts and nearby communities, encompasses a 650-mile driving loop within twenty-nine counties. Not all Texas forts are within this designated region, but the ones included exemplify the military posts of the nineteenth century. For the most part, no soldiers are buried at the forts. To save personnel and maintenance costs, the US government ordered soldiers' remains to be removed from fort cemeteries and reinterred at the National Cemetery in San

Antonio. Nevertheless, a few soldiers were not moved and others have memorials dedicated to them. The fort cemeteries became civilian burial grounds after the soldiers' remains were removed.

FORT BELKNAP

Established in 1851 as a northern anchor on the Texas frontier line of defense, Fort Belknap, now a state park near the present town of Graham, is 130 miles northwest of Dallas. This fort safeguarded travelers along a network of frontier trails, most notably the Butterfield Overland Mail route. Abandoned by federal troops in 1861, state troops of the Frontier Regiment under Colonel James M. Norris occupied the fort at various times throughout the Civil War. Federal troops re-occupied it in 1867, before it was finally abandoned the same year. A handful of buildings remain in the park-like setting, and a museum in the old commissary chronicles frontier history.

Belknap Cemetery, established in 1855, is across the street from Fort Belknap State Park on Highway 61. The remains of the twenty-eight soldiers interred in this cemetery were removed by order of the federal government in 1907 and reinterred at the National Cemetery in San Antonio, and it became a civilian cemetery. However, **Major Robert Simpson Neighbors** (1815–1859), born in Virginia, came to Texas in 1836 and is buried in Belknap Cemetery. A historical marker stands at his grave, a rectangular false crypt covered in mold and lichens. He was an Indian agent who reputedly had more influence over Texas's Indians than any other man of his era. A quartermaster in the Texas Army from 1839 to

1841, he was also a Texas Ranger. In 1842, Neighbors was taken prisoner by Mexican General Adrian Woll in San Antonio, along with many other Rangers and San Antonio officials. He spent eighteen months in Perote Prison in Veracruz, Mexico. After gaining his freedom, he began service in 1845 as an agent to various Texas tribes. Major Neighbors, who learned the Comanche language, later became the supervising agent for all the Indians in Texas. As a result, he was the target of much hostility from frontier civilians and soldiers.

After relocating several Texas Indian tribes to the Indian Territory in Oklahoma, he returned to Fort Belknap to write his report. As he left the courthouse on September 14, 1859, he was shot in the back. Sympathies, except among the Indian tribes and government officials, were with the killer, Edward Cornett, despite his reputation as a "drinking, blustering, dissolute desperado," who was also known to have murdered another man. Although several witnesses testified that Cornett had killed Neighbors, he initially was not held accountable for the crime. Eight months later, the law caught up with him. The local sheriff, along with a posse that included Texas Rangers (as the legend goes), shot and killed him in the hills near Belknap while trying to arrest him for the attempted murder of another man. Leading newspapers throughout the nation vindicated Neighbors's accomplishments and especially his quest for peace. He left a wife and two small children, one a newborn he never saw.

Three granite ledger markers in a row commemorate the burials of early Texas Rangers **Abraham Trigg Smith** (1798–1841), **Harvey Staten "State" Cox** (1839–1864), and **Thomas Fitzpatrick**

(1834–1864). Smith died in an Indian ambush while out with his ranging company. He'd served only three days before he was killed, leaving a wife and six children. Cox, who'd served in a Minute Men Texas Ranger troop in 1860, was the sheriff of Young County and well known on the western frontier when he was killed in 1864 by Indians during a cattle drive in the county. Thomas Fitzpatrick was also killed in 1864. In Charles Neuhaus's Company of Rangers, Thomas was working as a cowhand on the Young County ranch of Elizabeth Ann Sprague when he became the widow's third husband (see Fort Griffin Cemetery, Elizabeth Ann Carter Clifton). They married at Fort Belknap on August 26, 1862. Elizabeth's first husband had been murdered under mysterious circumstances; her second husband "disappeared," and Thomas himself was murdered eighteen months after the wedding, according to Company B Muster rolls. He was twenty-nine when he was buried at Belknap Cemetery.

FORT CHADBOURNE

Fort Chadbourne, named in honor of Second Lieutenant Theodore Lincoln Chadbourne, killed at the Battle of Resaca de la Palma during the Mexican War, was established in 1852. Located between Abilene and San Angelo on US Highway 277, twelve miles north of Bronte, several of the buildings of the old fort have been restored and are open to the public. A safe stopover for the Butterfield Overland Mail Company stagecoach four times a week, the fort had a fluctuating roster of as many as 450 or as few as fifty men stationed there. At the outbreak of the Civil War, federal troops left and the Texas Regimental Forces took over, some of whom were mustered into the Confederacy at the post. Following the Civil War, the Fourth US Cavalry re-occupied Fort Chadbourne. Because of the lack of water and supplies, along with deterioration of the buildings, the troops were moved to an area along the Concho River, where they established Fort Concho. Fort Chadbourne was decommissioned and used as a picket post until 1873. The land passed into civilian hands in 1877.

Fort Chadbourne Cemetery, also called the Old Fort Chadbourne Cemetery, is located south of US Highway 277, 2.2 miles east of the junction of that highway and State Highway 70 and is 1–1/2 miles from the historic site of Fort Chadbourne. According to resident historian Ann Pate, "out of thirty-one soldiers who were on our muster rolls and died or were killed only two are in the San Antonio National Cemetery."

Thomas Lawson Odom (1825–1897), who served in the Texas Legislature in 1882 during the time of the Fence Cutting Wars, was pivotal in passing the law making it a felony to cut another's fence in Texas. His marble pillar monument upon which stands a cloth-draped urn within a large fenced plot is one of the most imposing in Fort Chadbourne Cemetery. Born in Alabama, Odom moved to Texas in 1853. He enlisted in the Confederate service in Bexar County, serving in the San Antonio and Fredericksburg areas until the close of the war. He moved to old Fort Chadbourne, and in 1877, purchased land that included the fort and became a stock raiser. He and his wife **Lucinda Odom** (1829–1882) were the first of eight generations to call Fort Chadbourne home.

Texas Ranger **Private Benjamin Goodin Warren** (1843–1885), born in Tennessee, was shot and killed in Sweetwater, Texas, to keep him from testifying in a trial involving fence cutting. Warren had obtained warrants against several men for cutting barbed wire fences around ranches so they could graze their cattle on property belonging to other cattlemen. While he was in a hotel office talking with friends, a shot was fired from outside striking him in the head, killing him instantly. Three men who had been charged with fence cutting were accused of Warren's murder. Two of them were convicted and sentenced to life in prison. However, one of the convictions was overturned. It is unknown if the third suspect was ever charged. Private Warren had served as a Texas Ranger for Company E, Frontier Battalion, for ten months. He was survived by his expectant wife and eight children. His ninth child was born eight months after his murder. His marble tombstone, a small pillar on a pedestal, etched with the Masonic emblem, is inscribed: "Farewell my wife and children all. From you, a Father Christ doth call."

William Harrison Robinson (1842–1910) was shot and killed by a longtime neighbor. A newspaper article describing the murder of the sixty-eight-year-old man indicated that the shooting took place in Robinson's own field near Fort Chadbourne. The killer, George Moore, a neighbor who Robinson had known for more than twenty years, refused to give a reason for the shooting, although later it was revealed to have been about a "fence dispute." Robinson's tablet tombstone is simple, carved with his initials and last name and the dates of his birth and death. He left a wife and ten children.

FENCE CUTTING WARS

Several of the individuals buried at **Old Fort Chadbourne Cemetery** were involved in the Fence Cutting Wars, a conflict between cattlemen who wanted to retain the practice of occupying open range and those who purchased barbed wire to be able to fence their land within permanent ranches. While enclosing their own land, some ranchers also enclosed public land, while others strung wire around farms and ranches belonging to others. In some cases, the fenced land prevented access to roads and schools; this led to armed bands of "fence cutters" who roamed about at night, destroying fences. Damage due to the wrecking of fences by 1883 was estimated at $20 million. After heated debates, the legislature in 1884 made fence cutting a felony punishable by one to five years in prison, while the fencing of public lands or lands belonging to others knowingly and without permission was made a misdemeanor. Other measures were put in place, which ended most of the fence troubles, with sporadic outbreaks of cutting continuing for several decades, especially during droughts.

FORT CONCHO

Fort Concho, now Fort Concho National Historic Landmark, was established in 1867 along the banks of the Concho River to protect frontier settlements and quell hostile threats. Soldiers were also tasked to map West Texas as they patrolled. That same year, the town of San Angelo had its beginning when a trading post "over the river" from Fort Concho was established. The fort and the city became synonymous. Constructed of native limestone, Fort Concho consisted of at least forty buildings, covered more than 1,600 acres, and served as regimental headquarters for the Fourth and Tenth Cavalry. Elements of all four regiments of the Buffalo Soldiers were stationed at the post during its active period. At full strength, Fort Concho supported 400–500 men made up of companies of infantry and troops of cavalry, staff officers, and support personnel. In June 1889, the last soldiers marched away from Fort Concho and the fort was deactivated.

Today, Fort Concho National Historic Landmark, 630 S. Oakes Street, San Angelo, encompasses most of the former army post and includes twenty-three original and restored fort structures. The old frontier army post is now a historic preservation project and museum owned and operated by the City of San Angelo, Texas.

MEDAL OF HONOR HEADSTONES

The bodies of 137 Fort Concho soldiers and military dependents who died at the fort during the Indian Wars era were disinterred in 1884 and 1889 and reburied at the National Cemetery in San Antonio. However, between the fort's Headquarters and Quartermaster building stand a stone interpretive marker and five Medal of Honor headstones, the only ones in the nation that are not in a federal, state, or local cemetery. The Medal of Honor, the highest US military decoration, is awarded in the name of Congress for achievements above and beyond the call of duty. The memorial headstones were erected in this place because the burial ground for these Indian Campaign Congressional Honor of Medal recipients was unknown at the time of the dedication in 1992. The tombstones memorialize **Sergeant Edward Branagan** (1846–?) for gallantry in action at Red River, Texas, September 29, 1872; **Private Gregory Mahoney** (1850–?) and **Corporal William McCabe** (1848–?) for gallantry in attack of a large party of Cheyennes near Red River, Texas, September 26–28, 1874; **Private William O'Neill** (1848–?) for bravery in action at Red River, Texas, September 29, 1872; and **Private John O'Sullivan** (1850–1907) for gallantry in a long chase after Indians at Staked Plains, Texas, December 8, 1874.

FORT GRIFFIN

Fort Griffin, now Fort Griffin State Historic Site, 1701 North US Highway 283, fifteen miles northeast of Albany, was established in 1867 along the westernmost border. First named Camp Wilson, the outpost was renamed Fort Griffin in honor of the late Major General Charles Griffin who had been the commander of the army's Department of Texas and designed plans for the new fort. Set on a hill above the Clear Fork of the Brazos River, most of the buildings were rough log houses, tents, and frame buildings with earth and canvas roofs. With the threat of Indian depredations gone and civilization pushing even farther westward, Fort Griffin was no longer necessary. The bodies of fifty-one soldiers and six children were removed from the fort military cemetery before it was closed, and reinterred at the National Cemetery in San Antonio. At sundown, on May 31, 1881, the US flag at the fort was lowered for the last time.

The town of Fort Griffin, also called "The Flat" and "Hide Town," developed simultaneously with the fort, providing soldiers with gaming tables, saloons, restaurants, livery stables, and bordellos. With the closing of the fort, the town of Fort Griffin—once a den of rabble-rousers, gamblers, outlaws, and buffalo hunters—was left as a small rural community with a school, post office, and a general store. A Texas Historical Marker stands at the entrance of the frontier town of Fort Griffin and there are several restored buildings, including a saloon, jail, blacksmith, and general store. Within the vicinity of this town and the Fort Griffin Historic Site are three cemeteries, one for "negroes" and two other civilian cemeteries.

Fort Griffin Cemetery is on a hill near the old frontier town of Fort Griffin (US 283, then west on CR 184 for ¾ of a mile). Turn right into the town at the historical markers and then take a left on the gravel road between the Fort Griffin Lodge Hall and the farmhouse. You will pass a creek. Go through the first cattle guard and almost immediately turn left onto a fork in the road that will take you up a hill. There is another fork in the road. Stay right and continue until you reach the top of the hill where the cemetery will be on your left. From the town, the cemetery is about 1.2 miles. A forlorn and abandoned cemetery with more than twenty-five tombstones dating from 1878 to 1900, there are also many more graves that are unmarked. The

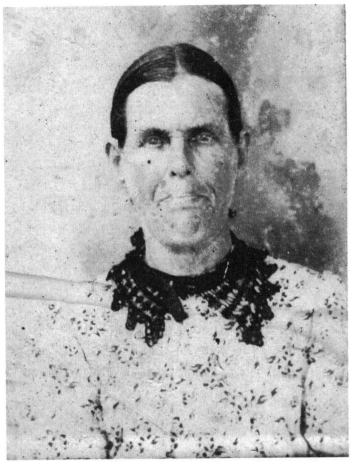

The most renowned person in the Fort Griffin Cemetery, Elizabeth Ann Carter Clifton, is buried in an unmarked grave.
Fort Belknap Historic Site, Commissary Museum.

families buried here include several prominent families in Fort Griffin history and in that of Albany, where many of the families moved when the railroad bypassed the town.

The life of **Elizabeth Ann Carter Clifton** (1825–1882) illustrates the tragedies that often befell women in the Indian territories of Texas. Born in Alabama, at age sixteen Elizabeth married a free black man, Alexander Carter, the first of four husbands. They had two children when they moved near Fort Belknap, where she managed a ranch and ran a boarding house while her husband and father-in-law operated a cargo business. In 1857, her husband and his father were murdered. A year later, Elizabeth was briefly married to Lieutenant Owen A. Sprague, a soldier stationed at Fort Belknap, who "disappeared" eight months later.

She continued to be one of the most successful women on the frontier. Her boarding house prospered after the Butterfield Overland Mail began stopping in Fort Belknap in 1858. When she was thirty-six years old, she married her third husband, Thomas Fitzpatrick, one of three cowhands working on her ranch, on August 26, 1862. He was murdered eighteen months later (see his profile under Fort Belknap).

Two years later, her Young County ranch was attacked by Plains Indians—an event that became known as the Elm Creek Massacre, the inspiration for the 1956 John Wayne movie, *The Searchers*. Her daughter Mildred and Mildred's infant son were murdered. Elizabeth; her son Elijah, age thirteen; and two granddaughters, Lottie, age five, and Milly, age two, were taken captive. Elijah was killed two days later. Elizabeth was held captive for a year at a Kiowa camp in northwestern

Kansas. She was found on November 2, 1865, by Indian Agent Jesse H. Leavenworth with a small white girl, Alice Taylor (see Junction Cemetery), working as slaves in the camp of Kiowa Chief Sun Boy. She was told that Milly had frozen to death earlier that year, but Elizabeth believed she was alive, which proved to be correct, although she did not live to see her granddaughter again. Lottie was released after nine months with tattoos on her arms and a dime-sized moon on her forehead (see Boy's Ranch "Old Tascosa," Casimero Romero Cemetery).

Two years after her capture, Elizabeth returned home and was reunited with Lottie. In 1869, she married her fourth husband, **Isaiah Clifton** (1814–1880), a Parker County farmer and widower. They moved to Fort Griffin with Lottie and Clifton's youngest four children to manage the landholdings inherited by Lottie after her mother's death.

Elizabeth outlived her fourth husband by two years. She remained at Fort Griffin until her death on June 18, 1882, at age fifty-seven. She was buried beside Isaiah in the mesquite-covered cemetery near the Clear Fork of the Brazos. Both of their graves are unmarked.

Samuel James Ward Sr. (1846–1881), owner of the two-story rock house now enclosed within Fort Griffin State Park, is buried within a rock enclosure with a tablet tombstone inscribed "Father at Rest." From his obituary: "He came to this country a poor cowboy in 1868 or 1869 and by his own industry and frugality he accumulated a competence, but like most of us he labored hard to add to his possessions and it is believed that overexertion, exposure, and mental labor were the prime cause which led to the disease which proved fatal to him. He has gone to join one of his children in another world, leaving a wife and five children, and a host of friends to mourn his death. He will be buried today by the Masonic fraternity, he being an honest member of that body."

On a ridge on CR 184, approximately a mile west of the old town site is a **Negro Cemetery,** indicated by a Texas Historic Cemetery Marker, which contains about twelve graves, none visible from the road. Three individuals buried in this cemetery are **Elijah Earls,** who died in 1880 and was described as a "tonsorial artist" or barber; **Marriah McKay Williams** (1781–1891), who came to Texas before the Civil War as a free black; and **James Lowe,** who died in 1880. The other burials are unknown.

Old Fort Griffin Cemetery is a civilian cemetery across the street from the historic fort site and within the state park land on the east side of US 283. Located not far from the military cemetery that was abandoned and displaced by the highway, it is visible from US 283 within the fenced park. It has approximately fifty gravesites, most marked with a single stone or stacks of stones. A few graves are enclosed by rock walls in the form of a crypt. Two such rock enclosures, topped with large stone slabs are inscribed: "I. H. S./**Virgil J. Hervey**" and "**Little Lula Hervey.**" Virgil, according to a May 10, 1879, *Fort Griffin Echo*, was killed at age twenty-two by A. L. "Long John" Mont, and the June 1880 issue of the same paper included the following about Little Lula, the infant daughter of Mr. And Mrs. Julien F. Hervey, who died at age ten months: "Little Lula had from birth been sickly and now, before the troubles of this world can be known to her, her spirit has been called to the God who gave it." Lula's father Julien had once been an acrobat in a circus and was working in the town of Fort Griffin as a restaurateur and as a barkeep in a saloon. He was reported to have been killed by a buffalo and may have been buried next to his brother Virgil. An upright tombstone for Virgil, dated 1855–1877, was removed from the cemetery by park officials and is stored with another intact tombstone found in this cemetery—that of the infant son of J. P & C. J. Taylor, who died in 1883 at age one month.

FORT MCKAVETT

Fort McKavett is forty-one miles northwest of Junction at 7066 FM 864. One of the best preserved among Texas frontier forts, it was established in 1852 for the protection of newly arrived immigrants and as a way station for California-bound travelers. Initially called Camp on the San Saba, it was renamed in honor of Captain Henry McKavett, killed in the 1846 Battle of Monterrey during the Mexican-American war. Seven years later it was abandoned because the need for Indian protection waned and travelers to California found a more southerly route. However, in 1868, the army reopened the fort as a military post because of increased hostilities between local Comanche Indians and settlers after the Civil War.

For the next fifteen years, until 1883, Fort McKavett served as a major supply depot providing food and provisions for West Texas forts, military campaigns, and scientific and mapping explorations. After the military operations ended and soldiers left, settlers began to move into the vacant buildings, and the town of Fort McKavett was founded.

Eighty-five years later, on May 17, 1968, the fort, which encompasses 140 acres, was designated a state historic site, and five years after that, in 1973, the last residents moved out of the original buildings.

The historic **Fort McKavett Cemetery** is located in a tree-studded field, about a quarter mile northwest of the entrance to the Fort McKavett State Historic site at FM 245 (Fort McKavett Cemetery Road). The post cemetery was established at the time of the founding of Fort McKavett, but a community graveyard was already on site. Soldiers, their families, and area civilians were buried there during the heyday of the fort. According to fort records, ninety-one soldiers were buried at Fort McKavett Cemetery between 1852 and 1883. Of these, at least twenty-nine were Buffalo soldiers—the first black Americans to serve in frontline regular units of the Army infantry and cavalry. The remains of military personnel and some family members who died at the fort were moved in 1883 and reinterred in the San Antonio National Cemetery. However, most of the civilians were not removed.

One cannot read the grave marker for **John Westlyn Vaden** (1849–1886) under a large tree at Fort McKavett Cemetery without feeling a tinge of outrage at his obviously senseless murder: "Shot in Cold Blood While Unarmed in Ft. McKavett by the Gunfighter, Ben Daniels." However, the reality of what happened to Vaden—who once served as a Texas Ranger, was elected justice of the peace in Menard County, and was a deputy sheriff there at the time of his death—is quite different from what the marker, placed years after his death, implies.

An article in the November 1924 issue of *Frontier Times*, titled "Killing of John Vaden at Ft. McKavett," by John Warren Hunter, tells

The grave marker for John Westlyn Vaden evokes a sense of outrage until one learns the whole story.

the tale. Hunter, who was acquainted with Vaden, wrote: "This is a fascinating account of the son of a good man, who turned rotten. Possessing a hot temper and a furious desire for violence, Vaden wreaked terror and murder wherever he went. Finally, at Fort McKavett he got his comeuppance."

While it is true that Vaden was not in possession of a gun at the time of his death (his wife having hidden it, knowing that he was raging drunk), he did have a weapon. He went back to town, stormed into a mercantile, and picked up a long wooden pole with a sharp iron hook attached to the end. He went around town terrorizing townspeople with the pole. He came upon Daniels, with whom he'd had an altercation earlier in the evening, and began to prod him with the pole. Daniels, a Menard County deputy sheriff who also worked as a bartender at the local saloon, asked him to desist several times, but Vaden continued his advance. Finally, Daniels opened fire. Four shots went wild. The fifth killed Vaden. According to Hunter, the community was relieved that they no longer had to deal with the likes of Vaden, whose violence was often fueled by liquor. He was buried the following day in Fort McKavett cemetery with only his widow, his children, and a few others in attendance. Hunter wrote, "He sleeps in an unmarked grave." The grand jury, after hearing the evidence, decided not to prosecute Daniels for the killing.

Mrs. Annor Braddocks (1854–1872), an African American laundress and a soldier's wife, is buried at Fort McKavett Cemetery. Marking her grave is a simple but substantial tablet tombstone covered in lichens. It is inscribed: "Mrs. Annor Braddocks of Pulaski, Tenn, Died Jan 27th 1872, Aged 18 years." Laundresses at Fort McKavett often did laundry for nineteen men for $1 per soldier a month, including housing and food. While they made $19 or more a month for this labor-intensive work, army privates made $13. All residents of the fort, whether black or white, were buried together in this cemetery.

All posts had morgues. At Fort McKavett, bodies were taken to the Dead House, which was connected to the infirmary. The body was washed and dressed for viewing by family and friends. A military procession escorted deceased soldiers to the cemetery for a gravesite ceremony.

FORT PHANTOM HILL

Fort Phantom Hill, fourteen miles north of Abilene and thirty-five miles southwest of Albany, was a US Army and Confederate Army installation on the Clear Fork of the Brazos River. In the Comancheria, the area was long inhabited by Comanche Indians who called the area Ghost Dance Hill. Studded with a large grove of post oak, two or more feet in diameter, visible up to ten miles away, the hill appeared like a mirage in the prairie and seemed to tremble in the heat waves of bright mornings.

The fort, originally known as the Post on the Clear Fork of the Brazos River, was an active military post from 1851 to 1854. An inadequate water supply and little timber for buildings contributed to its closure after only three years. A few years later, fire destroyed most of the buildings. In 1858, the old fort became a Butterfield Stagecoach stop and a way station on the Southern Overland Mail route. During the Civil War, the Confederacy's Frontier Battalion inhabited what was left of the fort. By 1871, it was used as a subpost of Fort Griffin, near Albany, Texas, and by troops engaged in Indian campaigns. In 1875, a town grew up around the ruins of the old fort. The town became a buying and shipping point for buffalo hides and eventually had more than 500 residents. By the 1890s, Fort Phantom Hill was for the most part abandoned. An 1892 letter written to the *San Antonio Express* related that Fort Phantom contained nothing but "one hotel, one saloon, one general store, one blacksmith shop, and 10,000 prairie dogs."

Today, the thirty-eight-acre site is owned by the Fort Phantom Foundation, which has done much to develop the remnants of the fort—an intact stone powder magazine, a stone guardhouse, an almost-intact commissary, and several stone chimneys from the original buildings. A cemetery with five graves, each surrounded by stone, was about 100 yards west of the commissary and a grave for the son of Lieutenant W. W. Burns was sixty yards southwest. The infant died in January 1852; part of his gravestone was stolen and used as a grindstone.

Phantom Hill Cemetery, also referred to as Fort Phantom Hill Cemetery, is on Farm Road 600, 1–1/2 miles north of its intersection with Farm Road 1082, near a new Fort Phantom Baptist Church building. The cemetery, which contains more than 600 graves on flat prairieland, is still being used. The earliest existing marker is dated 1880, for **J. B. Carpenter**, a local rancher born in Texas, who took ill and died at age thirty-seven. A broken tablet stone lying on the ground marks his grave, near that of **Thomas Fletcher "Phantom Hill" Scott**.

Scott, born in Alabama in 1830, was a grocery merchant who settled with his family in Phantom Hill in Jones County in 1879 after learning that the town was a railroad station for the Texas and Pacific Railway and that many stockmen were raising livestock in the area. He set up his mercantile in the old Fort Phantom magazine building, a room in which ammunition and explosives had been stored. Scott became the town's first postmaster the year he arrived. People in the community called him "Phantom Hill Scott."

Scott wrote a memoir a few years before his death in which he mentioned some of the earliest burials in the area being near Deadman Creek, originally called Willow Creek, not far from the post. By the time the Scott family arrived, it was already being called Deadman Creek because of deaths that had occurred either in or near the creek. The first, according to Scott, was a soldier, surname Morehead, who froze to death when a norther hit in late December 1850. A man Scott described as a "settler for troops" told him the story of the soldier's death.

An Apache Indian guide had advised the commanding officer not to move the garrison from its camp because a terrible norther was brewing. The officer did not heed his advice and ordered the military caravan to break camp and start the trek toward Phantom Hill. They were on open prairieland when the norther hit that evening, with freezing wind, sleet, and snow. The mules and oxen pulling the soldiers' wagons were stuck in muck and snow for hours. By the time they straggled into Willow Creek crossing, where they found shelter among the trees lining the creek, and timber to build fires, they realized Morehead was missing. Some soldiers went back along the route and found him frozen to death. They buried him near the creek crossing where they had assembled, covering his grave with a two-foot-high wall of rock and cement. According to Scott, that was when locals began referring to the area as Deadman Creek. Scott lamented that Morehead was not reinterred in the Fort Phantom cemetery, which by 1879 had five or six graves, each surrounded by stone, although each grave had sunk into the ground "about a foot or more." Instead, the soldier was left by the creek, his gravesite a visible reminder of his tragic death for years to come.

Captain William J. Maltby, who was with the military caravan, gave a similar account of the man's death with a few differences. The man's name was James Morehead. He was a teamster and "died of the cold despite efforts to save him" and was buried near the camp. His death was recorded as being in November 1851. Also lost in the norther were "twenty-seven mules and oxen—frozen to death."

Scott himself passed away on December 5, 1913, at age eight-three, according to his death certificate. His flat granite marker is no longer visible, covered by weeds, flowering plants, and a thorny bush. An early photo of his marker shows the following inscription: "Father, T. F. Scott 1831–1914," etched with the incorrect years of his birth and death.

FORT RICHARDSON

Sixty miles northwest of Fort Worth, Fort Richardson, named after Union General Israel B. "Fighting Dick" Richardson, who died at the Battle of Antietam during the Civil War, was the northernmost army outpost in Texas and the anchor of the defensive line of fortifications in West Central Texas. Located in Jacksboro at 228 Park Road 61, this fort was seventy miles from Indian territory when it was established in 1867. From 1868 to 1873, Fort Richardson was strategically the most important post in Texas, facilitating settlement in the north-central region. In 1872, it housed more than 650 officers and soldiers, the largest garrison among military installations in the United States.

When the army defeated the remnant Comanche and Kiowa Indians at Palo Duro Canyon in 1874, a victory that permanently settled the tribes onto reservations in Oklahoma, army leaders saw no need to continue maintaining the post. It was abandoned in May 1878 and used as an Indian school for a few years. The fort was declared a state historic site in 1963 and came under the management of the Texas Parks and Wildlife Department. In 1973, it reopened as "Fort Richardson State Historic Park," comprising seven restored original buildings, including the post hospital, officers' quarters, powder magazine, morgue, commissary, guardhouse, and bakery.

Behind the officer's quarters in what is now Fort Richardson State Park is a remnant of the **Fort Richardson Cemetery**, with only two marked graves, that of **William E. Stanton** (1871–1874) and his brother **Robert F. Stanton** (1873–1874). The children, who both died of whooping cough, were the sons of a teamster who hauled supplies to the post.

The remains of thirty-seven soldiers and a few civilians were moved to San Antonio National Cemetery in 1883. The burial register for this military post, a record of the US Office of the Quartermaster General, indicates that the soldiers all died between 1869 and 1873 of various causes, including drowning, gunshot wounds, dysentery, meningitis, consumption, murder, acute alcoholism, congestive fever, typhoid, remittent fever, chronic diarrhea, delirium tremors, Bright's disease, and pleuropneumonia. Some were simply "found dead."

LOYAL VALLEY

An unincorporated farming community (pop. 50) off FM 2322, Loyal Valley is halfway between the cities of Mason and Fredericksburg via US 87 N—eighteen miles southeast of Mason and twenty-four miles north of Fredericksburg. Established in 1858, Loyal Valley became a stagecoach stop between San Antonio and the western forts. John O. Meusebach, founder of Fredericksburg and famous for his treaty between the Comanche chiefs and German settlers, named the new settlement Loyal Valley, moving there with his family in 1859. According to his granddaughter, he named the area for his personal loyalty to the Union during the American Civil War. Meusebach operated a general store and stage stop, served as justice of the peace, as notary public, and as the community's second postmaster in 1873. Today, only a few old buildings exist in what was once the town of Loyal Valley.

The **Loyal Valley Cemetery** is on House Mountain Road off FM 2322 across the road from a small nineteenth-century stone church. Within a fenced field behind a large metal storage building, the cemetery contains about sixty marked and many more unmarked graves, and has an eerie atmosphere. A large dead tree, its naked branches reaching to the sky, stands next to a false crypt of crumbling stone and concrete within which a large shrub is growing. Rusted wrought-iron fences surround graves that no longer bear markers. The markers in others are moldy and hard to read. Nevertheless, the history of the people interred makes it a must-see cemetery.

Stonemason **Philip Buchmeyer** (1820–1891), buried in the cemetery next to his wife **Augusta** (1833–1911), built the church across the street from the cemetery. Augusta Lehmann was a widow when she married Philip in the early 1860s. Only their married surname is etched on the top of the tombstone they share, along with the inscriptions "Father" and "Mother" and their birth and death dates. Augusta was the mother of two of the most famous children kidnapped in Texas, **Herman Lehmann**, age ten, and **Willie Lehmann**, age eight, both also buried in Loyal Valley Cemetery. A State of Texas Historical Marker erected at the entrance of the small cemetery chronicles the boys' capture.

Herman and Willie were kidnapped by a raiding party of Apache Indians on May 16, 1870, as they were scaring birds

One of the most poignant memorials in the Loyal Valley Cemetery is this double marker of white marble inscribed in German for a mother and baby daughter.

away from wheat fields near their home at their mother's request. Five days after the kidnapping, soldiers from Fort McKavett caught up with the raiding party. Willie was released, but the Apaches fled with Herman, who lived with Apache and Comanche tribes for the next eight years, culminating in a move to an Indian reservation near Fort Sill, where he lived with Comanche Chief Quanah Parker and his family. After Herman's return to his family, whom he thought had been killed during the initial raid, he had a hard time adjusting. His autobiography, *Nine Years among the Indians* (1927), details his life during his captivity and was called "one of the finest captivity narratives in American literature" by Texas folklorist J. Frank Dobie.

The pink Texas granite tombstone for **F. Herman Lehmann** (1859–1932) is small and simple, with a palm leaf etched at the top, along with his name, birth and death dates. A small curb surrounds the perimeter. The tombstone of **William F. Lehmann** (1861–1951), also small and simple, is of gray granite titled with "Father," his name and birth and death dates. It is also surrounded by a small curb.

Bertha Lehmann (1860–1885), who died at age twenty-five, was the wife of **Gustave Lehmann** (1855–1940), elder brother of Herman and Willie. **Emma** (1885–1885) was their four-month-old daughter. The translation for Bertha's inscription is; "Love that unites us on Earth/Blooms continuously forever in Heaven,/Where no eye weeps over separation any longer/And [love] unites sinless souls there." The baby's inscription reads: "A white rose blossom/A friend plants on thy grave/Sleep, since with loveliness and God/Thou art rocked in its fragrance."

MASON COUNTY HOODOO WAR

Tim Williamson, murdered on May 13, 1875, by masked vigilantes who accused him of cattle theft, is in an unmarked grave in **Loyal Valley Cemetery**. He was a victim of the Mason County Hoodoo War that erupted over cattle rustling and pitted Germans against American-born residents. Armed bands, taking the law into their own hands, raided settlements and conducted midnight hangings throughout the county. Seeking revenge, Williamson's adopted son, Scott Cooley, a farmer who'd been in Texas Ranger Company D, assembled a gang of desperadoes who rode through the countryside creating chaos and terror. Cooley killed almost a dozen men, scalping one of them, and was arrested in the spring of 1876 in Burnet, Texas. He escaped soon after his arrest with the help of his gang. Nevertheless, he was dead by the summer at age twenty-four. Some say he died of "brain fever," while others say that he was poisoned. By the fall of 1876, the feud had waned, although several legal proceedings were still ongoing. A fire at the Mason County Courthouse on January 21, 1877, destroyed all the records related to the feud, in effect ending the Mason County Hoodoo War.

MENARD

Menard (pop. 1,300), once known as Menardville, was formed in 1858 and became the county seat in 1871. Thirty-seven miles west of

Mason and twenty-three miles east of Fort McKavett and situated on the banks of the San Saba River, the town was founded on the site of the Spanish Mission San Sabá and the Presidio of San Luís de Amarillas, both established in April 1757. The presidio was built to protect New Spain's northern frontier from Comanche raiders, but because of its isolation, it suffered repeated attacks and was finally abandoned in 1770. Menard settlers used stone from the old presidio to build homes and fences. By the mid-1880s, the town had a church, a school, several stores, and 150 residents, with livestock, wool, and hides as its principal products.

The **Opp-Bihl Cemetery**, off Highway 190 on Dunagan Road, between Menard and Fort McKavett, is a small family cemetery on private property established in the 1880s on a bucolic hilltop setting with a backdrop of the San Saba River. Rancher **John D. Sheen** donated the small parcel for the cemetery and started with the burial for "Baby Sheen" who died after twelve days on April 5, 1882. This grave is in the front section within a fenced plot, a large cactus growing inside. Only a few tombstones and one unmarked grave are in the front section.

The rear portion of the cemetery, separated by a fence, has the graves of seven members of the Bihl family, five children who passed away between 1888 and 1902, and their parents **Frank Edward Bihl** (1850–1929) and **Mary Eastwood Bihl** (1847–1918), and Mary's brother, **William L. Eastwood** (1844–1890).

The patriarch of the clan, **Frank E. Bihl**, a Texas Ranger, was well known in Menard County and beyond, and his life is indicative of the fortitude and resilience necessary to survive in that tumultuous time. His parents were immigrants from Alsace, France, part of the Castro

William Eastwood's tablet tombstone, with the unusual carving of a hand pointing up with a cigarette, is inscribed, "He died as he lived, a brave cowboy."

Colonists who established the town of Castroville in 1844. Frank's tombstone is inscribed with a birth year of 1848. His death certificate indicates a birth year of 1847; nevertheless, Frank was actually born in 1850, according to his baptismal certificate (the most reliable source for birth year), and the 1850 San Antonio census, where he is listed as being five months old.

Frank was an orphan by the time he was eight, both his parents having passed away in 1858. He lived at St. Mary's Academy in San Antonio, where he was schooled to become a Roman Catholic priest, and his facility for languages was nurtured. According to a *Menard County History* account, he could read and write nine languages, seven fluently. His calling to the priesthood ended when he saw "A little girl in a red calico dress."

Beginning at age fourteen, he worked as a freighter between San Antonio and the Texas forts and often served as an interpreter for the government. In 1872, Bihl joined Texas Ranger Minute Company V stationed out of Castroville to help protect farms and ranches from Indian depredations. After his one-year term ended in 1873, he entered the cattle business, ranging his stock between Bandera and San Antonio. Around this time, he met Mary Eastwood Zimmerlie, a married woman with two sons who lived in Castroville. She and her husband divorced and she married Frank in 1876. By 1883, they'd settled near Fort McKavett, where Frank was employed as a cowboy at the SXS Ranch, eventually acquiring his own ranch in Sutton County. By 1900, Mary had had eighteen children, only six still living, and in 1910, Frank retired, moving the family back to Fort McKavett. Frank and Mary had been married for forty-one years at the time of Mary's death in 1918.

A few years after his first wife's death, Frank met Annie K. Seaton Haney (1887–1982), a widow with four daughters, who worked as a housekeeper for a friend. He proposed in 1923; he was seventy-two and she was thirty-six. When they went to get the marriage license, he is said to have quipped to the clerk, "I'm a little young to be getting married, but I have permission from my parents." They married on October 8, 1923, and he brought Annie to Fort McKavett in a new 1923 Model T Ford. During their six-year marriage, they had three children, two daughters and a son, Frank Jr., born on February 14, 1929, when Frank was two months shy of seventy-nine. A photograph of him holding his youngest child taken on August 22, 1929, appeared in the *Dallas Morning News* with the header: "Daddy at 82 [*sic*], He's Pretty Proud!" Frank died just two months later. In the cemetery next to Frank's heart-shaped tombstone, is a Texas Ranger marker. His epigraph reads, "A friend to all, and a wonderful father."

Pioneer Rest Cemetery on US Highway 83 in Menard is a Texas Historic Cemetery established in 1863 with the burial of **William "Jack" Bradford**, born in Virginia in 1797. The city purchased the cemetery land from the Schleicher family in 1904. Rising into a steep hill, with terraces accessed with stone and cement steps, the cemetery contains a variety of unique headstones and memorials, several covered in sea shells, and is the final resting place for many pioneers, soldiers, cowboys, gamblers, preachers, Civil War veterans, Indian fighters, and Texas Rangers. Several children buried in this cemetery in the 1880s passed away from diseases such as influenza, measles, and pneumonia. Some succumbed in tragic accidents. A two-year-old girl died from a rattlesnake bite and a four-year-old

Eighteen-year-old Floyd Lee Thompson died in 1903 and is buried at Pioneer Rest Cemetery. His marker, a marble pedestal upon which rests a lamb and a tree trunk, indicates a life cut short. A domed cement grave decorated with large scallop shells covers his burial site.

girl burned to death when children, playing around an open fire under a wash pot, caught a stick on fire and accidentally touched her dress, which burst into flames. The rock fence surrounding the cemetery is the original stone from the presidio San Luis de las Amarillas.

The **Callan** family plot on one of the top terraces of Pioneer Rest Cemetery has four graves marked by large crosses on granite pedestals surrounded by a wrought-iron fence. Texas Ranger **James Joseph Callan** (1833–1917), from Ireland, immigrated with his parents, settling in the East. The family moved to Texas in 1855, where James joined the US Army, serving on the Mexican border. In 1859, he married **Margaret Sheen** (1844–1919), subsequently fathering fourteen children. At the onset of the Civil War, he joined the Texas Frontier Cavalry as senior captain in the Confederacy, and for the first two years remained along the frontier to protect it against Indian encroachments. He was later assigned to Bankhead's Brigade and served on the Texas coast under General Magruder. From 1868 until 1871, he and his family lived at Fort McKavett, where he served on the Ranger Force as a scout and guide for the federal troops at that post. He then established his permanent home at what was then called Menardville and worked briefly in the newspaper business as an editor. He served as a commissioner of Menard County and was Justice of the Peace at the time of his death.

SEASHELLS ON GRAVES

During the nineteenth century, a custom in Texas and in many Southern states, even those areas not close to the coast, was to cement seashells on grave mounds. The use of cockleshells or scallop shells on graves symbolizes a journey or pilgrimage; the shell is also a symbol of baptism, specifically the Baptism of Christ. In some churches, the baptismal font is shaped like a shell and sometimes a smaller shell is used to sprinkle water.

SAN ANGELO

San Angelo (pop. 103,000) was founded as a trading post in 1867 across the river from Fort Concho. About 220 miles northwest of San Antonio and seventy miles north of Fort McKavett, it is near the geographical center of the state. Named in memory of the late wife of founder Bartholomew "Bart" J. DeWitt, the town was called Santa Angela until 1883, when it was changed to San Angelo. The growth of the town, incorporated in 1903, was due to the nearby fort, an ample water supply, ranching, agriculture, and the railroad, which made it a major shipping center. By the turn of the century, with a new telephone company established, San Angelo was destined to be a major town within the region.

Established in 1893, **Fairmount Cemetery**, a Texas Historic Cemetery on 1120 West Avenue, today encompasses fifty-seven acres and has more than 33,000 burial sites, many reinterments dating to the Republic of Texas era. In the early twentieth century, city leaders noted that the Old City Cemetery, closed the year Fairmount opened, was impeding progress in downtown San Angelo. In 1921, the city purchased the early graveyard, sent out notices and began to relocate the graves to other cemeteries, Fairmount being the recipient of the majority of the burials. The remains of pioneer ranchers and oilmen, civic leaders, merchants, saloon owners, veterans of wars, former slaves, and Buffalo soldiers were reinterred in the southeast corner of Fairmount, a beautifully landscaped cemetery with many impressive monuments.

As in many other Texas cemeteries, a substantial granite monument for Confederate Veterans was erected in Fairmont, this one memorializing "more than 140 Confederate Veterans" buried there. The national motto of the Confederate States, "Deo Vindice," or "God, our Defender," is engraved on the bottom of the monument.

Four Buffalo Soldiers from the Indian Wars era are buried in this cemetery, including **Jacob "Jake" W. Wilks** (1840–1922). His tombstone is a white marble tablet typically found in military cemeteries. Born a slave in Kentucky, Wilks escaped with his family through the "Underground Railroad." Raised in Ohio, he enlisted at Camp Nelson, Kentucky, on September 16, 1863. On July 17, 1862, Congress had passed two Acts for the enlistment of "colored troops," but it was not until after the Emancipation Proclamation in January 1863 that official enrollment began. Wilks served three years in Company C, 116th Regiment. He re-enlisted, joining Company F, Ninth US Cavalry, and was promoted to Sergeant. Serving until 1871, he re-enlisted again and was stationed at Fort McKavett from 1869 to 1874, and then at Fort Seldon in New Mexico, where he was honorably discharged on October 2, 1876, after contracting a chronic lung disease.

He met **Elizabeth "Lizzie" Moore** (1854–1930) at Fort McKavett. Her mother was a laundress there. In 1884, he and Elizabeth married and had six children. Jake purchased land and cattle at Fort McKavett and in San Angelo and became a successful rancher. In 1899, the family settled in San Angelo, where Jake died in 1922.

BUFFALO SOLDIERS

The Plains Indians gave the name Buffalo Soldiers to the African American regiments on the frontier. One theory for the nickname was because the soldiers had dark, curly hair that resembled the fur of a buffalo, and another is that they fought valiantly as the "mighty buffalo."

More than 180,000 black soldiers served in segregated regiments in the Union Army during the Civil War. Congress, recognizing the military merits of black soldiers, authorized two regiments of black cavalry, the Ninth and Tenth US Cavalry, and six regiments of black infantry. From 1866 to the early 1890s, the Buffalo Soldiers served at a variety of posts in Texas, the Southwest, and the Great Plains. Divided into small company- and troop-sized detachments at frontier posts, the Buffalo Soldiers patrolled the frontier, built roads, and escorted mail parties, among other typical garrison duties. They also participated in most of the major frontier campaigns against the Cheyenne, Kiowa, Comanche, Apache, Sioux, and Arapaho Indians.

The life-size statue of saloon owner Thomas McCloskey by noted sculptor Frank Teich looms over his family plot in Fairmont Cemetery on a ten-foot-high pedestal.

In 1892, **Thomas McCloskey** (1856–1914) a Canadian by birth, and his wife **Laura** (1855–1917), from Georgia, arrived in San Angelo. Thomas purchased a saloon on the corner of Concho and

Chadbourne Streets. He first called it McCloskey's Place and then changed the name to the Arc Light Saloon after electric streetlights were installed near it. The Arc Light gained a reputation as the place for businessmen to have a drink and make deals without worrying about the raucous and rowdy behavior usually associated with bars, although it was the scene of at least one shootout. The headline, "Tom McCloskey Friend of the Poor Is No More," appeared in the December 29, 1914, issue of the *San Angelo Daily Standard*, announcing his death.

Thomas's younger brother David joined him and Laura within a year of their arrival, but he died on November 14, 1893, of consumption (a term used in the nineteenth century for tuberculosis). Because of its dry, warm climate, San Angelo had been touted as a restorative place for consumptives, but David was in the last stages with "no hope for recovery." Inscribed on his tablet tombstone lying flat on the ground is, "Gone to Rest." Laura's small rectangular tombstone with a carving of a branch of lilies tied at the stems with a ribbon also notes her as "wife of T. H. McCloskey."

Texas bluebonnets blanket Fredericksburg's St. Mary's Catholic Cemetery in the spring.

CHAPTER 4

HILL COUNTRY TRAIL REGION

Rugged limestone and granite hills rise from 400 to 800 feet above the surrounding plains in this south-central Texas region. Live oak and ash juniper trees, yucca, and prickly pear cactus grow amid exposed rocks and boulders, with intermittent streams and springs that disappear into underground caverns and aquifers. In the southeast portion of the Edwards Plateau, the Texas Hill Country is a geographical region of faults and uplifts formed from marine deposits of sandstone, limestone, shales, and dolomites 100 million years ago during the Cretaceous period when this area was covered by an ocean. Because of its inherent beauty, and despite its rugged terrain and harsh climate, many early pioneers settled in this region.

AUSTIN

In the early 1830s, pioneers settled along the Colorado River in a townsite known first as Waterloo. Renamed after Stephen F. Austin, the "Father of Texas," Austin (pop. 1 million) was chosen as the capital of the new Republic of Texas in 1839 and was made the state capital after Texas was annexed as the twenty-eighth state on December 29, 1845. However, many Texans thought the town was too remote and small to be the state's capital. Officials in Houston and Waco offered their cities as better locations, and in 1872 voters cast their ballots in a statewide election to decide which of the three cities should be the capital. Austin was the winner. In 1888, the University of Texas was founded and the current capital building was completed (after a fire destroyed the original 1853 building). Its downtown district along Congress Avenue and Sixth Street is on the National Register of Historic Places.

Hornsby Cemetery is on FM 969 in East Austin, between FM 973 and Blue Bluff Rd. This family cemetery was founded by the first settler of Travis County, **Reuben Hornsby** (1793–1879), a surveyor with Stephen F. Austin's Little Colony, who brought his family here in 1832. The pastoral Hornsby Cemetery is meticulously kept and has more than 350 gravesites dotted with large shade trees. It is a reminder of the first permanent white settlement in Austin, Hornsby Bend, and is located near where the original Hornsby homestead and fort once stood before they were demolished in the early twentieth century. This cemetery is the final resting place of many generations of Hornsbys, including several Texas Rangers and **Rogers Hornsby** (1896–1963), a famous major league baseball player during the 1920s.

The Hornsby Cemetery began with the burials of Texas Rangers **Howell Haggett** (?–1836) and **John Williams** (?–1836) who'd been sent to the settlement to help guard Hornsby's fort. Scalped by Indians while working in the corn fields, they were buried on the spot, today at the back of the cemetery and separated by a rock wall. A 1936 Texas Centennial monument dedicated to them and Texas Ranger **William**

Atkinson (?–1845), also killed by Indians, and three Texas Ranger Memorial Crosses mark their gravesite. The monument also includes a memorial inscription for **Daniel Hornsby** (1826–1845), killed in the same Indian skirmish as Atkinson and buried on the opposite side of a rock wall from the others.

Reuben Hornsby (1793–1879) shares a granite tombstone with wife **Sarah Morrison** (1796–1862) upon which a Citizen of the Republic of Texas seal is affixed. A Texas Ranger Memorial Cross stands in front of the tombstone. Hornsby, originally from Georgia, received a grant of a league and a labor of land totaling 4,604.1 acres in 1832 from Stephen F. Austin in the new Austin Colony. The Hornsby home at that time was the northernmost on the Colorado and was often the target of Indian raids. In June 1836, Indians killed Reuben and Sarah's eighteen-year-old son **Daniel** and a companion while the boys were fishing in the Colorado River. The Hornsbys, parents of ten children, were noted for their hospitality and personal courage. By the end of Reuben's life, he'd become a prosperous planter.

Josephus Hornsby (1822–1862), another son of Reuben and Sarah, was a Texas Ranger who fought in several Indian battles. Josephus is buried next to his second wife **Eliza Ann Lane** (1830–1892), with whom he had six children. Their marble pillar tombstones feature carved clasped hands. When one of the cuffs appears masculine and the other feminine, as is the case for these carvings, the clasped hands symbolize matrimony. They can also symbolize a heavenly welcome or an earthly farewell. A Texas Centennial monument detailing Josephus's many Ranger activities in defense of the Republic stands prominently in front of the tombstones.

Texas Ranger crosses mark fifteen graves in the Hornsby Cemetery, although there are nineteen total, with four placed as commemorative markers for Hornsby Rangers buried elsewhere.

The epitaph on the pedestal of Josephus's tombstones reads: "A more nobler soul was never/lifted to heaven on angels' wings,/ than he who rests here. He was one of/the early settlers often engaged in/deadly conflict with the Indian foe./And never refused when duty or/country called upon him to go." The epitaph on Eliza's pedestal reads: "Borne by angels on their wings/Far from earth the spirit flies/ Finds her God and ever sings/Sweet songs in paradise./Asleep in Jesus blessed sleep/From which none ever wakes to weep."

Josephus's first wife, **Polly Strawn** (1827–1847), died at age nineteen during childbirth, before their first wedding anniversary. Her simple tablet tombstone reads: "Sacred to the Memory of Mrs. Polly B. Hornsby. Was Married on June 11, 1846, then was deceased in May 28th 1847, Aged 19 Years and 11 months." They had one daughter **Nancy**, who died of typhoid in 1861, at age fourteen. Josephus was returning home from a trip, traveling with Eliza's family, who were moving to Texas, when he received word of his first wife's death. He married Eliza a year later.

The Hornsby family donated the land adjacent to the Hornsby family cemetery and separated by a fence for Mexican immigrants. **Cementario Mexicano**, also called the **Hornsby Mexican Cemetery**, has more than 100 graves. The oldest graves are in the front and most of the tombstones have succumbed to the elements and are unreadable. According to the Austin Genealogical Society website, the earliest marked grave is that of sixteen-year-old **Francisa Rivera** (1880–1896). The decorations on the gravesites are typical of Mexican burial sites in the Southwest, where the November 1 Mexican holiday, "Dia De Los Muertos" or Day of the Dead, is still celebrated. Families decorate the graves of departed loved ones with flowers and garlands (sometimes fresh, often artificial), small statuary and figurines, wreaths, seashells, and other colorful knick-knacks, as a way of remembrance. In the *Labyrinth of Solitude*, Mexican poet Octavio Paz observed, the Mexican is familiar with death, "jokes about it, caresses it, sleeps with it, celebrates it; it is one of his favorite toys and his most steadfast loves." Although there is also fear, "at least he [the Mexican] does not hide it; he confronts it face to face, with patience, disdain, or irony."

The contrast between the Spartan gravesites at Hornsby Cemetery on one side and the colorful and decorated graves of the Hornsby Cementario Mexicano on the other is striking.

Oakwood Cemetery, 1601 Navasota Street, was established in 1839, in what was then the northeast corner of Austin. Originally called City Cemetery, the burial site consisted of ten acres. The land became city property in 1856 and was later called Austin City Cemetery until 1912 when the city settled on the name "Oakwood." Today this cemetery encompasses more than forty acres, with the oldest section (Section 1) designated as "Old Grounds." The cemetery was segregated by race, as was the prevailing custom of the era. Negros were buried in a large area in Section 4, designated as "Colored Grounds." Those of Mexican heritage and paupers (in unmarked graves) were buried along the fence lines on the outer boundaries of the cemetery. There is also an old Jewish section called Beth Israel I, in Section 1. Within the four sections of this cemetery are more than 10,700 marked graves and an unknown number of unmarked graves.

In 1939, **Mary "Mollie" O. Taylor Bunton** (1863–1952) published her memoirs, *A Bride on the Old Chisholm Trail in 1866*, as part of the Texas Centennial celebration. Her small book is the only description of a cattle drive ever told from a woman's point of view and is described by biographer Ana Carolina Castillo Grimm as "entertaining, lyrical. . . [and] delightful." In Section 2 of Oakwood, the Taylor family plot, anchored by a large ornamental crypt, is the final resting place for Mollie and her husband, **James Howell Bunton** (1854–1923). Her father, Matthew, had a thriving medical practice in Austin and a 50,000-acre ranch in Kinney County. Mollie was sent to a ladies' finishing school in New York. After she returned to Austin in the early 1880s, many young men courted her, but she ultimately chose as her beau a cowboy from West Texas who owned a ranch in Sweetwater. She and James Bunton married in 1885. After a series of blizzards in February 1886 killed thousands of cattle, destroying herds all over the western plains and into West Texas, including Bunton's, he restocked his herd with 5,000 head of cattle from South Texas with the intention of driving them up to market in Kansas. As a new bride, Mollie did not want to be left alone and convinced her husband to take her with him. In her memoirs, she depicts this trail ride, the only one she ever went on. When she and James arrived in Coolidge, Kansas, they attended a ball in her honor at the hotel in which they were staying. That night she was crowned "Queen of the Old Chisholm Trail." The couple did not have children. Her husband died of pneumonia in 1923. Four years later, Mollie was inducted as an honorary member into the Old Trail Drivers' Association. She died of a cerebral hemorrhage in 1952 at age eighty-nine.

Alice Driskill (1880–1881) was the first child of William W. Driskill and Louise M. Chambliss, and granddaughter of cattle baron **Jesse Lincoln Driskill** (1824–1890) who built the famed Driskill Hotel in Austin in 1886. Driskill was born in Tennessee. He and wife, **Nancy Day** (1829–1910), who met and married in Missouri, moved to Texas in 1851. In 1857, Driskill entered the cattle business. During the Civil War, he sold beef to the Confederate Army and the Texas Rangers. He became a colonel and made a fortune, which he lost after the war ended. He became successful once again in the cattle trade. In 1871, Driskill moved his family to Austin. He continued in the cattle business, establishing ranches in South Texas, Kansas, and the Dakota territories. In 1885, he purchased an entire city block in

The Driskill family plot in Oakwood Cemetery would not be noticeable except for the poignant marble statue marking the grave of "Little Alice."

downtown Austin and built the Driskill Hotel, which became the social and political center for Texas society. After the severe winter of 1887–1888 on the northern plains killed the majority of his cattle herd, he again lost his fortune. No longer able to settle his debts, he had to sell the hotel in 1888. Two years later, on May 3, 1890, Colonel Driskill died of a stroke. He was buried at Oakwood Cemetery in the family plot. The Driskill Hotel today is a historic landmark in Austin.

A marble scroll tombstone in Section 1 of Oakwood marks the grave of **Susanna Dickinson Hannig** (1814–1883), also referred to as "Mother of the Babe of the Alamo." Susanna was the sole adult Anglo survivor who witnessed the massacre. She is buried next to her fifth husband **Joseph W. Hannig** (1834–1890), whom she married in 1857. His unique marble tombstone features a tree trunk draped in ivy and perched on rocks. Although Susanna died before him, it appears she selected his marker before her death, as it is inscribed "My Husband."

Born Susanna Wilkerson in Tennessee, she was the wife of Captain Almaron Dickinson, stationed at the Alamo at the time of the massacre during the morning of March 6, 1836. Susanna and her infant daughter Angelina were within the Alamo mission with several other women and children of Mexican descent when the battle ensued, killing all the Alamo defenders. Following the fall of the Alamo, Susanna, with her baby and the other women and children were escorted from the Alamo and taken to General Antonio López de Santa Anna. He interviewed them all and then sent a letter of warning with Susanna to deliver to Sam Houston.

Susanna had a difficult time after her first husband's untimely death, marrying four more times before her union with Hannig, who was twenty years her junior. A native of Germany who became prosperous as a cabinet shop proprietor and owner of a furniture and undertaking parlor, he also owned a store in San Antonio. The couple had been married for twenty-six years at the time of Susanna's death and, although Joseph married again, he chose to be buried next to Susanna.

Ben Thompson (1843–1884), buried in Section 1 of Oakwood, was a notorious gunfighter and gambler who, nevertheless, was elected twice as Austin's City Marshal. His simple tablet tombstone, fronted by a Confederate cross and plaque, is one of the most visited at the cemetery. Born in England, Benjamin emigrated with his family to Austin in 1851. He served in the Confederacy and then joined Emperor Maximilian's forces in Mexico, fighting until the fall of the empire in 1867. Returning to Texas, he spent time in Huntsville prison over an altercation with his brother-in-law. When he got out, he became a professional gambler, also earning a reputation as a gunfighter, and was hired out to lawman Bat Masterson for a year to protect a railroad out of Leadville, Colorado. In July 1882, while still serving as marshal, Thompson quarreled over a card game at the Vaudeville Theater and Saloon in San Antonio. He killed Jack Harris, a prominent sportsman and owner of the saloon (see San Antonio, City Cemetery Historic District). Thompson was indicted for the murder and resigned as marshal. After a sensational trial and acquittal, he returned to Austin to accolades from an adoring public and resumed his life as a professional gambler. Almost two years later, on the evening of March 11, 1884, Thompson returned to the Vaudeville Theater with his notorious friend **John King Fisher**, deputy sheriff of Uvalde County (see Uvalde's Pioneer Park Cemetery). Within minutes of their arrival at the Vaudeville, both men were shot and killed from behind, presumably by Harris's friends. A coroner's jury in San Antonio ruled the killing as self-defense, and no one was ever charged with the murders.

The simple, granite tombstone **Elizabeth Johnson Williams** (1840–1924) shares with her husband, **Hezekiah** (1840–1914), in Section 1 of the old burial ground of Oakwood gives no indication of the fascinating life story of the educated woman who became a legend for her business acumen and independent spirit. At a time when women were relegated to domestic duties, Elizabeth, or "Lizzie," as she preferred to be called, had careers in teaching, writing, bookkeeping, ranching, real estate, cattle brokering, and financing. At age thirty-nine, she married Hezekiah Williams, a retired Baptist preacher working as a stock driver who was also a widower with four sons. Despite his Baptist background, he liked to gamble and drink, and this may be why she had him sign a prenuptial contract stating that her property, including all future financial gains she might make, belonged to her.

The couple owned a home in Austin and a ranch of several thousand acres in Hays County. Lizzie had more experience in the cattle industry than did her husband, having been a bookkeeper for cattlemen. She entered the cattle business with her own herd, registering her cattle brand, CY, in 1871. By the time of her marriage to Hezekiah eight years later, she was a woman of independent means. After their marriage, they drove cattle "up the trail" together several times and they enjoyed a friendly business rivalry.

After a thirty-five-year marriage, Hezekiah—who Lizzie called "Hess" and "the old buzzard"—died and Lizzie's joy for life apparently died as well. She retreated into widowhood, dressed in black, and lived frugally and alone for the rest of her life, until senility in her later years made it necessary for her to move in with a niece. After her death on October 9, 1924, Lizzie's family was surprised to learn she had an estate valued at almost $246,000, including cash found hidden throughout the building she owned in Austin. Within thirty years of her death, she was hailed as an early Texas "cattle queen" and is the first woman in Texas to ride the Chisholm Trail with a herd of cattle acquired under her own brand.

The **Texas State Cemetery**, 909 Navasota Street, is one mile east of the Capitol. Twenty-two acres of beautifully maintained grounds, enormous shade trees, and impressive monuments signify that people of importance are buried here. The first burial was that of **General Edward Burleson** (1798–1851). Burleson served with Sam Houston

Cattle Queen Lizzie Johnson Williams and her husband Hezekiah
Williams, on their wedding day, June 8, 1879.
[PICB 01491] AUSTIN HISTORY CENTER, AUSTIN PUBLIC LIBRARY.

in the Battle of San Jacinto and as the first vice president of the
Republic of Texas. Meant to be the final resting place for individuals
who have made a significant contribution to Texas, the Texas State
Cemetery by the end of the Civil War included a Confederate burial

ground. Later it was expanded to include the graves of prominent Texans and their spouses. Many of those buried here were reinterred from other cemeteries. With more than 3,200 graves and awe-inspiring monuments of notable Texans, the Texas State Cemetery is a "must-see" for anyone interested in Texas history. This cemetery has a Visitors Center and small museum, and tours can be arranged through contacts on the cemetery's website.

A larger-than-life-size bronze cast statue of **Stephen F. Austin** (1783–1836), his arm extended, marks the grave of the "Father of Texas" in the Texas State Cemetery. Pompeo Coppini went to Chicago to supervise the casting of the statue at the Florentine Brothers Foundry in 1912. Its position on the highest point of a hill signifies the prominence of Austin, after whom the city is named, in Texas history. Austin was originally buried in Gulf Prairie Cemetery at Jones Creek, Texas. In 1910, his remains were removed and brought to this cemetery. Sam Houston, sitting as the first governor of the Republic of Texas at the time of Austin's death, proclaimed in an official statement: "The Father of Texas is no more; the first pioneer of the wilderness has departed."

After his father Moses died in 1821, Stephen, who was born in Virginia but lived most of his early life in Missouri, traveled to San Antonio, taking over what had been his father's dream: the Anglo settlement of Texas, then part of Mexico. Stephen took over the Spanish grant of 200,000 acres, bringing in 300 families of settlers. He was the first to colonize, the most successful of all the *empresarios*. At first loyal to Mexico, he later went to Mexico City with a petition requesting the creation of an independent state government for Texas, for which he was placed in jail. After his release, he returned to Texas where the revolution had already begun. He served as commander of the region's volunteer army before going to the United States to gain support for their efforts. When he returned in June of 1836, the fight was over. He ran for president of the new republic but was defeated by Sam Houston, who appointed him secretary of state. Austin served for two months before he caught a cold and died of pneumonia.

The epitaph on the pillar tombstone of **William Alexander Anderson "Big Foot" Wallace** (1817–1899) is inscribed: "Here lies he who spent his manhood defending the homes of Texas/Brave, Honest, and Faithful/Born Apr. 3, 1817 Died Jan. 7, 1899." Family lore was that Wallace, who was born in Virginia, was a descendant of Scottish highlanders William Wallace and Robert the Bruce. When he learned about the deaths of his brother and a cousin in the Goliad Massacre in 1836, he set out for Texas to avenge their deaths. Wallace was a big man, weighed 240 pounds without surplus fat, and stood six feet two inches "in his moccasins." The most common story for the reason of Wallace's nickname is that a large Indian who stole livestock from settlers was named "Bigfoot" because of the large footprints he left at the scenes of his crimes. One of Wallace's friends jokingly told him that when the Indian wasn't around, Wallace—being a man of large stature with big feet himself—could easily take his place.

After the war with Mexico was over, Wallace tried farming, but that life didn't suit him. He joined the Texas Rangers and was a participant in many battles over the years. In the 1850s, as a captain, he commanded a Ranger company, fought border bandits and Indians, and was so expert at trailing that he was often called upon to track down runaway slaves trying to get to Mexico. During the Civil War, he helped guard the frontier against the Comanche Indians and led scouting details. In his later years, he lived on a small ranch on the Medina River on land granted him by the State of Texas. A single man who never married, he died at age eighty-one in Bigfoot, Texas, a small town named after him, forty miles southwest of San Antonio. First buried at the Longview Cemetery, his body was moved to the Texas State Cemetery.

The life-size, white Italian marble sarcophagus of **Albert Sidney Johnston** (1803–1862) sculpted by Elisabet Ney in 1903, won a bronze medal at the St. Louis World's Fair, where it was shipped from Seravezza, Italy, in 1904. The carved figure of General Johnston, attired in formal military dress, lies upon his crypt surrounded by a wrought-iron fence and a Plexiglas dome.

Johnston, born in Kentucky, was a graduate of the US Military Academy at West Point in 1826. During his long military career, he took part in three major wars and served as a general in three separate armies: the Republic of Texas Army, the US Army, and the Confederate Army. Johnston came to Texas in 1836 and served in the Texas Army, quickly rising to the position of brigadier general and later serving as secretary of war. Texas became his newly adopted home state, even as he spent time traveling all over the country for his military duties. At the beginning of the Civil War in 1861, he resigned his commission in the US Army, refused the federal government's offer of a command, and returned to Texas.

"Big Foot" Wallace, frontier Texas folk hero, is buried in front and to the right of Stephen F. Austin.

Confederate President Jefferson Davis appointed Johnston a general in the Confederate Army and assigned him command of the Western division, a vast region of the South from the Appalachian Mountains to Texas. Considered one of the South's senior officers,

Johnston was highly respected by Davis, a former classmate at West Point, and became one of only eight Confederate officers to receive the rank of full general. Many of his contemporaries considered Johnston to be the finest soldier on either side of the conflict, even though by early 1862, he was forced to abandon Kentucky and Tennessee and fall back into the Deep South after losing some decisive battles. On April 6, 1862, he was killed while leading his forces at the battle of Shiloh. He was temporarily buried at New Orleans. By special appropriation in 1867, the Texas Legislature had his remains transferred to Austin for burial in the State Cemetery. His memorial monument was installed in 1905.

CASTROVILLE

Called the "Little Alsace of Texas," Castroville (pop. 3,200) was founded on the Medina River twenty-five miles west of San Antonio on a Republic of Texas land grant contract made with Empresario Henri Castro in 1842. Castro, after whom the town is named, was descended from Portuguese Jews who had fled to France after the inception of the Spanish Inquisition. He arranged transport for the mostly Catholic farmers from the Haut-Rhin region of Alsace in northeastern France who spoke an Alsatian dialect of German. From 1843 to 1847, Castro brought 2,134 colonists to his land grants, which became the towns of Castroville (1844), Quihi (1845), Vandenburg (1846), and D'Hanis (1847).

Castroville was the first and most successful town despite initial struggles. Raids by Comanches and Mexicans, droughts in 1848 and

1849, an invasion of locusts, and a cholera epidemic in 1849 did not deter the settlers who laid out the town, patterned after European villages with small town lots surrounded by individual farming plots. By 1856, Castroville supported two churches, a school, three large stores, a post office, a brewery, and a water-powered gristmill. The community raised corn, cattle, horses, hogs, and poultry, and sold produce to the military posts in the area. Today, Castroville has more than 200 historic structures and has been recognized as a national and Texas historic district. Many descendants of the early settlers still make Castroville their home.

CHOLERA

Numerous epidemics stalked Texans in the nineteenth century. Cholera, yellow fever, smallpox, dengue fever, measles, diphtheria, and whooping cough afflicted residents throughout the state. Cholera first appeared in 1833, but it was most destructive during an epidemic in 1849. In San Antonio that year, 500 succumbed to this disease. Cholera is a highly contagious intestinal ailment with symptoms including vomiting and diarrhea that quickly depletes body fluids. Within five days, the dehydrated victim went into shock and often ended up in the graveyard. Numerous home remedies were tried—wearing copper charms, a German practice; black pepper and opium with a brandy and water chaser; peyote; and bloodletting. In 1854, Dr. John Snow, an English physician, discovered that a water source was the cause of a cholera outbreak in London that resulted in 500 deaths in ten days. The pump handle of the affected well was removed and cholera deaths slowed and then stopped. The Broad Street pump is still a landmark in London. That same year, Filippo Pacini isolated the bacteria that caused cholera, but his discovery was not widely known until almost thirty years later, when German bacteriologist Robert Koch publicized the knowledge and means of fighting the disease. Cholera bacteria enter the body through the mouth, either in food or in water that has been contaminated with human waste. Treatment consists of large volumes of water mixed with sugar and salts either by mouth or intravenously replaced. Antibiotics may be used in severe cases. In 1873, a cholera epidemic hit the United States, but it was not widespread. Sporadic outbreaks occurred until the turn of the century, when improved sanitation helped to alleviate cholera epidemics as a threat.

St. Louis Cemetery, on a hill on the northwest end of Castroville between Jackson and Alsace Streets off Highway 90 West, has served the parish of St. Louis Catholic Church since 1844 and many Castro colonists are buried here. A stone wall built in 1860 surrounds the original burial ground. On the north side and adjacent to this graveyard is the Zion Lutheran Church Cemetery. Like many cemeteries of the era, St. Louis is, for the most part, segregated, with Hispanics buried in a section on the south side of the graveyard. At the back of the cemetery, on the summit of Cross Hill, stands a thirteen-foot-tall concrete and marble crucifix (the fifth to be erected at this site since 1844). At the base of the crucifix is a statue of a kneeling Mary, the Mother of Jesus, at her son's feet. With more than 2,400 graves, the cemetery has many interesting tombstones.

The grave marker for Benedictine Brother **Michel Bohm** (?–1862) is carved with a cherub's head and a cross with the initials CSPB, which stands for *Crux Sancti Patris Benedicti*, the Cross of our Holy Father Benedict. Encircled around the cross is a faint inscription that may have been the words, *Eius in obitu nostro praesentia muniamur!* "May we be strengthened by his presence in the hour of our death!" The Benedictines considered St. Benedict of Nursia (Norcia, Italy) the patron of a happy death.

At the foot of the slab gravesite of **Amelia Mathias Castro** (1790–1871) is a small plaque identifying her as the wife of **Henri Castro**, "founder of Castroville, born in 1786, died in 1864, and buried in Monterrey, Mexico." Castro was on a trip back to France via Monterrey when he became severely ill and died on November 31, 1865. He was buried at the foot of the Sierra Madre in Monterrey. Amelia was a wealthy widow when Castro married her in 1813. She brought him a dowry of 50,000 francs, and four foster children came with them to Texas. A similar slab adjacent to Amelia's covers the gravesite of **Augustine Castro** (1841–1886), wife of Lorenzo, Amelia and Henri's adopted son,.

A broken tablet stone lying flat on the ground marks the grave of **Jean Jacques "Jacob" Haby** (1795–1854 [*sic*]). Born in Oberentzen, Haut-Rhin, Alsace, France, Jacob and his wife, **Marthe Kempf** (1804–1878), arrived in Galveston as part of the first Castro colony immigrant group on May 29, 1844, along with their children, Jacob's sister Catherine, and her husband Michel Gsell. The Habys were part of an extended family group that also included a brother, Francois Joseph Haby II and his family. When Francois arrived, he purchased 1,500 acres along the Medina River, now a town called Rio Medina, near Castroville, where his brother Jacob had put down roots for his own family. Over the years, the brothers divided the land among their children. The area came to be known as the Haby Settlement, and at one time included a church, a school, a small store, and two butcher shops.

Marthe died twenty-five years after Jacob and they are buried three rows apart, her grave in front. Her pillar tombstone with a barely discernable inscription stands in contrast to her husband's simple marker. Jacob died December 6, 1853, and although he lived less than ten years after he emigrated, he and his wife and their extended family left hundreds of descendants.

CENTER POINT

On the Guadalupe River eight miles southeast of Kerrville, Center Point, an unincorporated community (pop. 4,500), became a small settlement with the arrival in 1852 of Elizabeth Denton, her children, and slaves. Austrian immigrant Dr. Charles de Ganahl opened a post office on the north side of the river in 1859. First called Zanzenburg, the name was changed in 1872 to Center Point by the new postmaster who moved the post office to the south side of the river. The settlement was halfway between the hill country towns of Kerrville and Comfort, Fredericksburg, and Bandera, hence the name change.

Center Point, which by 1900 had about 500 residents, was a farming and stock-raising center. With a railroad depot nearby, it became a trading hub for the region.

Center Point Cemetery, on FM 480 and 1099 East, was established in 1872. The five-acre cemetery has 1,452 graves, with the oldest marked burial from 1875. The cemetery has become famous as the unofficial cemetery of the Texas Rangers because so many are buried here—thirty-two known. Researcher Bobbie J. Powell, whose great-grandfather Texas Ranger **Robert J. Lange** (1860–1936) is buried here, believes there are several more Rangers in unmarked graves. How Center Point cemetery became the final resting place for so many Rangers is unknown, although the town has long been known as a retirement spot. What is known is that Rangers from other parts of Texas started requesting to be buried beside their comrades in Center Point. Mike Cox, an author and authority on Texas Ranger history, calls the little cemetery the "unofficial Arlington of the Texas Rangers."

TEXAS RANGERS

From their earliest days, the Rangers had an aura of mystique and invincibility. Although some were criminals wearing badges, the majority were decent, brave, and law-abiding. In August 1823, Stephen F. Austin created a Ranger force of ten men tasked with the protection of the colonists. These men are regarded as the first ancestors of the modern Texas Rangers. In 1835, as Texas Independence loomed, the legislature created a "Corps of

---

Rangers" to protect the frontier from hostile Indians. Their pay was $1.25 a day; they could elect their own officers; and they were to furnish their own arms, horses, and equipment. Abolished by the Reconstruction government after the Civil War, the Ranger service was reinstated in 1874 as the Frontier Battalion, a permanent military force to protect the Texas frontier. After the threat of Indian raids ceased, the Rangers were tasked to protect the frontier from lawlessness and crime. Today's Rangers, approximately 150, are selected from the ranks of the Texas Department of Public Safety. They are an investigative law enforcement agency with statewide jurisdiction.

The most famous Ranger buried here is **Andrew Jackson "A. J." Sowell** (1848–1921), primarily because of his books, which have become classics in the study of early Texas: *Rangers and Pioneers of Texas* (1884), *Early Settlers of Southwest Texas* (1880), *Life of Big Foot Wallace* (1899), *History of Fort Bend County* (1904), and *Incidents Connected with the Early History of Guadalupe County Texas* (n.d.).

Sowell was born in Seguin in 1848. His namesake uncle, Andrew Jackson Sowell (1815–1883), with whom he is sometimes confused, was also a Texas Ranger. A. J. joined the Rangers in 1870 and took part in the campaign against the Wichita Indians in 1870–1871. His activities as a Ranger are recorded in his writings. Sowell married **Mary Lillian Tinsley** (1855–1902) in Seguin in 1872, and they had five children. After two of their daughters died of consumption

Andrew Jackson Sowell, Texas Ranger, 1871.
[AR-X-016-J274] Austin History Center, Austin Public Library

(tuberculosis), Mary contracted the disease and also succumbed. She was buried next to one of her daughters in the Uvalde Cemetery. Although he traveled extensively around Texas, Sowell in his later life lived near his daughter, Adaline Sowell Hill Rogers, in Center Point, hence his burial there. Sowell's pink granite tombstone, with a Masonic symbol, has the inscription: "Blessed are the dead which die in the Lord and their works do follow them. Rev. 14.13."

CHERRY SPRING

Cherry Spring (pop. 75), sixteen miles northwest of Fredericksburg, an unincorporated farming and ranching community, was settled in 1852 by two German immigrants from Fredericksburg. En route from San Antonio to El Paso, the small community was moderately successful as a way station for travelers. Sheep ranching and farming were the primary occupations. A post office was established in 1858 and closed in 1912. The 1860 census for Gillespie County listed 117 residents in Cherry Spring, mostly German immigrants.

Despite the community's small population, there are at least eight cemeteries within eight miles of Cherry Spring. The most renowned is the **Marschall-Meusebach Cemetery** off Highway 87 and a quarter mile down South Cherry Spring Road. In a field under a copse of large live oaks and enclosed within a rock fence are the graves of twenty-six individuals, members of the families of two former German noblemen related by marriage.

Meusebach, also known as **Baron Otfried Hans Freiherr von Meusbach**, brought 5,257 German emigrants to Texas from 1845 to 1847. He negotiated a peace treaty in 1847 with twenty Comanche chiefs who protected the German frontier settlements from Indian raids and opened more than three million acres of land to settlement. Because of his efforts, Germans became the largest ethnic group emigrating from Europe, and by 1850 comprised 5 percent of the population of Texas.

The gray granite pillar tombstone marking Meusebach's grave is the centerpiece of the cemetery. One side is inscribed with his anglicized name, the dates of his birth and death, and the motto: *Tenax Propositi*, Latin for "Firm of Purpose." On the opposite side is his German name, along with the years of his birth and death. On top, underneath a circle with an unusual emblem, are the words, "Texas Forever."

D'HANIS

A small, unincorporated community twenty-five miles west of Castroville, D'Hanis (pop. 920) was founded by Henri Castro in 1847 when he brought twenty-nine families from the Alsace region of France to settle along the San Antonio-Rio Grande Road. Named after William D'Hanis, a manager of Castro's colonization company, the original town was bypassed by the railroad in 1881. The majority of residents then moved one-and-a-half miles west to be closer to the depot, calling the new settlement, "New D'Hanis" and the old site "Old D'Hanis." The only thing left in Old D'Hanis after a few years was St. Dominic's Catholic Church, abandoned in 1914, and the church graveyard.

The limestone ruins of St. Dominic's Catholic Church loom eerily over **St. Dominic Cemetery** in Old D'Hanis at the corner of County Roads 5226 and 5231. Designated a Texas Historic Cemetery, the old graveyard was in use from 1847 until 1893. The cemetery has 146 graves, many unmarked, and several unique French-German-style tombstones with epitaphs that provide the history of the original town and its settlers.

The first burial was that of **Mary Ann Rudinger**, age eighteen years. Her marker, a flat stone on the ground, is inscribed: "The first death upon arrival of settlers at Dhanis, May 25, 1847, Carrying smaller children over streams she became ill and died on above date. Her Father and Mother also buried here, Joseph—Maggie (nee Brown)." The inscription on **Alexander Hoffman's** substantial monument reads, "Born in Bohemia, Killed by Indians in Uvalde County, March 23, 1860, Served in Mexican War, First Sheriff Bandera County." Born in 1822, Hoffman was about thirty-eight when he died.

Catharina Zuercher Gartieser (1805–1861) emigrated with her husband **Jean Baptiste Gartieser** (1800–1850) and three children as part of the Castro Colony group in 1846. Five years after her husband's death, she married her second husband Andres Brieden. Some sources say Brieden was a stonemason who helped build St. Dominic's Church and he may have carved Catharina's tombstone. However, on the bottom of the tombstone is inscribed, "by Joseph Rudinger, 1861." Rudinger was Catharina's son-in-law. Whoever carved them, the images are striking and beautifully rendered.

FREDERICKSBURG

Fredericksburg (pop. 12,000), seventy-five miles west of Austin and seventy miles northwest of San Antonio, was founded in 1846 under the leadership of John O. Meusebach of the Society for the Protection of German Immigrants in Texas (see sections on Loyal Valley and

One of several bas-relief tombstones in this church graveyard was fashioned from a large slab of limestone with the inscription: "Hier Ruht (Here Lies) Catharina Garteiser." This side shows the Sacred Heart of Jesus. On the other side is the image of the Blessed Virgin.

Cherry Springs, Marschall-Meusebach Cemetery). The settlement was named in honor of Prince Frederick of Prussia. Because of Meusebach's treaty with the Indians, the town grew quickly with fewer depredations than the Anglo settlements had. The 1850 census shows 754 residents. The quaint German historic district has more than 700 historically significant structures.

Fredericksburg has two main historic cemeteries—**Der Stadt Friedhof**, German meaning "The City Cemetery" and **St. Mary's Catholic Cemetery**. The perils of frontier life—cholera epidemics, victims of Indian raids, and Civil War casualties—are reflected on the tombstones.

Der Stadt Friedhof, 300 block of North Lee Street on the east side of town, was established in 1846 along Barons Creek and is the oldest cemetery within Fredericksburg, the final resting place for a number of the original German colonists. The earliest graves have limestone markers. Later, white marble and Texas red granite became popular. Cast-iron fences imported from Cincinnati and other industrial centers surround many of the graves. At the back of the cemetery separated by a large field is the final resting place of some black residents of Fredericksburg.

There are more than 5,500 graves in this cemetery, among them the gravesites of the maternal grandparents of President Lyndon Baines Johnson, thirty-sixth president of the United States—**Joseph Wilson Baines** (1846–1906) and **Ruth Ament Huffman Baines** (1854–1936). Joseph Baines was born in Louisiana and came to Texas in 1850. He and his wife lived in other Texas towns most of their lives, with a family farm and law office in Blanco. Financial losses forced

Joseph to sell the farm and close his business. The couple moved into a modest house in Fredericksburg in early 1905. Joseph died there after a three-month illness, on November 18, 1906. Joseph and Ruth are buried next to each other, red granite tombstones marking their graves.

The grandparents and many other family members of US fleet admiral **Chester Nimitz Sr.** (1885–1966), who played a major role in World War II, are buried in **Der Stadt Friedhof.** His German-born paternal grandfather, **Charles Henry Nimitz,** aka **Karl Heinrich Nimitz Jr.** (1826–1911), was a great influence on Chester, whose namesake father died before he was born. Charles was a former seaman in the German Merchant Marine. His family first immigrated to South Carolina from Bremen, Germany. Fascinated with stories about Texas, Charles joined the Meusebach immigrant group and settled in Fredericksburg in 1846. He became a Texas Ranger in the Texas Mounted Volunteers in 1851, later served as captain of the Gillespie Rifles Company in the Confederate Army, and after the war was elected to the Texas Legislature. In 1852, he built the Nimitz Hotel, referred to as the Steamboat Hotel because the shape of the front resembles a ship's bow. Today it houses the National Museum of the Pacific War in Fredericksburg.

In 1848, Charles married **Sophie Dorothea Mueller** (1824–1877) and they had twelve children, nine of whom lived to adulthood. Charles was buried next to his wife. A small rough-hewn red granite marker for both stands upon a large elevated concrete slab.

Born in Frankfurt, Germany, **Elizabeth Emma Schnerr** (1827–1903) fell in love with **Friedrich Wilhelm Schnerr** (1825–1908). Friedrich was also in love with Emma. However, his wealthy family did not approve of the match as she was beneath their social class. The couple married anyway and immigrated to Texas in the early 1850s, settling in Fredericksburg. They had four children. When Emma died in 1903, Friedrich was grief-stricken. After her burial, he left her grave unmarked for several years because he could not find a tombstone to adequately memorialize the love of his life. He ordered a tombstone but threw it away after he saw it believing it did not adequately express his deep love for Emma. Elisabet Ney heard their story and offered her services. Out of marble, Ney carved a small cherub, a look of contemplation on its face, eyes peering up, chin rested on folded arms. Friedrich was touched and accepted the tribute to his wife. In 1906, Elisabet traveled to Fredericksburg to see the angel in place; she died a year later in her studio in Austin (see Liendo Plantation Cemetery for Ney's gravesite).

Three young men, two of them brothers, are buried next to each other under a large concrete slab, small rectangular markers describing the tragic manner of their deaths. The inscription on the marker for **Heinrich Arhelger** (1833–1863) reads, "Von Indianern Ermordet" (Killed by Indians). The markers of brothers **Heinrich Itz** (1844–1863) and **Jakob Itz** (1830–1863) are inscribed, "Von der Duff Bande Ermordet" (Killed by the Duff Band). All three were killed in February 1863, but only Arhelger's marker gives a date of death, February 14.

Arhelger, riding a mule, and his brother-in-law, on a horse, had gone out to look for their ox team for a freight-hauling trip when they were ambushed by a small group of mounted Indians. While his brother-in-law was able to escape, Arhelger was not. The Indians on horses easily overtook his mule. When he was found the next day, he was lying dead in a dense thicket, arrows piercing his body. An arrow

The Der Stadt Friedhof is known for the Schnerr Memorial, a cherub statue by renowned Texas sculptor Elisabet Ney, reputed to be her last work before she died.

in his neck had pierced his artery. In his right hand, he gripped his revolver with one chamber still loaded. Arhelger was thirty at the time of his death and the father of four children. Although a posse went after the marauding Indians, they were never found.

The Itz brothers' deaths were more sinister. They were murdered by a company of the so-called Partisan Rangers under the command of Captain James Duff. Squads led by Duff terrorized men of fighting age who would not pledge allegiance to the Confederacy. The Germans call them *Die Hangerbande*, the "Hanging Bandits." A freight-hauler and wagon-master before the war, Duff was in charge of a Confederate troop that was sent to Fredericksburg to keep order. He became the most hated man in the county, arresting people on suspicion of treason and sedition for undue cause.

Another brother, **Karl Itz** (1838–1908), survived the Nueces Massacre, a violent confrontation between Confederate soldiers and German Texans who supported the Union and were opposed to slavery. That battle had taken place on August 10, 1862, and Karl went into hiding. Duff sent a detachment of his troop to search for him near the family home north of Fredericksburg. Unable to find him, they instead seized his two younger brothers Heinrich and Jakob. They were taken to Fredericksburg on the pretext of forcing their enlistment into the Confederate Army. Instead, the troop murdered them in the middle of Main Street, a warning of the fate that would befall draft dodgers and deserters. Karl, devastated by the deaths of his brothers, lived in hiding until the war ended. He eventually married and had many descendants. He is buried next to his wife at Der Stadt Friedhof, a red granite monument tombstone marking their graves.

St. Mary's Catholic Cemetery at the corner of Catholic Cemetery Road and West Travis on the west side of Fredericksburg has more than 3,800 graves. Established in 1875, it is associated with

St. Mary's Catholic Parish but is not located near the church. Also referred to as St. Mary's Garden Cemetery, it is the second parish cemetery and most picturesque, especially in the spring when bluebonnets are in bloom.

Two of the most photographed memorials are statues of cherubs. One stands atop a pedestal for **James D. Becker** (1918–1923), son of Henry and Cora Becker, who died at age five from scarlet fever. He was the great-grandson of Franz Becker and Barbara Zenner Becker, who arrived in Fredericksburg in 1850. The "guardian angel" above the boy's monument holds a bouquet of flowers, a symbol of remembrance signifying the beauty and brevity of life. The other statue of a cherub holds roses on a pedestal tombstone over the grave of **Mary M. Weinheimer** (1921–1923). The granddaughter of Fredericksburg pioneers, she was "one year and twenty-five days" when she was laid to rest.

Some of the graves are domed and covered in sea shells, while others have interesting symbols typically seen in Catholic cemeteries.

CHRISTIAN SYMBOLS

One of the most unique Christian symbols usually engraved within a cross are the letters IHS. They are interwoven, which makes the symbol look like a dollar sign. The three letters are derived from the first three letters of Jesus's name using the Greek alphabet: Iota, Eta, Sigma. Among other Christian symbols often used in Catholic cemeteries are various renditions of the cross of

Christ; a monstrance—a receptacle in which the consecrated Host is exposed for veneration—usually marking the grave of a priest; a chalice; a crown; a scallop shell symbolizing baptism and the hope for Resurrection; the Holy Ghost depicted as a dove flying down from the heavens; a lamb depicted with a cross, banner, and halo; and a heart surrounded by thorns often with flames leaping above it, depicting the Sacred Heart of Jesus.

Within an iron fence in the old section of St. Mary's Cemetery are three tablet tombstones. The small tombstone in the middle is unreadable except for the initials "A. B" but is likely the child of the husband and wife on either side of it. The larger tombstones for **John Becker** (1828–1884) and his wife **Anna Heiken Becker** (1827–1899) feature clasped hands, the symbol of matrimony, with a cross in the background, indicating their Christian faith. The couple was from Hanover and immigrated to Fredericksburg in the 1850s. John's German epitaph is translated: "So, rest then in that peace/that Death has so soon/written for us./Take my hand./Till we see each other again." Anna Becker's German epitaph is translated: "In the land where there's such parting/God unites those who've loved each other here."

HELOTES

Twenty miles northwest of downtown San Antonio, Helotes (pop. 10,000) incorporated in 1981, was settled in the 1850s by immigrants primarily from Germany and Mexico. Helotes was derived from the

Spanish word *elotes*, meaning ears of corn. In 1873, it became a stage-coach stop and remained a farming and ranching community for decades and was a frequent site of cattle drives between San Antonio and Bandera in the late nineteenth and early twentieth centuries. Today, Helotes is a thriving town with a quaint historic district and is often referred to as the "Gateway to the Texas Hill Country."

Zion Lutheran Cemetery #1, originally **Helotes Lutheran Cemetery #1,** at 9944 Leslie Road started as a family burial ground when Swiss immigrant **Anton Gugger** (1807–1881) became the first interment on September 29, 1881. His tablet tombstone, broken but pieced together and cemented upright into a rectangular stone block, features a carved hand, finger pointing up. Etched in German are the words: *zum Andenken an,* "In Memory of." The grave of his wife **Marie** (1819–1911) is marked with a gray granite pillar monument, engraved with the well-known epitaph: RIP "Rest in Peace." Gugger's wife and descendants donated the acreage that included Gugger's grave to Zion Lutheran Church in 1906.

Zion Lutheran Cemetery, a Texas Historic Cemetery with more than 900 graves, contains several unique markers, including trapezoid-shaped slabs encrusted with scallop shells. Some tombstones are engraved in German and others feature oval photographs of the deceased embedded in the stone. Some of the stone markers in the cemetery are memorials for people who were buried at their farms or places of death before the cemetery was established. There are also some reinterments—remains from other burial sites reburied at Zion Lutheran Cemetery.

Among the early pioneers buried in Zion Lutheran Cemetery are **Amalie Mueller Boegel** (1835–1928) and her first husband **Carl Mueller** (1832–1878). The couple operated the Helotes stagecoach stop and established the first post office. Carl was shot and killed over a boundary dispute, and his killer, a neighbor, although charged with murder and going through several trials, was eventually acquitted. Amalie married **Adolph N. Boegel** (1848–1891) a year after Carl's death. She is buried between both husbands under a large shade tree. A flat rectangular tombstone for the trio with the epitaph, "Rest in Peace," marks their graves.

A prominent pioneer ranching family, **Jacob Hoffmann** (1838–1903) and **Carolina Ernst Hoffmann** (1842–1927) and several of their six children are buried here. Son **Frank** (1870–1919), a cowboy, was accidentally shot and killed when a gun fell over and went off as he got out of his vehicle to open a gate near the entrance of their ranch. Their eldest son **Jacob Jr.** (1866–1941) had a mental breakdown, purportedly caused by spending weeks alone in the hills tending sheep. In 1900, he was committed to the State Mental Hospital in San Antonio, where he lived until his death, forty-one years later.

Patriarch Jacob Hoffmann's July 1903 obituary described him as "a wealthy German farmer," who "by hard work and thrift . . . accumulated considerable valuable hay land near the Helotes settlement . . . a stock raiser and farmer" with an "estate . . . estimated to be worth some $80,000," about $2.4 million in today's currency.

The Hoffmann ranch included 12,667 acres. Today, much of the original ranch remains intact within Government Canyon State Natural Area.

KYLE

Twenty miles south of Austin on Interstate Highway 35, Kyle (pop. 52,000) was founded in the early 1880s by Captain Fergus Kyle as a depot for the International-Great Northern Railroad line. Pulitzer Prize–winning author Katherine Anne Porter (1890–1980) was sent to live in Kyle in her formative years. After her mother died in 1892, Katherine moved in with her paternal grandmother, with whom she lived for nine years, until her grandmother's death. Many of Katherine's stories are set in locations in and around Kyle, a farming and ranching community at the time. Incorporated in 1928, the city had the distinction in the 1940s of being the only Texas town with an all-woman government.

The **Kyle Cemetery**, 2601 South Old Stagecoach Road, established in 1849, is a Texas Historic Cemetery. The fifteen acres upon which the cemetery is located belonged to **Colonel Claiborne Kyle** (1800–1867) and wife **Lucy Bugg Kyle** (1801–1863), both from Tennessee. Two burials had already occurred by 1849. The first was that of an unidentified man whom the colonel's ranch hands found hanging from a large oak tree within this acreage. He was buried on the spot underneath what became known as the "Hanging Tree." The other burial was that of Kyle's adopted son, **Willie Parks**, who died in 1849. With more than 1,800 graves, this cemetery holds the remains of some of the earliest Hays County settlers, including Claiborne and his wife Lucy who share a simple granite bevel marker within a curbed plot that is inscribed, "Donors of this Cemetery."

Many Kyle descendants, such as their son **Fergus Kyle** (1833–1906), after whom the town was named, and the grandparents of Katherine Anne Porter, **Catherine Anne Skaggs Porter** (1827–1901) and **Asbury Porter** (1814–1879), are buried here. There are a number of remarkable tombstones in the old section—obelisks with symbolic carvings, pillars topped with urns, and arched memorials, such as the one for Civil War Confederate **Brigadier General Sydney Drake Jackman** (1826–1886) and his first wife, **Martha Rachel Jackman** (1824–1870).

Major Edward Burleson (1826–1877), veteran of the Mexican War and one of the most prominent men in the history of this area, and his wife **Emma Kyle** (1832–1877) share a marble obelisk monument. On one side at the base are clasped hands with the inscription of the couple's wedding date, "Feby 15, 1854." Burleson's obituary appeared in the *Austin Statesman* and was picked up by the *New Yorker*. A report of his burial printed in the May 15, 1877 edition of the *Galveston News* includes the following: "Major B. was a son of General Ed Burleson of the Texas Army and Vice President of the Republic. He was a Delegate from this district to the last Constitutional Convention and was more recently a member of the Commission for the Location of the Branch Penitentiaries. In him Hays County has lost her most valuable citizen and the State one of her most devoted and patriotic sons."

His wife Emma was also a formidable person. As described by a friend who had known her since 1865: "She was a tall woman of commanding appearance, wonderful character and unusual executive ability. When her husband was absent on public affairs, she managed their farm and was the counselor and guide for three daughters and seven sons. She was a model of industry, frugality, and fine judgment. She instilled these characteristics into her children by precept and example."

The **Kyle Family Pioneer Cemetery**, once known as the "Slave Cemetery," adjacent to the Kyle Cemetery on its southern border, is separated by a wrought-iron and limestone entrance gate. Shaded under a grove of large cedar and oak trees, it had been long neglected, overgrown with weeds, and covered in debris. In 1989, Hays County Historical Commission members found sixteen tombstones, mostly broken and fallen over. A restoration project took place in the 1990s. In 2015, this burial ground was awarded Texas Historic Cemetery status. According to the marker text, the 1850 census for the area indicates that Claiborne Kyle owned twenty-eight slaves, ranging from two years to eighty. Burials took place from 1850 to 1938. Few headstones remain and most were carved by hand.

The obelisk tombstone of Vinie Kyle, born a slave, is the most substantial in the Kyle Family Pioneer Cemetery and best preserved. In unmarked graves beside her are her husband Samuel (b. 1839) and several of their children. According to the historical marker at the cemetery, Samuel is believed to be the son of Colonel Claiborne Kyle and slave Kitty Kyle, whose unmarked grave is within this cemetery.

This obelisk tombstone marking the grave of Vinie Kyle, who was born a slave, is the best preserved in the Kyle Family Pioneer Cemetery.

LLANO

Seventy-five miles northwest of Austin, Llano (pop. 3,500) was established in 1856 on the river that bears the same name. A frontier trading center into the 1870s, the town grew after iron deposits were discovered in northwestern Llano County in 1886. Business leaders planned for an iron furnace and foundry and other supportive infrastructure, fully expecting the town to be the new "Pittsburgh of the West." The 1890 population reached 7,000. In 1892, at the peak of the boom, the town was incorporated and a bridge was erected over the river for the railroad. Because of the improved transportation, several granite cutting and finishing businesses moved to town. As for other infrastructure, only a small dam and street lighting were completed. As it turned out, the iron deposits were not large enough for commercial exploitation, so the boom ended. However, granite was available in abundance and that industry flourished. Farming, ranching, and the granite industry remained the foundations of the town's economy into the twentieth century.

The **Llano City Cemetery** at 1410 Hickory Street began with the interment of one-year-old **Tina Miller** in August 1862. A few weeks later, seventeen-year-old **Emily Young Wright** was interred and their two tablet gravestones are the earliest marked burials. Today, this cemetery has more than 5,100 graves. Since 1907, the city of Llano has maintained and enlarged the burial ground and a map and list of burials is available on the city's website. A Texas Historic Cemetery, this burial ground is the final resting place of Llano's civic leaders, elected officials, military veterans, and business owners, as well as **Frank Teich** (1856–1939), a stonecutter and sculptor known as the father of the Texas granite industry. Teich sculpted several cemetery monuments mentioned in this book, such as those of Richard

Coke and David Richard Wallace in Waco's Oakwood Cemetery and the Grief monument over the grave of William Scott Youree in the Scottsville Cemetery.

Teich was born in Lobenstein, Germany. He started painting at age eight. After graduating from the University of Nuremberg, he

Famed sculptor Frank Teich is buried in Llano City Cemetery.

was apprenticed to sculptor Johannes Schilling. He immigrated to the United States in 1878, traveling throughout the country working on monuments. He settled in San Antonio, Texas, where he opened a marble yard in 1885. Not long after, he moved to Llano to take advantage of the readily available granite. In 1901, he opened Teich Monumental Works two miles from town. He was responsible for or worked on hundreds of monuments and statuary, many of them Confederate, throughout Texas and in southern states. His funeral on January 28, 1939, was widely attended and publicized. According to the *Llano News*, "As the funeral rites were conducted, Saturday, in the sunshine of a warm winter day, newspapers and the radio throughout America recorded his passing."

Teich is buried next to his wife **Elvina Lang Teich** (1859–1942), whom he married in 1887 and with whom he had three daughters. The couple each has small bevel granite markers engraved with vines, along with their names and dates of birth and death. They are simple in comparison to the extraordinary statuary and monuments for which Teich was known. However, a larger granite monument that stands within the Teich-Foster family plot is a worthy memorial. **Linden Foster** (1898–1980) was Teich's son-in-law and owner and manager of R & W Granite Monuments in Llano. The gray granite monument erected by Foster's company is framed with vines carved in bas-relief and features a carved oil lamp with a flickering flame ascending from the spout. The oil lamp symbolizes the Bible verse, II Samuel 22:29: "For thou art my lamp, O LORD: and the LORD will lighten my darkness." The light from the lamp represents the pathway to Truth and Knowledge.

$\mathcal{P}_{OLLY}$

Once known as the J. P. Rodriguez settlement, Polly is a rural, unincorporated community founded in the 1850s six miles northeast of Bandera and twenty-eight miles north of Helotes off State Highway 16/Bandera Highway. Named after the famed Indian scout and rancher **José Policarpio (Polly) Rodriguez** (1829–1914), the community had a school, a Methodist Church founded in 1882, a post office established in 1888, a general store, and 300 residents. The post office was discontinued in 1912. The school was consolidated with the Bandera Independent School District in 1942. A church, several scattered houses, and a cemetery marked the community on county highway maps in the late 1940s, but by the 1980s, only the cemetery remained. Today, this area is best known for the chapel built by Rodriguez and its historic cemetery.

Polly's Cemetery, off Privilege Creek Road at 359 Polly's Chapel Road, was established by Polly Rodriguez as a community cemetery on his ranch in the 1890s, although burials began taking place much earlier. He donated one acre for the interment of his family and area residents, and this cemetery is his final resting place underneath a cedar tree. Included on his large granite tombstone is the inscription: "By nature strong, fearless, daring, by grace an apostle to his people winning many souls to Christ. He suffered privation, persecution, sorrow. Unmoved he went with joy and singing to the end." There are about 160 graves, many with markers so old and worn that inscriptions are no longer legible. The majority of those buried here are of Mexican descent and many of the markers are inscribed in Spanish.

Indian scout and rancher José Policarpio (Polly) Rodriguez became a Methodist preacher. A medallion indicating his affiliation with the United Methodist Clergy is affixed on his grave.

Polly was born in Zaragoza, Coahuila, Mexico, in 1829 to a family of means and education. In 1841, his family moved to San Antonio, where he learned gunsmithing and surveying. In 1849, Polly was hired as a scout for the government-contracted Whiting-Smith expedition to establish a westward road from San Antonio to El Paso. The expedition established Polly's reputation as an able and reliable scout. He continued to serve the government in this capacity for the next twelve years. In 1852, he married **Nicolasa Arrocha** (1829–1890), with whom he had five children. Working out of Camp Verde, he had occasion to travel through the hill country of Bandera County, where he purchased 360 acres along Privilege Creek in 1856. He built a home and started a ranch, adding more land. During the Civil War, he volunteered as a private in the Bandera Home Guards. In the 1870s, Polly renounced his Catholic faith and became a Methodist. He was widely ridiculed and condemned. Nevertheless, he embraced his new faith and was granted a license to preach in 1878. In 1882, he built a small chapel where he acted as minister. In 1897, he published his autobiography, *The Old Guide*. His wife Nicolasa died in 1890. Thirteen years later, at age seventy-four, he married **Anastacia Salinas** (1887–?) who was one month shy of sixteen. She bore him four children. He died at age eighty-five on March 22, 1914, in Poteet, Texas.

QUIHI

Twelve miles west of Castroville, Quihi (pop. 100) is a small unincorporated settlement along the perimeter of Henri Castro's land grant. The name comes from the word for a Mexican eagle buzzard, the *quichie* or *keechie*. The first ten families arrived in 1846 and Indians promptly killed two families. Nevertheless, other families followed and the settlers founded Bethlehem Lutheran Church in 1852. The town's small population remained steady. Today the town consists of scattered farms with the church and cemetery comprising the town center.

The Medina County Historical Marker at the cemetery site indicates that there are 104 marked and unmarked graves in the **Bethlehem Lutheran Cemetery** at 3901 Farm Road 2676 in Quihi. Many are enclosed within rusted wrought-iron fences, tombstones askew from shifting ground. The cemetery was consecrated next to the original church building in 1864. The first recorded burial was that of **Frederick Boehle** in 1867, while the last burial in 1936 was of **Anna Heichmann Neumann** (1849–1936). Many of the tombstones have touching inscriptions in German, such as that of **Ernst August Bohlen** (1842–1915), whose obelisk red granite marker enclosed within an ornamental iron fence is here translated: "The still grave does not scare the believer./He hopes in God and has/no fear of judgment."

The graves in this cemetery were arranged chronologically and numbered that way in church records, which were inscribed in an old German dialect that few people could translate. Many of the early graves had wooden markers lost to time. Twelve children died in the 1918 influenza pandemic. They were buried in the southeast part of the cemetery and their unmarked graves can be seen by aligned surface depressions made by rotting wooden caskets. Two graves just outside the original cemetery boundaries are those of individuals who could not be buried in consecrated church grounds because of their manner of death. **Herman Gerdes** (1842–?) committed suicide. His grave was dug in a lane between the cemetery and a field. He had a tombstone, but it was lost and the area where he was buried plowed over.

The other grave outside the cemetery and still prominently visible is that of **August Mumme** (1851–1879). Buried across a road that runs through the far side of the cemetery, his grave, with its prominent tombstone within a concrete enclosure, is situated on a north-south axis, rather than the traditional east-west orientation. Linda Gilliam Vereen, a Mumme family descendant, reported two stories regarding his death. The first is that August, twenty-eight at the time of his death, got involved with a band of local cattle rustlers. He became fearful of his involvement and resolved to turn his cohorts in to the authorities. Before he could do so, they murdered him. Another version is that August turned outlaw and was killed in the act of cattle rustling. The German inscription on his tombstone indicates he was murdered at the hands of his acquaintances, and three sets of initials are inscribed. Here is the English translation: "Murdered by a known hand. J.M. M.G. C.W./Am I dead? Oh no, thou Loved Ones./Life flows freely above./All death is left below./ All dying is past./Do you know how that happens?/Come higher,/ Come and see."

August Mumme was refused burial at his home church cemetery. His family then applied to Bethlehem Lutheran Church, whose minister agreed to bury him but not within the consecrated burial grounds.

CHRISTIAN BURIAL PROHIBITIONS

Rules that apply to burial in consecrated church graveyards have been in effect for thousands of years, although today these prohibitions may be applied less stringently than in the past. To consecrate means to "set aside" and make holy as a tribute to God. Burying someone who has not met established Christian standards in consecrated ground renders that ground "unholy" and "unsanctified." Prohibitions for exclusion from Christian burial include those not baptized and individuals who have proved themselves unworthy, such as pagans, infidels, heretics, and apostates. The prohibition against Christian burial for suicides—except in cases that the act was committed when they were of unsound mind or unless they showed signs of repentance before death—is as old as the fourth century. Christian burial has also been withheld from those who have been killed in a duel and notorious sinners who died without repentance. Ordinarily, the local church clergy has the final say in whether the deceased can be buried in a church graveyard. The burials of **Herman Gerdes**, a suicide, and **August Mumme**, an outlaw murder victim, outside the boundaries of Bethlehem Lutheran Church Cemetery but within range indicate a compromise, likely to help ease the heartache of the families.

UVALDE

Eighty-three miles west of San Antonio and sixty-two miles from the Mexican border, Uvalde (pop. 16,000), first called Encina, was founded by Reading W. Black in 1855. He and Nathan L. Stratton operated a ranch here. Black opened a store, two rock quarries, and a lime kiln and established a permanent home. In 1856, when the county was organized, the town was chosen as the county seat and renamed Uvalde after Spanish governor Juan de Ugalde (1729–1816), a captain in the Spanish Army and famed Indian fighter in Texas.

Lawlessness and border warfare continued into the late 1880s; nevertheless, in 1888, the town was incorporated and two years later had a population of 2,000 and sixty businesses, with agriculture as its primary economic base. Guajillo honey dating back to the 1870s continues to be an important export. Uvalde was also the home of John Nance "Cactus Jack" Garner, former Speaker of the House and vice president of the United States.

When the city of Uvalde put a street through its city cemetery, graves on the east side were moved to a new section, which they designated **Pioneer Cemetery**, 500 North Park Street. In a large open field with a few large oaks scattered throughout, the cemetery has more than forty marked and unmarked graves with timeworn and intriguing tombstones and gravesites. The manner and/or location of death are etched on at least three of the tombstones: "Killed by Indians," "Assassinated by Indians," and "Killed in Mexico." Although Uvalde's founder is buried in the Uvalde City Cemetery, a unique and imposing memorial for him was erected in the center back of Pioneer Cemetery underneath the shade of a large oak. Concrete and rocks were fashioned to look like a large tree trunk surrounded by logs. A plaque attached to the trunk monument reads: "In Appreciation of **Reading Wood Black** (1830–1867), Who Came to Texas from New Jersey in 1852 and Founded Uvalde in May 1855."

This cemetery is known as the final resting place of **John King Fisher** (1854–1884), known as **King Fisher**, a notorious frontier outlaw turned lawman. Born in Collin County in North Texas, Fisher and his family moved to Florence in central Texas, where his career as an outlaw began when he was fifteen. A neighbor accused him of stealing a horse and then changed his mind, helping the boy escape. Fisher fled to Goliad, where he was arrested for breaking into someone's house. This time he was sent to prison. He was released after four months and established a ranch on Pendencia Creek, forty-five miles southwest of Uvalde and about forty miles east of the Mexican border. This region was known as the Nueces Strip, where cattle rustling was a major business. Fisher became one of the leaders of the Strip. Drifters, criminals, and rustlers were protected at his ranch. An imposing figure, he often wore an ornamented Mexican sombrero, a black Mexican jacket embroidered with gold, a crimson sash, and boots, with two silver-plated, ivory-handled revolvers swinging from his belt.

Fisher was arrested at various times for murder, and horse and cattle theft, managing to avoid conviction. However, these legal ordeals took their toll and Fisher decided to give up his lawless life. In April 1876, he married **Sarah Elizabeth Vivian** (1856–1946), with whom he had four children. He later bought a ranch near Eagle Pass. His reformed life and reputation as a gunslinger spurred Uvalde County leaders to appoint him deputy sheriff in 1881. He was efficient and popular. As a result, after the sheriff was indicted in 1883, Fisher became acting sheriff. He made plans to run for the office in 1884, but in March of that year, fate intervened. He was on a trip to San Antonio and met up with the noted gunman and Austin City Marshal **Ben Thompson** (see Austin, Oakwood Cemetery). They went to the Vaudeville Variety Theater in San Antonio, where they were involved in a shootout. Both Fisher and Thompson were killed in the melee. Fisher's body was returned to Uvalde. According to one newspaper account, a large number of citizens met the train carrying his casket. They expressed "great regret at his death."

Fisher's original grave was located after one of Uvalde's senior citizens remembered marking an old oak tree at the time of the lawman's burial. When the grave was opened, Fisher's cast-iron coffin with its glass viewing panel and welded lid was still intact. His body and fancy clothing were still well preserved. He was reburied beneath a large oak tree within an iron fence enclosure in Pioneer Cemetery. A Texas Historical Marker about him was erected at Pioneer Cemetery in 1973.

Pompeo Coppini sculpted this angel that stands prominently in the Hutchings family plot in Galveston's Trinity Episcopal Cemetery.

CHAPTER 5

INDEPENDENCE TRAIL REGION

The struggle for Texas Independence was an epic saga that, almost 200 years later, continues to reverberate throughout the world. Who doesn't "Remember the Alamo?" The twenty-eight-county Independence Trail Region stretches more than 200 miles, from San Antonio to Galveston along the Gulf of Mexico coastline, encompassing a rich historical tapestry of towns and settlements, battlefields, and missions that tell the story of this epic struggle for freedom and its aftermath.

GALVESTON

When French pirate Jean Lafitte, Galveston's first European settler, arrived on the island in 1817, he encountered the native Karankawa Indian tribe. By the next year, the tribe was all but annihilated when a battle broke out after Lafitte's men kidnapped a Karankawa woman. Initially, under Lafitte's leadership, the colony grew to 2,000 inhabitants and 120 structures, funded by stolen currency and goods. Storms destroyed most of the colony, and in 1821, Lafitte burned down his island fortress and was on the run. Galveston (pop. 50,500), fifty miles southeast of Houston, became the Mexican port of entry. In 1836, the

Texas Army retreated here before their victory at San Jacinto. After the revolution, the island became a popular seaport and by the 1880s, the business district was booming and grand Victorian homes were being constructed.

On September 8, 1900, a devastating hurricane and tidal wave destroyed much of the island, leaving 6,000 dead, becoming the worst natural disaster in the history of the United States. In 1902, city leaders authorized the construction of a seawall to help lessen damage from future storms. The new seawall, fortified over the years, has protected the island from subsequent storms.

A monument to commemorate the thousands who perished was commissioned and installed on 4800 Seawall Boulevard in 2000, the 100th anniversary of the hurricane. Artist David Moore created the impressive 1900 Storm Memorial, a ten-foot-tall bronze statue of a small family, the man reaching one arm to the sky, his other arm around his wife who is cradling a child in her arms. With a backdrop of the Gulf, waves crashing against the shore, the statue is a striking memorial and reminder of the tragic loss of life in the 1900 storm.

The earliest burial grounds in Galveston were the large sand dunes covered with grass and trees on the side of the island facing the Gulf of Mexico. In 1839, 250 victims of a yellow fever epidemic were buried in the dunes. Storms and the natural cycle of rain and wind gradually swept the sand away, exposing bodies and caskets. Realizing this burial system would never work, city leaders donated four city blocks that same year, establishing Old City Cemetery and a Potter's Field for the indigent. This burial ground was well outside the city limits at the time. Many of those previously buried in the sand dunes were exhumed and reinterred at the new city cemetery, and, as others were exposed by the elements, they too were reburied in the new cemetery, their identities often unknown. As the years went by, more acreage was added. Today, this area is known as the **Broadway Cemetery Historic District.**

On Broadway between 40th and 43rd Streets and bisected by Avenue K, the **Broadway Cemetery Historic District** encompasses six city blocks and seven burial grounds, plotted between 1839 and 1939. Collectively the cemeteries resemble a city of stone, their monuments and statuary grand, expansive, and awe-inspiring. The architectural styles include Greek, Italian, and Renaissance, and a variety of symbolic carvings adorn the tombstones. Because of erosion, settling, and extreme weather, grade raisings have occurred periodically. Between 1904 and 1910, many of the mausoleums and monuments were elevated. Nevertheless, today only the top portions of many of the mausoleums are visible.

Kathleen Maca, an expert on the history of the cemeteries and author of *Galveston's Broadway Cemeteries,* said that the last grave raising was in the 1920s and today what people see is only the top of three layers of burials: "The cemeteries have been raised two or three times in different areas, and when the stones were lost during the raisings, they just resold the plots and did another burial on top." About 6,000 grave markers are visible, but that figure is only a fraction of the bodies actually buried. By 1939, an estimated 28,000 people were buried in Oleander Cemetery alone.

The entire complex of tombstones, monuments, and statuary is paved with walkways and each cemetery is delineated and indicated with a sign: **Old City Cemetery** (1839); **Potter's Field** (1839), renamed **Oleander Cemetery** (1939); **Trinity Episcopal Cemetery** (1844); **Old Catholic Cemetery** (1844); **Old Cahill Cemetery/ Yellow Fever Yard** (1867), renamed **New City Cemetery** (1900); **Hebrew Benevolent Society Cemetery** (1868); and **New Cahill Cemetery** (1900), renamed **Evergreen Cemetery** (1923).

Major General John Bankhead Magruder (1810–1871) was a West Point graduate from Virginia, a career soldier who served in the US Army and the Confederate States Army. Magruder's ornate marble obelisk marker stands near the wrought-iron fence that borders **Trinity Episcopal Cemetery**. Famed sculptor Pompeo Coppini designed the monument, but it was carved by a monument maker from Galveston. The obelisk features carvings of four branches of the military forces active in the Battle of Galveston during the Civil War.

Magruder, said to have been "the wittiest man in the old army," resigned from the US Army on April 20, 1861, was commissioned a brigadier general in the Confederate service, and was quickly promoted to major general. Magruder, who spoke with a lisp, was assigned to the Texas District by General Robert E. Lee. He was six feet tall and was said to have been "the handsomest soldier in the Confederacy." Although he was married, few people knew he was. According to a friend, "He was a born soldier. . . . He would fight all day and dance all night." His wife, whom he married in 1831, lived in Baltimore and he saw her only on occasional furloughs, but long enough to have three children, the last born in 1841. Although he made his home in Houston, he was buried in Galveston, the city he victoriously recaptured on January 1, 1863.

The **Alberti** monument, a block of gray granite, also in Trinity Episcopal Cemetery, has a list of nine names engraved upon it. Five have the same year of death—1894. The tragic story of those buried here begins with a mother—**Elize "Lizzie" Roemer Alberti** (1858–1898)—wife of the local butcher **Louis G. Alberti** (1852–1915). After her eighth child **Caroline** was born in 1894 and then promptly died in April of that year, **Elize** began to exhibit strange behavior and had violent outbursts. She'd experienced the death of another child ten years earlier, when her first child, **Louis Jr.**, died of lockjaw at age seven. Her neighbors later told news reporters they first noticed her "mental affliction" then, but she wasn't violent. The death of Caroline was apparently more than she could take. In May, relatives intervened and she was sent to live with her parents who also resided in Galveston. They believed a change of scenery would help her. After a few weeks, she returned home and resumed her duties.

On December 4, 1894, while her husband was at work next door, she called her six children downstairs and made them drink wine mixed with morphine. Four of them—**Willie**, age four; **Dora**, age six; **Elize**, age eight; and **Ella**, age ten—passed away in great agony within hours. One daughter didn't hear her call, so she didn't go downstairs. Another survived. Mrs. Alberti, who'd previously told her children she was going to poison them, was taken to a mental hospital in San Antonio, where she stayed for four years. She was released and a few weeks later, on

September 30, 1898, she committed suicide from an overdose of morphine. She was buried with her children. Her husband Louis, left to raise their two surviving daughters, died in 1915, and is also buried in the family plot, along with Mrs. Alberti's younger sister **Dorothea Roemer** (1870–1895) who died of lung congestion a year after the tragedy.

Not far from the Alberti plot, a Coppini Angel stands over the grave of **Frances Hutchings Byrne** (1867–1922). Frances was one of nine children of **John Henry Hutchings** (1822–1906), a prominent Galveston banker and businessman who was crucial in improving the local harbor, and wife **Minnie Knox Hutchings** (1838–1915), a

Celtic crosses mark graves in many cemeteries in Texas, but the addition of the carving of an Egyptian pharaoh in the Hutchings family plot is rare. Another exquisite statue is the Coppini Angel on the right, sculpted by Pompeo Coppini. In the background, far right is one of the many submerged mausoleums.

socialite. Frances was a widow at the time of her death, and her children commissioned Pompeo Coppini to sculpt the statue for her grave. The large Celtic cross over John and Minnie's graves in the center of the Hutchings plot is most unusual for the carving of an Egyptian pharaoh on the vertical bar. The Celtic cross, a long vertical bar and a shorter horizontal bar that intersects the vertical higher than half way with a circle surrounding the intersection, dates back 5,000 years to the Romans and the Egyptians. It is believed to be representative of the Latin cross and the Anka, an Egyptian symbol that represents "the key of life." The meaning of the circle stands for eternity.

INDIANOLA

An enormous granite statue overlooking Matagorda Bay on South Ocean Drive in Indianola, memorializes French explorer René Robert Cavelier, Sieur de La Salle, who established a small colony here in 1685. La Salle was murdered two years later while on another expedition and by 1670, only fifteen of 200 colonists left in Indianola were still alive. This port, 156 miles southwest of Galveston Island, became a debarkation point for German colonization in 1845. However, more than 4,300 immigrants were stranded that year because their agents had gone broke. Mosquito-borne illnesses, cholera, and other diseases claimed many lives. Several settlers decided to walk to their destinations of New Braunfels and Fredericksburg. When they arrived, they infected more people, causing hundreds of deaths.

Despite this early calamity, Indianola flourished for thirty years as a port supplying forts on the western frontier. For a time, it was a thriving second port on the gulf. Several natural disasters changed all that. In 1867, a fire ravaged the town and that same year a yellow fever epidemic caused a number of deaths. With a population in 1875 of more than 5,000, Indianola was ravaged by a hurricane on September 16, 1875, which caused great loss of life and destroyed the port. The town rebuilt on a smaller scale and then was almost obliterated by the hurricane of August 20, 1886. That storm demoralized the population and forced them to move inland. Today, Indianola is called "The Queen of Texas Ghost Towns," a small, unincorporated fishing village with three small cemeteries, one of them featured here.

Old Town Cemetery, a **Texas Historic Cemetery** on Zimmerman Road, is on an elevated ridge overlooking a marsh and Indianola Beach. About fifty stone tombstones and a few well-preserved zinc obelisks are spread across the ridge. The oldest burial is that of **James Chilton Allan** (1810–1851), a judge and lieutenant in the Confederate Army. Also buried here are some of Calhoun County's earliest settlers who came in the first wave of German immigration to Texas. Many of the original tombstones, including Allan's, were lost during the hurricanes of the late nineteenth century. Markers with the inscription "Known Only To God" have been placed on several graves.

Angelina Bell Peyton Eberly (1798–1860), known as the heroine of the Archives War, was born in Tennessee in 1798. A small ledger marker with a Citizen of the Republic of Texas medallion commemorates her burial at the Old Town Cemetery as her original tombstone was lost during the 1875 hurricane. A Texas Historical Marker about her was also erected at the intersection of State Highway 316 and Zimmerman Road.

When Angelina was twenty, she married her first cousin Jonathan Peyton. They came to Texas in 1822, moving to San Felipe de Austin, the capital of Stephen F. Austin's colonies, forty-eight miles west of Houston. Together with their three children and several slaves, they operated an inn called Peytons [*sic*] Tavern. Two years after Peyton died in 1834, Angelina married widower Jacob Eberly. They made their home in Austin, where Angelina opened a tavern called the Eberly House, a popular eatery for politicians.

In 1842, Angelina, again a widow after her second husband's death the year before, became aware of the controversy involving President Houston's desire to relocate the government to Houston. She woke one night and saw twenty men secretly removing records from the capitol and loading them into wagons. She ran to a nearby cannon staged downtown to alert residents in case of Indian attacks and lit the fuselage. A six-pound cannonball exploded, crashing into the side wall of the Land Office Building, waking the town's residents. This started what was called the "Archives War," and resulted in the "rescue" of the original records of the Republic of Texas and the preservation of Austin as the capital. Already a respected businesswoman, she became a Texas patriot and heroine to Austinites. Four years later, Angelina moved to Lavaca (Port Lavaca today) and leased a tavern house there. In 1851, she opened the first hotel in Indianola, where she died in 1860.

In Austin, a bronze, life-size sculpture of Angelina firing the cannon stands on the northwest corner of the intersection of 6th Street and Congress Avenue, just south of the capitol—the exact location of the original cannon.

The **Rahtgens** family plot within a rusted iron fence enclosure in Old Town Cemetery provides a sobering glimpse into the tragic past of this seaport ghost town. Underneath a zinc obelisk monument with removable panels are graves of a mother, father, and seven children.

John Henry Rahtgens (1827–1879) was born in Lubeck, Germany. A seaman, he arrived in the United States in 1845. He met **Alice Owen** (1830–1909), an orphan who'd immigrated to the United States the same year with a group of other Irish immigrants. In 1852, they married in Cameron, Texas, and after the birth of their first child, a son, they moved to Indianola. Several more children were born, five of whom died in the various epidemics and storms that plagued the port town in those early years. One son, John, escaped the calamities of Indianola, only to die in a train wreck near El Paso in 1886, ironically the same year the hurricane wiped out Indianola, taking his sister Nettie. **James Augustus**, age three, died in 1858; **Richard**, age ten days, died in 1859; **James Jefferson**, age three, died June 1867; **William**, age one, died in September 1867; **John**, age twenty-eight, died in March 1886; **Henrietta "Nettie,"** age twenty, died October 1886. On the monument in bas-relief is the year 1886, presumably the year the marker was erected.

Their firstborn, **Thomas Henry** (1853–1923), also buried here, survived and moved to Port Lavaca with his mother after Nettie's death. Another sister **Alice Ellen** (1861–1905), who married W. H. Smith and is buried in a Port Lavaca Cemetery, is the only Rahtgens who married and had descendants.

SAN JACINTO BATTLEGROUND STATE HISTORICAL PARK

This historic park is located in what was once the town of San Jacinto until the hurricane of 1885 wiped it out. This site is where the Texas Army, under the leadership of General Sam Houston, secured Texas Independence on April 21, 1836. The park, at the juncture of Independence Parkway and Park Road 1836, is adjacent to the Buffalo Bayou leg of the Houston Ship Channel in Harris County, five miles northeast of the intersection of State Highways 134 and 225, twenty-two miles east of downtown Houston.

The battle of San Jacinto lasted less than thirty minutes. According to General Houston's report, 630 Mexicans were killed and 730 were taken prisoner. Mexican General Antonio López de Santa Anna escaped but was captured the next day. Only nine Texans were killed in the battle. One, **Olwyn J. Trask**, who was wounded, went to Galveston, where he died several days after the battle. The other eight were buried next to each other at their campsite. Their resting place became the nucleus of the cemetery for the town of San Jacinto.

Mortally wounded during the battle of San Jacinto, **Sergeant Benjamin Rice Brigham** (1815–1836) was twenty-one years old when he died the night of April 22, 1836. In 1882, a blue marble obelisk memorializing the nine soldiers who died during the 1836 Battle of San Jacinto was placed at the head of his grave, chosen because his tombstone was the only one still there forty-six years after the battle. His name is inscribed above the names of the seven other soldiers buried near him and the soldier who died in Galveston. The others are **Lemuel Stockton Blakey, John C. Hale, George A. Lamb, Dr. William Junius Mottley, Mathias Cooper, Thomas Patton Fowle,** and **Ashley R. Stephens.**

The Texans' animosity toward the Mexican soldiers because of the massacres at the Alamo and at Goliad was so great that they left their enemy dead to rot on the battlefield. Instead of burying or burning the more than 600 bodies, the Texas Army just moved away, leaving the decaying corpses and resulting stench for the locals to deal with. The residents finally took action when they discovered their cattle were chewing on the bones of the dead, which according to one observer, imparted such a sickening odor and taste to the beef and milk that neither could be used. They gathered the remains and buried them in trenches in an unknown location at the battle site. There are no markers and no memorials for the Mexican soldiers who died here.

In 1883, the state purchased ten acres that included the cemetery grounds. By 1930, the state had purchased 402 acres surrounding the cemetery. The ten-acre historic **San Jacinto Cemetery** is now partially covered by a parking lot to accommodate visitors to the *Battleship Texas*, and several graves with tombstones are located on some of the bulb-outs. Throughout the nineteenth century, Texans revered the site as "hallowed ground" and "sacred soil." The battlefield became the first Texas state park in 1907 and a National Historic Landmark in 1960.

A small section of the San Jacinto Cemetery is cordoned off as the **De Zavala Family Cemetery. Lorenzo de Zavala** (1788–1836), who served as the interim vice president of Texas in 1836, is buried there, along with several of his relations. According to a Texas Historical Marker at the site, de Zavala was born in Yucatán and educated in the Seminary of Ildefonso. Jailed from 1814 to 1817 for political activities, he learned English and became a medical doctor while in prison. After Mexico won independence from Spain, he kept working for democratic reforms. Loyal to the 1824 Constitution of Mexico, he opposed Dictator Santa Anna and moved to Texas to seek freedom. On March 2, 1836, he signed Texas's Declaration of Independence. Later he signed the Republic of Texas Constitution. Married twice, he had six children. The Texas Legislature in 1858 named Zavala County in his honor.

Lorenzo de Zavala, many of his descendants, and some of their neighbors and friends were interred in the De Zavala Family Cemetery on the plantation across Buffalo Bayou from this burial site at San Jacinto. The original cemetery established in 1836 was located on the de Zavala estate at Zavala Point, about half a mile north across the Houston Ship Channel from where the *Battleship Texas* is docked in San Jacinto Battleground Park. Over the next 125 years, tides, erosion, subsidence, and powerful ship wakes caused serious deterioration of the property. Graves were dangerously close to falling into Buffalo Bayou. In the 1960s, the bodies were reinterred in their present location at the San Jacinto historic site, with a red granite marker placed at de Zavala's grave. The San Jacinto monument on the southeast end of the park, a 567.31-foot-high column topped with a 220-ton star, provides an inspiring backdrop to this cemetery.

COLUMBUS

Columbus (pop. 3,600) was founded in 1821 on the site of an old Indian village called Montezuma. At the junction of Interstate Highway 10 and State Highway 71, sixty-five miles west of Houston, the settlement was one of Stephen F. Austin's first colonies established by some of his grantees, often referred to as Austin's "Old Three Hundred." First called Beeson's Ferry, named after Benjamin Beeson who operated a ferry across the Colorado River, the settlement had a rocky start, suffering from frequent Indian attacks. Nevertheless, by the time of the Texas Revolution, the town, renamed Columbus, was home to more than twenty-five families. However, General Sam Houston ordered the town to be burned down as the Mexican Army approached. Residents fled in what was called the Runaway Scrape in the spring of 1836. By the next year, townspeople had rebuilt and in 1847 Columbus had twenty houses, three stores, two taverns, and a smithy. Horseracing, betting, drinking, and chewing tobacco were favorite pastimes. The town, with a nineteenth-century economic base of tobacco and cotton, prospered.

The ten-acre **Columbus City Cemetery**, also known as **Old City Cemetery**, at 1300 Walnut/US Highway 90 off Veterans Drive, was established in the early 1850s, although the city of Columbus did not formally purchase it until 1870. The cemetery, with more than 1,000 burials, was in wide use until December 1913, when a flood washed out many of the graves and carried off several markers. Most of the burials since then have been of indigent blacks, although a few blacks were also buried here earlier. The old section in the back shaded by a copse of large oak trees has an abundance of old and weathered tombstones. Buried here are several of Stephen F. Austin's first colony settlers, such as ferry owner **Benjamin Beeson** (1786–1837), town founder **William B. DeWees** (1799–1878), and Runaway Scrape memoirist **Dilue Rose Harris** (1825–1914), along with several notable German immigrants.

Although his burial place is not marked, it is likely that **Detlef Jordt** (1793–1847) who wrote the classic travel journal, *Journey to Texas* (1833), under the pseudonym Detleff Dunt is buried in the Jordt family plot in Columbus. Dunt's book, along with other glowing accounts of Texas, inspired a historic stream of German immigration in the nineteenth century. Jordt arrived in Texas from Germany in early 1833, and his subsequent observations about Texas were profusely positive: "It is a land that puts riches in his [the immigrant's] lap . . . a country just waiting for people so that our European industry can raise and elevate it to the most blessed country in all the known world." He went back to Germany and returned with his two sons in 1836 after the War of Independence. His wife and daughters joined him soon after, settling in Columbus.

Underneath an enormous old oak, the **Jordt family** plot is surrounded by a rusted iron fence. Several pillar and tablet tombstones identify the graves of Detleff's wife **Dorothea Heeder Jordt** (1802–1870), his daughters, sons, and several grandchildren, four who died as toddlers, and one who died at age eighteen during the yellow fever epidemic of 1873.

Phillip Kretschmer (1849–1897) was not related to the Jordts but was very close to the family and to one granddaughter, in particular. Phillip emigrated from Bohemia, settling in Columbus in 1876. In his last will and testament written three days before his death on August 19, 1897, he left his entire estate to Miss **Dora Harde** (1862–1919), granddaughter of Detleff and Dorothea Jordt. Dora was thirty-five at the time of Phillip's death. They lived next door to each other, and Phillip worked for Dora's father, a merchant in Columbus. His obituary states that he died after "a three weeks' illness of inflammation of the bowels and other maladies in his forty-eighth year." His monument is inscribed: "God, in his wisdom, has recalled,/ The boon his love had given;/And though the body/moulders here,/ The soul is safe in Heaven."

On another panel, under a bas-relief bouquet of flowers, is the following:

Upon our dreams their dying eyes/In still and mournful fondness rise;/What fond strange yearnings/from the soul's deep cell/Gush for the faces we may no more see;/How are we haunted in the wind's low tone/by voices that are gone:/ Looks of familiar love/that never on Earth/our aching eyes shall meet,/But they are where these longings vain/ trouble no more the heart and brain;/the sadness of this aching love,/Dims not Our Father's House above,/nor shall the love so purified be vain,/Severed on Earth, we yet shall/ meet again.

The angel monument marking the grave of Phillip Kretschmer in the Jordt family plot gives testament to a deep love.

Although Dora married Ferdinand Guenther in 1901, when she died eighteen years later, she was buried next to Phillip. Her grave is marked by a simple, but substantial, square tombstone.

OLD THREE HUNDRED

Between 1824 and 1827, Stephen F. Austin granted 297 families and some partnerships of unmarried men, 307 land titles—a minimum of 177 acres for farming or 4,428 acres to raise livestock. These settlers are often referred to as the "Old Three Hundred." They established a colony between the Brazos and Colorado Rivers from the Gulf Coast to the San Antonio Road with the proviso that the land must be occupied and improved within two years or the grants would be forfeited.

The majority of the Old Three Hundred colonists, almost all of British ancestry, were from the Trans-Appalachian South: Louisiana, Alabama, Arkansas, Tennessee, and Missouri. Austin chose settlers based on proof of industry, literacy (all but four of the men could read and write), and their economic status. About one-quarter brought slaves. Austin's criteria for his choice of colonists enabled them and their settlements to flourish. Despite Mexican law requiring immigrants to be Catholic, most of Austin's settlers were Protestant.

GOLIAD

The city of Goliad (pop. 2,000) originated as one of the oldest Spanish colonial municipalities in the state, established in 1749 as Presidio La Bahía. Built on a hill near the San Antonio River, it grew into the settlement of La Bahía and on the opposite bank of the river stood

Mission Espíritu Santo. Early in 1829, a Coahuila y Tejas state legislator petitioned the governor to change the town's name to Goliad, an anagram of the name of Father Hidalgo, the priest who instigated the Mexican independence movement. On February 4, 1829, La Bahía became Villa de Goliad.

Goliad played an important role in the battle for Texas Independence, becoming the first town to sign a document for independence and hoisting the first flag of independence. The town became known for the Goliad massacre, the infamous execution of Texas revolutionary **Colonel James Walker Fannin** (1804–1836) and his command of 342 soldiers. Occurring three weeks after the fall of the Alamo, this massacre inflamed the passions of Texans exponentially against Mexican rule.

After the Battle of San Jacinto a month later, many of Goliad's Mexican citizens fled to Mexico and Anglo-Americans moved north of the river to the present townsite. Throughout the nineteenth century, cotton-growing and the cattle industry were prominent.

After the executions of Colonel Fannin and his men, the bodies were burned, the remains left exposed. Several months later, in June 1836, General Thomas J. Rusk (see Nacogdoches, Oak Grove Cemetery) was passing through Goliad and ordered the remains to be gathered and buried with military honors. This common grave was unmarked until about 1858, when a Goliad merchant placed a pile of rocks on what was believed to be the burial site. A memorial was erected in town in 1885. Forty-five years later, in 1930, a troop of Goliad Boy Scouts found charred bone fragments that had been unearthed over the years by animals. This discovery attracted an investigation of the site by a University of Texas anthropologist and historians who verified the authenticity of the gravesite. In 1936, in celebration of the Texas Centennial, the Texas Legislature appropriated money to build a massive pink granite cenotaph, dedicated on June 4, 1938.

The forty-five-foot-tall **Fannin Memorial Monument**, etched with the names of the soldiers killed, stands behind and adjacent to Presidio la Bahía, one-and-a-half miles south of Goliad on US 183. One of the inscriptions reads, "Beneath this monument repose their charred remains. Remember Goliad."

A chapel was erected within the walls of the Presidio La Bahía for the local soldiers and Spanish settlers. Called "Our Lady of Loreto," it has been in continuous use since the 1700s. Several burials took place within and outside the chapel over the years. Through archeological excavations and oral history, some of the individuals buried in the **Presidio La Bahía Chapel Burial Grounds** have been identified. Within the chapel near the altar is the grave of **Carlos de la Garza**, who died before 1870. A mass grave of five unknown individuals is about halfway into the chapel from the front doors. Outside the chapel is the marked grave of **Annie L. Taylor** (1852–1880), a married Mexican woman who died of tuberculosis. Her grave, with its original tombstone, is one of several in the courtyard in front of the chapel, some of them noted by small crosses cut into the stone walls at the base of the church. During an excavation of the presidio, thirteen graves, including that of Taylor, were found outside the church. Although five of the individuals buried are unknown, the

Of the thirteen graves discovered in the courtyard of the chapel of the Presidio La Bahía, only the grave of Annie L. Taylor is marked. Inside and beneath the chapel floor are six graves.

other gravesites were identified by descendants as those of **Bernardo Esparsa**; **Benito Bontan** and his son **José**, both murdered in 1870; **Daria Dwyer** and her son **Santiago**, who died in the 1880s; and two **de la Garza** sisters.

THE STINKING RICH

For centuries, burials took place within churches under the floor beneath the apse, in underground vaults, or in crypts along the walls, but only for those who could pay for the honor. The stench from the decomposing corpses—many not entombed in coffins—was often so severe, especially on damp days that it permeated the stone floors and walls and wafted into the church gallery. The term "Stinking Rich" is said to have originated from this custom, which persisted into the nineteenth century, although by the eighteenth century Europe's monarchs had begun to actively promote the end of such burials. In 1787, the Catholic Church prohibited burials within a church, but the custom persisted after that date. In some countries, these measures met with resistance because they damaged the interest of the privileged. Spain, one of the last holdouts, finally came around in the nineteenth century, due to the fearsome cholera epidemic that killed 800,000 people. Nevertheless, the rich continued to demonstrate their wealth in the new cemeteries constructed outside the city erecting massive memorial monuments of stone.

GONZALES

Historic Gonzales (pop. 7,500), seventy-four miles east of San Antonio on Highway 90, became the capital of DeWitt's colony (named after Green DeWitt) in 1825 and was named after Rafael Gonzales, the governor of Coahuila and Texas. The westernmost point of the Anglo-American settlement, it was the closest town to San Antonio de Béjar and the center for much revolutionary activity. In October 1835, Mexican dragoons tried to retrieve the town cannon. Town residents refused and challenged the Mexicans to "Come and Take

It." The Texans assembled a group of volunteers numbering about 140 and the Mexican troop leader, finding himself outnumbered, ordered a withdrawal to Béjar. This episode was the first skirmish of the battle for Texas Independence. Gonzales was incorporated in 1880 and had a population of 2,900 by 1884. The Gonzales Memorial Museum houses the Come and Take it cannon and a replica of the flag.

The **Green DeWitt Cemetery**, a Texas Historic Cemetery, is on a hill two miles south of Gonzales on 2301 County Road 197 at its juncture with Highway 183 in JB Wells Park. It overlooks arenas, show barns, and a covered pavilion, part of the 169-acre park. The one-acre family cemetery of about fifteen graves within a wrought-iron fence started with the burial of **Jonas DeWitt** (1850–1851), grandson of **Green DeWitt** (1787–1835) and **Sarah Seely DeWitt** (1787–1854), who moved their family from Missouri to Texas in 1826.

Green DeWitt, who founded Gonzales, successfully petitioned the Mexican government for an empresario grant to settle 400 Anglo-Americans on lands southwest of Stephen F. Austin's colony. However, his colony struggled against Indian attacks, and by 1831, he had lost his contract. By that time, Sarah had successfully petitioned the Mexican government for a grant of one league in her maiden name. The cemetery is on her land grant.

Green died in Monclova, Mexico, in 1835 while there to purchase land for future settlements. He was buried there. A small memorial for him was placed at the family cemetery in Gonzales. Sarah is best known for making the "Come and Take It" flag. She cut up her daughter Naomi's wedding dress to create the famous banner. Buried next to her husband's memorial, she is described on her slab grave as "the Consort of Empresario Green DeWitt." A Texas memorial marker behind her slab is dedicated to both her and her husband. All of the original tablet gravestones are encased in concrete. There is also a tall pillar monument with an urn on top designating the graves of several DeWitt descendants.

HOUSTON

Today, Houston covers more than 620 square miles and is the fourth-largest city in the United States with a population of more than 2.3 million. The city began in 1836 when Augustus Chapman Allen and his brother John Kirby Allen ran an advertisement in a newspaper for the "Town of Houston," claiming it would become a "great interior commercial emporium of Texas," based on its close proximity to the Buffalo Bayou, a ship channel.

At the time, the area was little more than a humid, mosquito-infested swamp overgrown with sweet gum trees and coffee bean weeds. The brothers named their town after General Sam Houston and persuaded the Texas Congress to designate it the temporary capital of the Republic of Texas. By April 1837, 1,500 people lived in the new town, which was incorporated two months later. Yellow fever epidemics struck several times from 1839 to 1867, until coastal towns began to quarantine infected victims. In 1839 alone, the disease killed about 12 percent of the population. Since many of the first Houston settlers were from the South, they supported the slavery-plantation system and used urban slaves for menial tasks. After the

Texas government moved to Austin in 1839, the city settled into an economy based on agriculture and commerce, becoming a major seaport for exporting cotton.

Founders Memorial Cemetery at 1217 West Dallas and Valentine Street is the oldest cemetery in Houston. Originally known as "City Cemetery," it opened in 1836 with the founding of the city in what is now the Fourth Ward near the edge of downtown. The two-acre cemetery, with more than 850 burials, many unmarked, is owned and operated by the Houston Parks and Recreation Department. Most of the burials here occurred in the early nineteenth century. There are several mass graves because of the recurring yellow fever and cholera epidemics. A triple pillar monument, each pillar cut off at the top indicating a life cut short, gives a glimpse of the toll of such epidemics for one family. The Morris brothers were all in their twenties when they died in the 1850s. This Texas Historic Cemetery contains the graves of citizens of the Republic of Texas and veterans of the Texas Revolution, along with twenty-eight Texas Centennial monuments.

John Kirby Allen (1810–1838), cofounder of Houston, was twenty-eight when he died of congestive fever and was buried at Founders Memorial Cemetery. Born in New York, he moved to Texas in 1832 with his older brother, Augustus Chapman Allen, a professor of mathematics. Their parents, four brothers, and a sister moved to Houston in 1837. John was an astute businessman and natural leader with a magnetic personality. At the start of the Texas Revolution, he and Augustus provided supplies, guns, and ammunition to the militia, often at their own expense. After the war, John was elected a representative from Nacogdoches to the new Texas Congress. He and his brother saw that the area around Buffalo Bayou could readily become a major seaport. In August of 1836, they purchased 6,642 acres originally granted by Mexico to a pioneer colonist. That land purchase started the city of Houston.

John's Texas Centennial monument is in a small plot including that of his brother George, who passed away in 1854, and his parents **Rowland** (1787–1841) and **Sally Chapman Allen** (1787–1841). Their pillar tombstone, upon which sits a carved lamb, is intricately carved with a cherub head and scroll, and a depiction of the female Virtue leaning on an anchor, the symbol of hope. John's brother Augustus moved to Mexico in the 1840s. After traveling to Washington D.C. on a business trip, he contracted pneumonia and died in January 1864. Unable to secure passage for his return to Texas, his wife sent his remains to Brooklyn, New York, where he was buried in the Greenwood Cemetery.

LIENDO PLANTATION

This historic plantation is recognized as a Texas historic landmark and is listed on the National Register of Historic Places. Fifty miles northwest of Houston, the plantation in Waller County was named after José Justo Liendo, the original owner of the land. Leonard Groce purchased the property in 1841 and established the plantation using slave labor, building a colonial-style home in 1853. The plantation became a convenient stopover between the Houston-Galveston area and Austin, with a stream of guests, including Sam Houston. The plantation, operating with 300 slaves, brought in between $80,000 to $100,000 annually. During the Civil War, it was used as a camp for troops as well as a prisoner-of-war camp. During Reconstruction, General George A. Custer and his command encamped here for three months.

The plantation was a money-losing venture after the war. In 1873, Groce's son sold 1,100 acres to famed German sculptor **Elisabet Ney** (1833–1907) and her Scottish husband **Dr. Edmund D. Montgomery** (1835–1911). Both were famous in Europe, she for having sculpted heads of states, famous artists, and politicians, Edmund for practicing medicine and experimental research. They decided to move to America, immigrating in 1871. Edmund was diagnosed with tuberculosis and had been told the climate in Texas would be better for him. Their two sons were born in the United States: Arthur in 1871 and Lorne in 1872. Arthur became ill with diphtheria and died in 1873. A distraught Elisabet "grabbed the child in her arms . . . rushed to her boudoir and locked herself in during the night," according to the doctor who treated the toddler. When she finally emerged, she'd created a death mask of the child. The doctor told her that the body needed to be cremated because of the contagiousness of the disease. He then quarantined the house. No one knows for sure how the actual cremation took place, since the parents never spoke of it. However, many people believe that Ney placed the body in the parlor fireplace of the Liendo plantation house and burned it herself, while others said his father built a funeral pyre in the back of the house and cremated the child. Whichever way it occurred, residents of the nearby town were

Elisabet Ney at her Austin studio, c. 1895.
[PICB 18956] AUSTIN HISTORY CENTER, AUSTIN PUBLIC LIBRARY.

said to have been outraged at this "un-Christian" method of disposal of a body. The little boy's ashes were kept in an urn above the fireplace.

For the next several years, Elisabet devoted herself to running the plantation, but was pulled back into sculpting. In 1892, she built a fortress-like studio in Austin (today the Elisabet Ney Museum) and began commuting the 110 miles on horseback. In these last years of her life, she completed several portrait busts, as well as statues of Stephen F. Austin and Sam Houston, now in the state capitol and her exquisite memorial to Albert Sidney Johnston in the Texas State Cemetery. Her husband became known as the "Hermit Philosopher of Liendo."

The couple is buried in the **Liendo Plantation Cemetery**, a small burial ground with nine graves enclosed by a fence, not far from the house. Edmund died in 1911, four years after Elisabet. Their son Arthur's ashes are said to have been buried with him. Edmund's upright tombstone has the following inscription: "Hermit Philosopher of Liendo/Eminent Scholar Gifted Experimental Biologist and/ Brilliant Speculative Philosopher."

Elisabet's grave marker is a full-size slab with a small insert that includes her name and the following inscription: "Sculptress, 1834–1907." Docents at the plantation say she did not like the term "sculptress" and referred to herself as a "sculptor." The date of her birth is also incorrect. She was born in 1833. Her plain and obscure gravesite belies the beauty, grandeur, and artistry of her own sculptures.

Panna Maria

Panna Maria, which means "Virgin Mary" in Polish, is the first permanent Polish settlement and the oldest Polish Catholic parish in the United States. Fifty-five miles southeast of San Antonio, the village was established on Christmas Eve in 1854 when 100 Polish families arrived there following a grueling nine-week voyage from their Upper Silesian homeland and a three-week trek across southeast Texas. They left the port of Bremen, Germany, on September 26, 1854, arriving in Galveston harbor on December 3. From Galveston, they secured another boat to Indianola, and from there, they traveled by oxcart to San Antonio, arriving on December 21.

Father Leopold Moczygemba, a Franciscan priest from their homeland who was in charge of arrangements for their stay, was waiting in San Antonio for the immigrants, which included four of his brothers. He led them back almost sixty miles to Panna Maria. Known as the patriarch of American Polonia for his work with the Polish communities in Texas and in the Midwest, the priest led a prayer after their arrival under an oak tree that still stands next to Immaculate Conception Catholic Church at 13879 North Farm Road 81. The historic church was erected in 1855 and rebuilt in 1877 after a fire.

With church funds, Father Leopold purchased 238 acres within the confluence of Cibolo Creek and the San Antonio River, set aside twenty-five acres for a church, and divided the remainder to those who could not afford to buy farms. Things did not go well for the new immigrants who suffered through droughts, epidemics, grasshopper infestations, Indian raids, and rattlesnake infestation—having settled on rattlesnake nesting ground. They turned on the priest, who'd painted a much too rosy picture about life in this wilderness called Texas. One Silesian wrote: "What we suffered here when we started! We didn't have any houses, nothing but fields. And for shelter, only brush and trees. There was tall grass everywhere, so that if anyone took a few steps, he was lost from sight. Every step of the way you'd meet rattlesnakes!"

Aware of the unrest, Father Moczygemba hosted a meal at his home where the settlers were given the opportunity to air their grievances. Just as everybody settled down to eat, a rattlesnake fell from the rafters onto the table. Everyone scattered, and threats on the priest's life intensified. He fled from Panna Maria in October 1856, and by 1857, he'd left Texas altogether. Families began to move to larger settlements, and those who stayed remained isolated as the railroad bypassed the village.

Today, Panna Maria is an unincorporated settlement with a rural population of about forty people. Many descendants of the original pioneers moved to nearby Karnes City. In 1976, the settlement was included on the National Register of Historic Places. The Panna Maria Historic District encompasses 3,500 acres and twenty-five historic structures. Located across the parking lot from the historic Immaculate Conception Catholic Church, a 16,500-square-foot Polish Heritage Center was scheduled to open in early 2021.

Time apparently does heal old wounds. On the front lawn of the historic Catholic church is the grave of **Father Moczygemba** (1824–1891). Originally buried in Detroit, Michigan, the priest was reinterred on October 13, 1974, underneath the oak where he said the first Christmas mass in Panna Maria in 1854. Descendants of the original settlers requested the reburial and helped to fund a new marker. A tall granite monument topped by a bronze bust and a full-sized slab marker memorialize the Polish priest. A long inscription detailing his life's work ends with the following: "Father Leopold Bonaventura Maria Moczygemba Patriarch of American Polonia./ Established Parishes, Founded Schools and Served as Pastor in Ten States and Performed/his Ministry in Latin, Polish, German, Italian, English, Czech and Spanish."

The **Panna Maria Cemetery** on County Road 242 off North Farm Road 81, about one mile northwest of the church, is the final resting place of many of the early Polish settlers: Biela, Czerner, Dziuk, Kowalik, Opiela, Pawelik, Moczygemba, and Wrobel, among others.

The grave of Father Leopold Moczygemba, "Patriarch of American Polonia," is in front of the historic Immaculate Conception of the Blessed Virgin Mary Church in Panna Maria.

The oldest tombstones—including intricately embossed metal crucifixes, such as the one that marks the grave of Polish immigrant **Jan Wrobel** (1827–1906) who settled in Panna Maria in 1868—are in the front right of the cemetery shaded by large oak trees. The well-kept cemetery of more than 900 graves is surrounded by a wrought-iron fence.

A marble statue of a little girl in period dress and shoes marks the grave of five-year-old **Lizbieta Biela** who died on March 9, 1888 and her baby brother Alexander, born on January 12, 1888. His tombstone etching on the pedestal of the marker is hard to read and is in Polish, but it appears that he died in April, about a month after his sister. Another sibling, Joseph, died in 1880, at age one month. His burial location is unknown. Of the five children born to John and Susanna Biela who were married in Panna Maria in 1877, just two survived to adulthood.

A beautiful statue of the Virgin Mary holding Jesus, similar to Michelangelo's "Pieta," is in the front commemorating the Seraphic Sisters, the Franciscan Sisters of Our Lady of Sorrows, an order founded in Poland in 1881.

Josef Moczygemba (1818–1912) and his second wife **Karolina** (1832–1917) are buried in the same plot and share a granite, double tombstone monument with a crucifix on top inscribed in Polish. Josef, one of Father Leopold's four brothers, traveled with the first group of Polish immigrants, along with his wife **Tekla Zienc** (1821–1854) and their five sons, ranging in age from infant to eleven years old. Tekla died on the voyage and was buried at sea. With five children to raise, Josef found a new wife within a year, marrying twenty-three-year-old Karolina Szyguda, who bore him four more sons and a daughter. They stayed in Panna Maria, despite the taint of their relationship with the disgraced priest.

RICHMOND

Fifteen miles southwest of Houston on the Brazos River, Richmond (pop. 12,500) started as a camp site in 1822 for a group of Stephen F. Austin's "Old Three Hundred" colony. The community evacuated during the Runaway Scrape, and in early 1837, two businessmen returned and began selling lots. They named the new city Richmond, after a town in England. The town became a railroad stop in 1855 and a prosperous shipping center for cattle and cotton. As other towns sprang up around Richmond, residents began to move out at the turn of the century, but beginning in the late 1940s, the town became a bedroom community for people working in Houston and the population grew. The town has been described as having "the air of the Deep South."

The beautifully landscaped and shaded **Morton Cemetery** at 401 N 2nd Street in Richmond was established on a portion of a Mexican land grant issued to William Morton, one of the early settlers of 1822. The cemetery's name and ownership changed several times, for a while operating as the Richmond Masonic Cemetery. In the early 1840s, the cemetery was renamed Morton Cemetery to honor its founder. Today, the cemetery, with more than 3,200 graves and many unique nineteenth-century crypts, statues, and monuments, stands as a memorial to him and is the final resting place of illustrious pioneers, including 1838–1841 Republic of Texas president **Mirabeau B. Lamar** (1798–1859), one of the state's first women settlers, **Jane Long** (1798–1880) known as "The Mother of Texas," and seventy-two Confederate veterans.

This brick tomb in Morton Cemetery is the first known Masonic landmark in Texas.

Robert Gillespie (1780–1825), a native of Scotland, was traveling through the area when he was mortally wounded by unknown assailants. He arrived at William Morton's cabin, where the family put him up and cared for him until his death on November 7, 1825, at age forty-five. It is unknown how long Gillespie lingered, but it was long enough for Morton to learn that the stranger was a Mason, like himself, and for Morton to develop an admiration for him, as indicated not only by the tomb he erected for him but also by the inscriptions on it:

"An honest craftsman moulders here,/Remote from friends and home./His widowed wife and orphans dear,/How sad must be their doom./His morals pure, his soul refined./He acted by the square./In him those virtues were combined,/

Which time cannot outwear." On another side of the tomb is inscribed a Masonic symbol and a hand holding a plumbline, along with the following paraphrased Scripture verse, Amos 7:8: "Behold I will set my plumbline/In the midst of my people Israel/I will not again pass by them any more [sic]."

Morton himself drowned in an 1833 Brazos River flood and his body was never found. A memorial marker for him was placed in front of the tomb.

When Santa Anna's army encamped in Richmond on its way to San Jacinto, some Mexican soldiers started to destroy the tomb. A Mexican officer, who was himself a Mason, ordered them to stop when he saw that it was a Masonic tomb. Over the years, the tomb deteriorated until it was restored by the Masonic Lodge in 1936 during the Texas Centennial.

SAN ANTONIO

San Antonio (pop. 1.6 million) is best known for the Alamo and the tragedy that occurred on the morning of March 6, 1836, when a band of Texian soldiers fighting for independence from Mexico were slaughtered by Santa Anna's troops after thirteen days of intermittent fighting. "Remember the Alamo!" along with "Remember Goliad!" galvanized the Texas revolutionary forces, spurring them on to victory at the Battle of San Jacinto. Nevertheless, the city's history began 100 years earlier, when Spanish missionaries and presidio settlers founded the settlement on May 1, 1718, with the establishment of

Mission San Antonio de Valero, known as the Alamo, one of the five eighteenth-century San Antonio missions that still stand today.

By 1821, San Antonio was the seat of the Spanish government in the northern province. In 1836, San Antonio had a population of about 2,500. The town grew rapidly after independence, bringing a large number of immigrants from Germany. During the last decades of the nineteenth century, San Antonio, starting point for the Chisholm Trail, became a major cattle center and commercial hub of the Southwest. The arrival of the railroad in 1877 brought migrants from the American South. Today, the Alamo City is a multicultural blend of Mexican and Texan culture, with three-fifths of its population of Hispanic/Mexican heritage.

San Antonio's Mission Graveyards and City Cemeteries tell a story of anguish, travail, courage, and resilience. The earliest cemeteries called *camposanto* (Spanish for sacred burial ground) were located in and around the missions. The five San Antonio missions established by Spanish priests of the Franciscan order were built along the San Antonio River approximately two-and-a-half miles apart. They flourished between 1747 and 1775, despite periodic raids by Apache and Comanche Indians. By 1824, the San Antonio missions were secularized, the lands were redistributed among the inhabitants, and the churches were transferred to secular clergy. All the missions had burial grounds within and outside their churches.

From 1724 to 1749, the Alamo was the burial ground for both the mission Indians and the presidio soldiers and their families. Church archives show that 422 Indians and twenty-six Spaniards were interred here during this period. Burials at San Fernando Cathedral (founded as a parish church in 1731; designated a cathedral in 1874) began as early as 1749. Burials were inside the church and immediately in front of it, surrounded by a stone wall. By 1807, the cemetery, populated with hundreds of shallow graves, had become so crowded that the parish priests complained that "the stench and vermin made it impossible to conduct services."

ALAMO DESIGNATED HISTORIC CEMETERY

Mission San Antonio de Valero, also known as the **Alamo,** gained recognition as a historic cemetery (an honorary designation) by the THC on May 10, 2019, while the Alamo church was awarded "verified cemetery" status on June 17, 2020. The recognition was a long time coming as remains have been discovered within the Alamo church as far back as 1937. In subsequent years, burials were discovered inside the church, along the south transept, and within the Monks' Burial room. The THC historic cemetery designation encompasses much of the Alamo complex, including the church, long barracks, and grounds. The "verified cemetery" designation includes only the church at this time. Nevertheless, church records documented between 1721 and 1762 (the last entry) indicate 1,376 burials, including many indigenous people, at the Mission San Antonio de Valero.

The provisional Spanish governor of Texas selected an open area on the west side of San Pedro Creek for a new burial ground in the early nineteenth century. Starting in 1808, burials took place in the new *camposanto* at the downtown site of today's Santa Rosa Children's Hospital (Catholic burials) and Milam Park (Protestant burials), 501 West Commerce, less than half a mile west of the cathedral. In addition to the normal occurrence of death and burials throughout the nineteenth century were the mass burials attributed to the flood of 1819, the 1835–1836 War for Independence, and three cholera epidemics (1834, 1849, and 1866). During the War for Independence, the fallen officers of Santa Anna's army and the body of Gregorio Esparza (1808–1836), the only defender not burned in the funeral pyres by the Alamo, were buried in this Catholic *camposanto*.

As the city began to expand, officials decided the eight-acre burial ground was needed to accommodate growth. In the 1850s, the City Council voted to remove all the bodies, about 3,000, from the *camposanto* and relocate them to new cemeteries, one established in 1853 on the East Side as a City Cemetery and one further west, San Fernando Cemetery # 1, for Catholic burials.

Despite this order, burials at the *camposanto* continued. The last recorded burial at the City Cemetery was in 1880, and at the Catholic Cemetery in 1860. There is no record of a mass exhumation of grave sites and removal, according to a longtime archivist at the Archdiocese of San Antonio. However, the Archdiocese contends that many graves were exhumed and reinterred at San Fernando Cemetery #1 in a common grave, "as was a customary practice during the time," although its location has been lost to time. Graves found during construction and renovation of the children's hospital over the years indicated that exhumation was incomplete at best.

A burial that remained in what is now Milam Park is that of **Benjamin Rush Milam** (1788–1835), after whom the park is named. Milam joined the Texas Independence movement leading an attack on the Mexican Army in San Antonio in December of 1835. He was shot in the head by a sniper, dying instantly during the siege. His grave is marked by a granite monument upon which stands a bronze statue of Milam holding a rifle in the air signifying his challenge, "Who will follow Old Ben Milam into San Antonio?"

The **City Cemetery Historic District** off East Commerce, less than a mile east of its intersection with IH-35, spans 103 acres. It is listed on the National Register of Historic Places. In 1853, the City Council selected this new burial ground on Powder House Hill, named after buildings constructed there by the Spanish military to store gun powder. Because of its higher elevation between Salado Creek and the San Antonio River, the cemetery was not likely to be disturbed by the flooding that plagued the downtown area. The Council designated twenty acres for the new cemetery and began to sell individual lots. Land was also donated or sold to fraternal organizations, churches, synagogues, and military organizations to bury their dead. By 1854, Alamo Masonic Lodge and the IOOF had opened cemeteries adjacent to City Cemetery #1. Over the next fifty years, thirty-one cemeteries were established on Powder House Hill, including the San Antonio National Cemetery, a federal military burial ground founded in 1867. Many San

This granite pillar monument topped with an urn marks the Maverick family plot in City Cemetery #1.

Antonians responsible for the city's early development are buried in the East Side Cemetery complex.

One of the most renowned individuals buried in the **City Cemetery Historic District** is **Samuel Augustus Maverick** (1803–1870), to whom the term "maverick" is attributed. Maverick owned a herd of unbranded cattle that wandered around on Matagorda Island. Because locals knew he was the owner, the cattle were referred to as "maverick's." The term came to mean an unbranded calf or yearling, but also refers to an individual with an independent streak.

Born in South Carolina, Maverick graduated from Yale University in 1825 and studied law in Virginia before immigrating to San Antonio in 1834. He served with Ben Milam in the battle for San Antonio. In 1836, he married **Mary Ann Adams** (1818–1898) in Alabama and they returned to Texas in 1838 to make their home. He was a delegate at the Republic of Texas Independence convention, practiced law in San Antonio, and acquired more than 300,000 acres. Maverick served a couple of terms as mayor of the city and also as a legislator in both the Republic of Texas and the state.

He died after a brief illness on September 7, 1870, and was buried in the Maverick family plot in **City Cemetery #1** underneath a large oak near the graves of five of his ten children who had preceded him in death. Much of what is known about the early days of San Antonio is because of his wife Mary Ann, a diarist who in 1895 published memoirs about her pioneer experiences in Texas. Her eyewitness account of the Council House Fight in San Antonio in 1840 is often cited in studies of Texas pioneer life

Also in City Cemetery #1 is former policeman and Confederate soldier, **D. A. (Jack) Harris** (1834–1882), who opened the Jack Harris Vaudeville Theater and Saloon on West Commerce and Soledad Streets in 1872. The entertainment venue was the most popular saloon and gambling place in town and Harris was universally liked. His establishment attracted important politicians and

D. A. (Jack) Harris, a popular Vaudeville Theater owner, was gunned down in 1882 by Ben Thompson, Austin's city marshal.

the usual nefarious types. One of them, Ben Thompson (see Austin, Oakwood Cemetery), lost heavily during a gambling session. He caused a scene and was told that he was no longer welcome at the saloon. He left, threatening revenge. Nursing a grievance that lingered for two years, he returned to the saloon, where on July 11,

1882, the gunslinger-turned-Austin lawman shot Harris in the chest with a six-shooter through a lattice screen, killing him. Two years later, Thompson and his pal, King Fisher (see Uvalde, Pioneer Cemetery), returned to the Vaudeville Theater and were killed by Harris's friends in retaliation.

Across Palmetto Street from City Cemetery #1 is the site of a significant **Confederate Cemetery**, established in 1885 by the Albert Sidney Johnston Camp No. 1, United Confederate Veterans. According to a Texas Historical Marker at the site, the earliest documented burial in this plot, that of Charles Hutcheson, dates to 1855 and was already in place at the time of the camp's purchase. The grave of **Hamilton P. Bee** (1822–1897), Confederate general and Speaker of the Texas House of Representatives, is marked by a granite obelisk with etchings of the Confederate flag, Lone Star flag, and two swords crossed. There are more than 1,000 graves in the Confederate Cemetery, including those of Civil War veterans, their dependents, and later generations of descendants.

Among prominent Confederate veterans interred here is **John Salmon "Rip" Ford** (1815–1897), soldier, elected official, and newspaper editor who started his military career with the Texas Army in 1836. During the Mexican War, he served as regimental adjutant under Jack Hays. One of his main duties was to send out death notices. At the beginning of each message, he included the words, "Rest in Peace." As the number of fatalities increased and in the chaos of the battlefield, he substituted the abbreviation "R.I.P." Soon the men were calling him "Old Rip." In his later years, he wrote reminiscences and historical articles promoting an interest in Texas history. Several memorials, including a Texas Ranger cross in front of a Texas Centennial monument, mark his grave underneath a large cedar tree.

Odd Fellows Cemetery, diagonally across the street from City Cemetery #1, is the burial site of two renowned Mexican War veterans and also the "lost burial place of the Alamo Defenders," according to a marker erected in 2004 by the Alamo Defenders Descendants Association. Within a plot surrounded by chain are two obelisk monuments, one for **Robert Addison Gillespie** (1815–1846), a Texas Ranger and Mexican War volunteer who was the first to reach the summit of Independence Hill during the battle of Monterrey. Wounded in an assault at the Bishop's Palace there, he died the next day. Like fellow Texas Ranger **Samuel Hamilton Walker** (1817–1847) buried nearby, his remains were returned to San Antonio, where they were both reinterred at the Odd Fellows Cemetery on April 21, 1856, as part of a Battle of San Jacinto Celebration.

Walker assisted gun manufacturer Samuel Colt in designing what became known as the Walker-Colt pistol, an early six-shooter much favored by the Texas Mounted Volunteers. Captain Walker was one of the foremost American soldiers of the Mexican War. During the siege of Fort Texas in May 1846, he rode through the Mexican lines to carry messages into and out of the fort. In 1847, Walker was serving in central Mexico when he was killed in a skirmish with Mexican guerillas.

In a 1906 *San Antonio Daily Express* article, City Clerk **August Biesenbach** (1848–1915), buried in City Cemetery #1, gave an account of an incident that he said took place when he was eight years old. He used to play on the Alameda (Commerce Street). In 1856, he witnessed the exhumation of remains consisting of bones and fragments of bones that were victims of the siege of the Alamo who had been interred near the place where the bodies had been burned and originally buried. He said he saw their transfer from that place to the Odd Fellows Cemetery. He said they were buried midway between the monuments of Captain R. A. Gillespie and Captain Samuel H. Walker.

Between the monuments of Texas Rangers Robert Gillespie and Samuel Walker is a burial site of the victims of the siege of the Alamo.

THE MYSTERY OF THE ALAMO DEFENDERS BURIAL SITE

After the Battle of the Alamo, Mexican General Antonio López de Santa Anna ordered the bodies of the dead Texians to be burned. Those who died during the battle or were executed afterward—182, according to eyewitness Francisco Antonio Ruiz, Alcalde of San Antonio—were burned in three funeral pyres near the Alamo. There is much controversy among historians today about not only the location of the funeral pyres but also the disposition of the remains. On February 25, 1837, Colonel Juan N. Seguin (see Seguin, Juan N. Seguin Memorial Plaza), an officer in the Texas Army, gave the defenders a formal military funeral. A March 28, 1837 account of the funeral in the *Telegraph* and *Texas Register* describes the procession in detail. Ashes were found in three places and removed from the two smallest heaps. They were placed in a coffin "neatly covered with black," with the names of Travis, Bowie, and Crockett engraved on the inside of the lid. The coffin, along with a Texian flag, a rifle, and a sword laid upon it, were placed in the parish church (San Fernando). The coffin was then taken in procession from the church through "the principal street of the city, crossed the river, passed through the principal avenue on the other side, and halted at the place where the first ashes had been gathered; the coffin was then placed upon the spot, and three volleys of musketry were discharged by one of the companies; the procession then moved on to the second spot, whence part of the ashes in the coffin had been taken, where the same honors were paid; the procession then proceeded to principal spot, and place of interment, where the grave had been prepared, the coffin had been placed on the principal heap of ashes."

At the time, Seguin delivered a eulogy in which he predicted that a "towering fabric of architecture shall be reared by their grateful countrymen above their ashes." While many believe that monument to be the Alamo Cenotaph erected in 1939, that is not the case. Apparently, a monument was never erected at the actual burial site and so its location was lost forever.

Many years later, in 1889, Seguin wrote a letter saying that he'd filled an urn with a "few fractions" of the Alamo defenders' remains and "ordered a sepulcher opened in the cathedral . . . in front of the railing, but very near the steps," where the urn was buried. In 1936, remains were discovered by workmen making repairs at the Cathedral at the exact location mentioned by Seguin. They were placed in a new marble sarcophagus at the entry of the Cathedral in 1938. The memorial plaque next to the coffin is inscribed, "Here Lie the Remains of Travis Crockett Bowie and other Alamo Heroes."

It is possible that the remains of the Alamo defenders are in the various places mentioned and in other locations yet to be discovered. There were at least three large heaps of ashes after all. While historians continue to dispute about the disposition of the remains, the rest of us will simply "Remember the Alamo."

The **San Antonio National Cemetery** at 517 Paso Hondo Street, the oldest military cemetery in Texas, began as the burial ground for soldiers posted to the western frontier, veterans of the Indian Wars, Spanish-American War, and the Civil War. In 1873, eligibility expanded to include all Union veterans, and in the twentieth century included most honorably discharged veterans, their spouses, and dependent children.

In 1867, the city donated almost two acres for the cemetery to the federal government within the eastside City Cemetery District. Covering most of a rectangular city block, it is bound by Center Street to the north, South Monumental Street to the west, and Paso Hondo Street to the south and is surrounded by stone and wrought-iron fencing. A portion of the city cemetery marks the eastern border of the national cemetery. Many of its first burials were reinterments of Union soldiers from cemeteries in and around the city, from Texas forts, and from other Texas locations. The cemetery, with more than 3,350 graves, is the final resting place for several famous Texans, many Medal of Honor recipients, and more than 280 African American "Buffalo" soldiers.

Distinctive and orderly, the cemetery features two circular pathways, one each in the eastern and western halves, connected by a cross axis in the center. Predominant are rows of standardized cambered or slightly arched, marble, rectangular headstones set upright for identified remains, with the individual's name and military unit inscribed on the front side. Burials of unidentified remains are marked by a low marble block. There are also over 250 private monuments, the earliest of which dates to 1853. The cemetery is laid out in sections

The statue marking the grave of Raoul Violland stands in contrast to the standardized marble headstones in the San Antonio National Cemetery. Son of a major who worked at Fort Sam Houston, the twelve-year-old died in 1914 from an accidental discharge of his own gun while hunting at a ranch.

for officers, soldiers who died at the military post of San Antonio, unknown soldiers, including over 300 buried in an adjacent common grave, and soldiers of the Indian Wars who were buried as unknowns before being identified over a century later.

Among several Medal of Honor recipients at the San Antonio National Cemetery is **Sergeant William H. Barnes** (1843–1866). A farmer from Maryland, he joined Company C of the Thirty-eighth US Colored Troops as a private. The Battle of New Market Heights, also known as the Battle of Chaffin's Farm, on September 29, 1864, was the first major battle in Virginia in which African American troops led an assault. It was a brutal morning for these men, and the last for many.

Half of the black troops were killed, wounded, or captured. On April 6, 1865, Private William Henry Barnes was awarded the Medal of Honor for his valor at this battle. His citation reads: "Among the first to enter the enemy's works, although wounded." Fourteen of the sixteen recipients of the Medal of Honor awarded to black soldiers in the Civil War were for action at New Market Heights.

After the end of the Civil War in May 1865, Barnes came to Texas with his regiment to assist in Reconstruction. On July 1, 1865, he was promoted to Sergeant, the highest rank he could achieve as a soldier in the Union Army. He became ill in July 1866 with consumption (tuberculosis) while in Indianola. On Christmas Eve of 1866, he died at the city hospital and was buried in the town cemetery. Sometime later, his body was disinterred and reinterred in the San Antonio National Cemetery in a common grave. A Medal of Honor memorial marker for Barnes was placed in the cemetery.

San Fernando Cemetery #1 at 1100 South Colorado Street was established in 1840 when it became apparent that the *camposanto* closer to town was no longer adequate for burials for the city's Catholic population. The Archdiocese of San Antonio owns and operates this thirteen-acre cemetery, which has more than 8,000 graves. Interments ceased in the early 1920s when San Fernando Cemetery #2 opened three miles west. Many of the earliest Hispanic settlers and important figures in Texas history are buried at San Fernando Cemetery #1, including **José Antonio Menchaca** (1797–1879), a veteran of San Jacinto; **Confederate Lieutenant José "Joseph" Rafael de la Garza** (1838–1864), who died during the Civil War; and signers of the Texas Declaration of Independence **Colonel José Antonio Navarro** (1795–1871) and **Colonel José Francisco Ruiz** (1783–1840). The cemetery contains a number of nineteenth-century monuments, statues, and tombstones and several Texas Centennial markers.

Captain José "Joseph" Rafael de la Garza (1838–1864) was born to a prominent and wealthy San Antonio family with deep Texas roots. Educated at St. Joseph's College in Bardstown, Kentucky, he was described by one of his teachers as a young man of "fine disposition . . . very mild and cheerful, always in good humor and someone who never utters an improper word."

After Texas seceded from the Union on February 1, 1861, Captain de la Garza was one of 90,000 Texans who joined the Confederate Army. As a company commander in the Seventeenth Texas Infantry, he was killed leading a charge against Union forces at the Battle of Mansfield, Louisiana, on May 8, 1864. He was twenty-six years old.

In a letter written to Bartholomew "Bart" DeWitt (Joseph's brother-in-law), dated April 19, 1864, H. B. Adams described his death, "Joe Garza fell while gallantly fighting at the head of his company at the battle of Mansfield." De la Garza wrote many letters, preserved by family members, that provide a rare glimpse into the daily life of a soldier in the Trans-Mississippi. DeWitt returned Joseph's body to be interred. His grave is marked by a slab situated between two small pillar tombstones. In 1876, the Texas Legislature named Garza County in honor of de la Garza and his family.

Captain Joseph Rafael de la Garza was one of 90,000 Texans who joined the Confederate Army. He died at age twenty-six leading a charge at the Battle of Mansfield in 1864.
[073–1145] UTSA LIBRARIES SPECIAL COLLECTIONS.

Sunset Memorial Park Cemetery, established in 1928 at 1701 Austin Highway in San Antonio, is the burial site of nationally renowned Italian artist **Pompeo Coppini** (1870–1957), sculptor of the sixty-foot-high Alamo Cenotaph of gray Georgia marble and

A close-up of the full-sized, bronze bas-relief of Pompeo Coppini and his wife Elizabeth conferring with Father Time.

pink Texas granite and many other memorials featured in this book. Coppini grew up in Florence and studied at the Accademia di Belle Arte, graduating with the highest honors in 1889. In 1896, he immigrated to the United States and two years later married **Elizabeth de**

Barbieri (1875–1957) of New Haven, Connecticut, who was one of his models. He moved to Texas in 1901 to work with German sculptor Frank Teich (see Llano, Llano City Cemetery). He made his home in San Antonio and today his studio at 115 Melrose is a nonprofit arts organization called Coppini Academy of Fine Arts.

Unlike sculptors Frank Teich and Elisabet Ney (see Liendo Plantation Cemetery), whose tombstones are simple and obscure, Coppini's is massive—fifteen-foot by twenty-four-foot by ten-foot monument of bronze and Italian marble weighing 57,000 pounds shipped from Italy. Coppini began work on the memorial monument in 1945, concerned that his final resting place would be marked by an ordinary tombstone, which he feared could lack "individuality, originality, or real refined taste." He died twelve years after he completed his tombstone and his wife died a few months later and was buried beside him.

SEGUIN

Seguin (pop. 31,000), named in honor of Juan Seguin, a Tejano freedom fighter, was founded in 1838 by frontier rangers along the Guadalupe River. Thirty-five miles northeast of San Antonio, the town was incorporated in 1853. During the nineteenth century, the town's economy was based on agriculture, with cotton its primary export. The 1997 miniseries adaptation of the novel *True Women* (1993), by Texas author Janice Woods Windle, was filmed in the greater Seguin area.

The **Juan Seguin Memorial Plaza** at 789 South Saunders Street is the final resting place of **Colonel Juan Nepomuceno Seguin** (1806–1890), Texas patriot and statesman. A Spanish descendant of the Canary

Islanders who established the first municipal government in San Antonio in 1731, he assembled Mexican-Texan troops and fought in the 1835 Siege of Bexar. He provided horses and aid for troops of Colonel William B. Travis and was a courier during the siege of the Alamo, earning him the moniker the "Paul Revere of Texas." He defended fleeing settlers in the Runaway Scrape after the fall of the Alamo. He served as a commander during the battle at San Jacinto and was appointed military commander of San Antonio where he directed the burial of the remains of the Alamo combatants. The first Tejano to serve in the Republic of Texas Senate, he also served as mayor of San Antonio before and after the Texas Revolution. However, because of the hostilities between Anglos and Mexican-Texans, including threats on his life, he resigned his mayoral post in 1842 and fled to Mexico with his family. He returned six years later and settled on a ranch near Floresville. He died in 1890 in Nuevo Laredo, Mexico, where he was living with a son, one of his ten children.

Seguin was the last person of Hispanic descent to serve as mayor of San Antonio until 1981, when Henry Cisneros was elected, 139 years later. Seguin's remains were returned to Texas and buried at the town named in his honor during ceremonies on July 4, 1976. A simple memorial slab of Texas granite marks his grave in a fenced, oak-shaded hillside park.

VICTORIA

In 1824, Don Martín de León brought forty-one Mexican families to settle what he called Guadalupe Victoria, 100 miles southeast of San Antonio and twenty-five miles northwest of Port Lavaca. One of the important stops on the La Bahía Road, it was a stock-raising center and shipping point for the port of Linnville, destroyed in the great Comanche raid of 1840. Although a Mexican settlement, many of its residents volunteered to fight for the Texas Republic forces. Nevertheless, after Texas's victory at San Jacinto, the Mexican citizens were ostracized and fled. Anglos changed the name of the town to Victoria (pop. 67,000) and it was incorporated with that name in 1839. Despite Indian raids and cholera epidemics, the town grew as more people arrived—Germans, Bohemians, Italians, Jews, Southern whites and their slaves, and returning Mexicans. Ranching continued to be the town's major enterprise throughout the nineteenth century.

The first community cemetery in Victoria was established in 1846 and located at present-day Memorial Square, part of the original town site of Victoria. Two city blocks were used as burial grounds. Prior to May 9, 1846, bodies were buried in home yards, as this was a long-standing custom. In 1846, the city passed an ordinance stating that the dead could no longer be buried "at home" but must be buried in public burial grounds. Those defying the ordinance were fined $25 for each offense. The space was soon overflowing with graves and land for a new cemetery was purchased across town. As many remains as could be identified were moved to the new public cemetery; however, over 230 individuals are still interred in unmarked graves at Memorial Square. A stone monument there is inscribed as follows: "To the Memory of Texas Soldiers and Victoria Pioneer Families who still lie buried in this sacred soil."

Evergreen Cemetery at 1845 North Vine Street was established in 1850 as the new public cemetery on twenty-seven acres granted to the city by the Republic of Texas. In addition to those reinterred from Memorial Square are those reburied from the Old St. Mary's Catholic

Church, razed in 1868. Because of city neglect, local women organized the Victoria Ladies' Cemetery Association in 1876 and took over care of the cemetery. The name "Evergreen" was chosen in 1883 because of abundant trees in the area. Among the 9,000 graves here are those of **Don Martín de León** (1765–1833), early empresario and founder of Victoria; **Margaret Borland**, one of the first female cattle drivers in Texas; and veterans of the Texas Revolution, Mexican War, and Civil War. Evergreen Cemetery now spans thirty acres and has a number of large and impressive monuments, statues, and tombstones that tell stories in stone of so many of its early pioneers.

Don Martín de León (1765–1833), early empresario and founder of Victoria, and several of his family members are buried in a family plot surrounded by a beautiful wrought-iron fence in Evergreen. A Texas Centennial marker was placed at Don Martín's grave, and several Texas Historic plaques mark the graves of his wife and several descendants, also prominent Victoria citizens.

Martín was born to Spanish parents in Burgos, New Spain (Mexico), and married **Patricia de la Garza** (1775–1849) in 1795. Both came from aristocratic families of great wealth. The young couple established a ranch near present-day San Patricio in about 1800. In 1824, Martín petitioned the new Republic of Mexico for permission to settle forty-one Mexican families along the Guadalupe River. He was appointed empresario and named the capital of his colony Guadalupe Victoria. His colony expanded to include most of modern Calhoun County west of Matagorda Bay. Thousands of cattle carried the De Leon's first historic brand registered in 1807 in Texas, the E and J signifying the "Espíritu de Jesús." The de León's ranchland laid the foundation for what is today's cattle industry in Texas. De León's empresario grant was second only to Stephen F. Austin's in terms of success and helped carve the central Texas gulf coast out of the wilderness.

Don Martín fell ill and died, victim of the cholera epidemic of 1833, leaving his widow, four sons, and six daughters, and an estate of over a half million dollars. After his death, his family struggled against Santa Anna's Mexican Army and were forced off their land, fleeing to New Orleans for three years. The family returned to Texas to recover their property with minor success, but they persevered and endured many hardships.

Another person of renown buried at Evergreen is **Margaret Heffernan Borland** (1824–1873), one of the first women cattle drivers in Texas. Her parents immigrated to America from Ireland in the early 1820s, settling first in New York City, where Margaret was born. She was five in 1829 when they sailed to Texas, settling in San Patricio. Her father was killed during the Texas Revolution and her mother and siblings fled during the Runaway Scrape searching for safety. Soon after the battle of San Jacinto, they returned to their ranch. In 1843, Margaret married Harrison Dunbar, with whom she had a daughter. In 1844, shortly after their daughter's birth, he was killed in a pistol duel in the streets in Victoria. A year later, in 1845, she married Milton Hardy. A civic leader in Victoria, he had served on the town's city council and owned almost 3,000 acres and five lots in town. In their seven-year marriage, they had three daughters and a son. One daughter died in infancy and their son died during the same cholera epidemic that took Milton's life in 1852. His estate included 12,000 head of stock cattle, land, and four slaves. Margaret was left to care for her three surviving daughters. Four years later, in 1856, she married her third and last husband, Alexander Borland, one of the richest ranchers in Victoria County. They had four children together, three sons and a daughter. In the spring of 1867, Alexander, weak from a lingering illness, left for New Orleans to consult with the "imminent surgeon, Dr. Stone." He died there. His surgeon was the same Dr. Stone who conducted a surgery that resulted in the death of the young woman Edith Smith in Coldspring (see Coldspring, Laurel Hill Cemetery).

After Alexander's death, Margaret moved with her family to Victoria. The summer of 1867 was one of the hottest. By July, reports of yellow fever abounded. Death again stalked Margaret. By the end of that epidemic, she'd lost all of her children from the first two marriages and her youngest son. Only three of her seven children were still alive and one baby granddaughter.

Margaret faced the challenge of running a large cattle ranch, despite her overwhelming losses. Assisted by her brother, a nephew, and various ranch hands, she accepted responsibility and moved forward. In 1867, the Chisholm Trail opened leading to Kansas markets, where more money could be made from cattle. The year after the great blizzard of 1871–1872 killed tens of thousands of cattle, Margaret decided to drive a herd up to Kansas As trail boss, she drove 1,000 head of cattle, taking her two teenaged sons (fourteen and sixteen), a nine-year-old daughter, and a six-year-old granddaughter, her nephew, a black cook, and several hired hands. In two months, they reached their destination—Wichita, Kansas. Unfortunately, within a few weeks of arrival and before she was able to sell the cattle, Margaret was suddenly consumed by "trail fever," a congestion of the brain or

Studio portrait of Margaret Heffernan Hardy Borland, Victoria County, Texas, rancher, c. 1872.
[082–0710] UTSA Libraries Special Collections.

meningitis. She died on July 5, 1873, at age forty-nine. Her body was taken by train back to Victoria for burial. Her son-in-law wrote the following tribute to her: "Educated in the school of adversity, and an intimate acquaintance of trials, Mrs. Borland was a woman of resolute will and self-reliance; she was one of the kindest mothers." Her grave marker is a pink granite pillar monument topped by an urn. On the pedestal is the inscription: "Our Mama. . . . Gone, but not forgotten."

The "Jesus in Cowboy Boots" memorial for Willet C. Babcock who died in 1881 is the most visited in Paris's Evergreen Cemetery.

CHAPTER 6

LAKES TRAIL REGION

This region in North Texas encompassing the greater Dallas-Fort Worth metropolitan area up to the southern border of Oklahoma was where a great ancient sea met the land. Tall-grass prairies, scattered forests, and major rivers—the Red, Trinity, Brazos, Sabine, and Sulphur—are what nineteenth-century pioneers encountered as they settled the area. After the Republic of Texas became a state in 1845, an avalanche of people poured into this region. Cotton growers and enslaved workers turned the prairies into plantations. In the 1870s and 1880s, cowboys herded millions of longhorns from South Texas through this region along the Chisholm, Shawnee, and Great Western cattle trails. But it was the railroad that brought in the first real prosperity in the late 1800s. By the turn of the century, Dallas and Fort Worth were the centers of commerce and culture—where the Old South met the Wild West.

ACTON

This small, unincorporated community on the Brazos River is forty miles southwest of Fort Worth and five miles east of Granbury. Established as a trading post in around 1845, Acton has remained a bedroom community in the Granbury Micropolitan Statistical Area. The community is best known as being the burial site of **Elizabeth**

"Betsy" Patton Crockett (1788–1860), wife of David Crockett, hero of the Alamo. Her burial site at **Acton Cemetery** on Farm Road 167 was made a state park—the Acton State Historic Site—and is the smallest state park in Texas at 0.01 acre.

Elizabeth Crockett was a widow with two children living in Tennessee when she became David Crockett's second wife in 1815, having lost her first husband in the Creek Indian War in 1813. David himself

Elizabeth Crockett's twenty-eight-foot-tall memorial with a larger-than-life-size statue of a pioneer woman peering toward the western horizon was commissioned by the Texas Legislature in 1911 and is dedicated to all pioneer wives and mothers.

was a widower with three children after losing his first wife in June 1815. His second marriage produced three more children; however, the relationship soured and Crockett began spending most of his time away from home hunting, exploring, and politicking. By 1832, Elizabeth had had enough of his absences and moved with their eight children to live with her Patton relatives. Crockett, who'd been elected to the US House of Representatives in 1827, lost his final bid in 1834. In January 1836, he and an armed brigade arrived in Nacogdoches. He swore allegiance to the provisional government of Texas in exchange for land and in February arrived at the Alamo mission where he perished at age forty-nine during the battle against Santa Anna's troops on March 6, 1836.

Elizabeth came to Texas in 1854 with their first child, Robert Patton Crockett, his wife and children. They moved onto a league of land granted to David Crockett by the Republic of Texas and patented by Elizabeth as his surviving widow. She lived with her son and his family in a log cabin. After her death at age seventy-two on January 31, 1860, Elizabeth was laid to rest in the Acton Cemetery, dressed in the widow's black she had worn since hearing of her second husband's death.

DALLAS

A modern metropolis, Dallas (pop. 1.34 million) was founded in North Texas on the Trinity River as a trading post in 1841 by John Neely Bryan, described by Leon Harris in *The Merchant Princes* as "the first in a long line of expert promoters reluctant to use hyperbole if an outright lie might prove more effective." The origin of the town's name is unknown, although it may have been named after George

Mifflin Dallas, US vice president from 1845 to 1849. The town was granted a charter in 1856 and quickly became a service center for the rural areas surrounding it. One of the first rail crossroads with service starting in 1872, Dallas was in a strategic geographical location for the transport of regional products to northern and eastern manufacturing plants. Cotton was the region's principal cash crop and the world center for the leather and buffalo-hide trade. During the last quarter of the nineteenth century, banking and insurance emerged as major industries and by 1890, Dallas had 38,067 residents.

Freedman's Cemetery at North Central Expressway and Lemmon Drive was established in 1861 as a one-acre burial ground for Dallas's early African American population. By 1879, it had expanded to four acres and was in use until 1925. The site represents the remnants of the once-thriving North Dallas community, which from the Civil War to the 1970s was the largest segregated African American enclave in Dallas and one of the largest in the country. Construction in the 1930s eliminated most of the above-ground reminders of the cemetery and the few headstones that were left were vandalized and removed. In 1965, the city acquired the cemetery land and turned a portion of it into a park. In the late 1980s, during a highway expansion, the archeologist overseeing the project for the State Highway and Transportation Department noticed a sign that said "Freedman's Memorial Park." Looking into it, she learned that the park was over the site of a former cemetery. It is illegal in Texas to cover a burial plot without moving the bodies, so before road expansion could proceed, the area needed to be excavated. A team of archeologists, working with the Black Dallas Remembered Historical Society, eventually unearthed more than 1,500 bodies that had to be reburied at a cost to the state of between $6 million and $7 million. The archeologists contended as many as 10,000 were buried in the original cemetery from the era of slavery until the 1920s.

In 1992, the city of Dallas passed an ordinance establishing a Historic Overlay District for the Freedman's Cemetery and authorized a memorial to be built on a portion of the old cemetery grounds. An enclosed pocket park was erected in 2000 at a cost of $2 million and included a field where many of the remains were reinterred after being discovered during the 1994 excavations. Five larger-than-life-size bronze sculptures by Detroit sculptor David Newton depict images of slavery. Newton's sobering, yet magnificent sculptures are a profound memorial to those who suffered and yet triumphed over adversity.

A portal through the pink granite arch at the front of the memorial is flanked by two impressive figures—the Sentinel, an African warrior, and the Prophetess, a female oral historian of the people buried here. Just inside the arch on the back side is a black man struggling against chains who symbolizes the "Struggling Soul," and a black woman covering her face in shame who symbolizes the "Violated Soul."

Affixed to the back wall of the granite platform are the only remaining gravestones, small and of white marble, for two individuals: **Emma McCune** (1855–1903) and for an unknown child. The latter has the following epitaph: "How much of light, how much of joy, is buried with a darling boy." Several engraved plaques of poetry written by Dallas elementary school students to commemorate those buried here hang on the granite walls and brick pillars within the memorial.

Three prominent individuals buried in unmarked graves at the Freedman's Cemetery are the **Reverend Allen R. Griggs** (1850–1922), a Baptist minister born a slave in Georgia and brought to Texas

At the center platform of the Freedman's Cemetery memorial courtyard is a sculpture called *Dream of Freedom*, a man consoling a woman, their backs crisscrossed with flogging scars.

at age nine. He married **Emma Hodge** (1854–1919), a schoolteacher, in 1871 and they had eight children. A trustee of the cemetery, Allen became a prominent local church leader and champion of early public education for the African American community. At the time of his death, he was dean of North Texas Baptist College.

One of the couple's children, the **Reverend Sutton Elbert Griggs** (1877–1933), was an author, Baptist minister, and social activist. Living in Virginia serving in his first pastorate, he wrote his first novel, *Imperium in Imperio* (1899), which may be the first black nationalist novel. Griggs, who wrote in a very direct and stilted style, wrote more than a dozen books, including five novels, five social tracts, his autobiography, a short biography of John L. Webb, and *The Kingdom Builder's Manual* (1924), a booklet of biblical quotations. At his own expense, he published and distributed these works, written for "the aspiring classes of the black south." He was one of the few Southern members of the Niagara movement, a civil rights group which had a platform based on the issues of racial and social justice and which eventually evolved into the National Association for the Advancement of Colored People.

Pioneer Park Cemetery, a Texas Historic Cemetery at 1201 Marilla Street on a hill in downtown Dallas, is composed of the remnants of four early graveyards. The graves include many of Dallas's early settlers and civic leaders. The first burials, those of two small children, took place sometime between 1846 and 1849; however, the oldest recorded grave is dated 1853. Two of the graveyards that now make up Pioneer Park Cemetery were associated with two early

Dallas fraternal organizations—Masons and Odd Fellows. Some of the land nearby was once used as a cemetery by the Hebrew Benevolent Association. Those graves were moved and reinterred in the Temple Emanu-El Cemetery next to the Freedman's Cemetery. The fourth section, known as Old City Cemetery, was formally deeded to the City of Dallas in 1871. Its oldest marked grave, that of John Henry Long, is dated 1870. The last burials in what is now called Pioneer Park Cemetery took place in the latter part of the 1920s. A stone memorial marker for Dallas founder **John Neely Bryan** (1810–1877) was erected in 1954. Bryan, called the "First Citizen of Dallas," is buried in an unmarked grave in Austin.

Anchoring the **Eakins** family plot in Pioneer Park Cemetery is an impressive monument featuring a life-size statue of Hope, an allegorical figure wearing a Roman stola, holding a broken chain attached to an anchor symbolizing the cessation of life. Her right hand held over her heart symbolizes faith. The monument was erected for early Dallas pioneer **John J. Eakins** (1822–1886) and five of his children who died between 1859 and 1874, the youngest five days old, the oldest eight years old. Eakins, a farmer and president of a paving and pipe company at the time of his death, was a Mason who served as a captain in the Mexican War from 1847 to 1848 and in the Confederate forces. Born in Kentucky, he settled in Dallas on 640 acres that encompassed the southern part of the city. He married **Ophelia Crutchfield** (1831–1903) in 1850. Ophelia and her family settled in Dallas in 1845. Her father erected one of the first hotels ever built in Dallas, known as the Crutchfield House. Of the eight children born to Ophelia, only one survived childhood. The couple donated land for the City Park (now known Dallas Heritage Village) and also gave more than an acre of land for a school.

Juliette Abby Peak Fowler (1837–1889) is buried in the Fowler family plot near her husband and two children. One of thirteen children born to Dallas pioneers **Jefferson Peak Sr.** (1801–1885) and **Martha M. Reser Peak** (1812–1890), Juliette left a lasting legacy to the city of Dallas. A historical marker at her gravesite extols her contributions. Juliette wed Fort Worth lawyer Archibald Young Fowler in 1859. Over the next three years, their two children—a son and a daughter—were born and passed away before their first birthday, and Juliette's husband died in 1861 after being shot during an argument with a sheriff in Fort Worth, where the couple had settled. Juliette moved back to Dallas after his death.

Sometime later, she adopted a seven-year-old boy who had been abandoned at her church and this act of charity sparked her subsequent commitment to the care of orphans and elderly women. Before her death in 1889, she purchased fifteen acres in East Dallas that would become the Juliette Fowler Communities. She provided for its care in her will, and under the direction of her sister, **Sarah Peak Harwood** (1833–1914), also buried at Pioneer Park Cemetery, the Juliette Fowler Homes began in 1892. The homes were transferred to the Disciples of Christ Church in 1903. Over the decades, orphanages gave way to foster care and the property trended toward caring for the elderly more than children, though it remained intergenerational. Today, the Ebby House, part of the Juliette Fowler community, supports teenage women who have aged out of foster care. A total of 450 residents live in this intergenerational community.

CONFEDERATE MEMORIAL CONTROVERSY

One of the largest monuments in Dallas, the sixty-five-foot-high **Confederate Memorial** was moved to **Pioneer Park Cemetery** in 1961 when construction began on a nearby freeway. The monument of Italian marble and Texas granite, designed by Frank Teich, was originally unveiled at Old City Park on April 29, 1897 at an all-day event attended by 400 Confederate and sixty-five Union veterans—"an event so extravagant that the Texas Legislature closed to allow its members to attend," according to Carol Morris Little, author of *A Comprehensive Guide to Outdoor Sculpture in Texas*. The monument includes a central obelisk with a Confederate soldier standing atop and four life-size statues at each corner: General Albert Sidney Johnston, General Robert E. Lee, General Stonewall Jackson, and Confederate President Jefferson Davis.

On February 13, 2019, the Dallas City Council voted to remove the monument in response to a growing controversy in the country over the propriety of monuments "honoring" the Confederacy. Legal appeals over the decision prevented removal for more than a year during which time the monument was covered in a black tarp. On June 12, 2020, a state appeals court approved the removal of the monument, "for archival storage pending resolution of the appeal."

Temple Emanu-El Cemetery at 3430 Howell Street and Lemmon Avenue is adjacent to Freedman's Cemetery. Established in 1884, this cemetery, rich with unique stories of Dallas's oldest Jewish congregation and great merchants whose names are nationally well known, is beautifully landscaped under a shaded canopy of trees and contains distinctive tombstones and markers, many inscribed in Hebrew. The graves of early Jewish pioneers originally buried in the Pioneer Park Cemetery were reinterred here.

Temple Emanu-El Cemetery is the final resting place of **Simon Linz** who, with his four brothers, started the Linz Brothers jewelry business in 1891, and German-born **Alexander Sanger** (1847–1925), who, along with several brothers, established "Sanger Brothers," a pioneer Texas dry-goods wholesale and a retail empire. Sanger Brothers, which opened its Dallas store in 1872, became nationally known for its innovative marketing and merchandising techniques and played a major role in the city's commercial development.

Dallas's arbiter of taste and fashion for fifty years, **Carrie Marcus Neiman** (1883–1953), who served as chairman of the board of the trendsetting store she started with her husband, Al Neiman, is buried here in the Marcus family plot with her brother Herbert (she and her husband were divorced). Her modest marker features just her name and dates of birth and death in relief, giving testament to her taste for simplicity.

Also buried here in the Harris family plot is **Adolph Harris** (1842–1912), founder of A. Harris & Company, a family-owned department store founded in Dallas in 1886. This company and Sanger

Brothers merged in 1961 to create the Sanger-Harris Department store, in operation until 1987, when it became Foley's. Also in the Harris family plot is son **Leon Abraham Harris** (1886–1935), whose tombstone features an elegant mosaic framed within an arched niche. Made of small pieces of pastel glass, the mosaic depicts a rural springtime scene of flowering purple irises and pink magnolias in front of a lake and a backdrop of mountains. The Sanger-Harris stores were known for their singular artistic mosaics on every storefront, some of which wrapped around three sides of the building. Harris's son, Leon Jr., commissioned the mosaics for the stores from the 1950s to the 1980s and no doubt did the same for his father's grave marker. Inscribed beneath Harris's memorial mosaic are the words *plus qu'hier moins que demain*, French for "More than yesterday, Less than tomorrow."

FORT WORTH

Established in 1849 as a US Army military post on a bluff overlooking the Trinity River, Fort Worth (pop. 942,000) was abandoned in 1853 when a new line of forts was built farther west. Settlers took possession of the site and established stores, school, churches, and mills. A stop on the stage line, Fort Worth, thirty-three miles west of Dallas, also became the place where cowboys could rest on their long cattle drives to Abilene, Kansas, although "rest" is a relative term. During this period, saloons and bawdy houses mushroomed and lawlessness prevailed. Starting in the 1860s, Fort Worth became known as "Cowtown," developing a thriving cattle industry. Northern cattle buyers established headquarters in the town. Stockyards and beef-packing plants rose around the railroad line when it arrived in 1876. By the turn of the century, with a population of almost 27,000, the town was a leading packing house center. Its ninety-eight-acre Fort Worth Stockyards National Historic District provides an extraordinary look into the city's livestock heritage.

Oakwood Cemetery at 701 Grand Avenue was founded in 1879 by John Peter Smith who donated the first twenty acres to the city of Fort Worth to create a cemetery in which to bury his stepson. The cemetery, which has a number of large mausoleums, grew to 100 acres with three separate cemeteries known as Oakwood, Calvary, and Trinity. Cattle barons, oilmen, politicians, bartenders, bankers, gamblers, and "women of the night" are buried here. Their stories are spelled out on monuments and historical markers. Plots are owned by lodges, unions, Catholics and Protestants, blacks and whites. Tracts are dedicated to both Confederate and Union soldiers.

Reflecting the colorful history of Cowtown is "Bartenders' Row," two rows of tombstones for eighteen local members of the Bartender's International League, who worked in Hell's Half Acre, Fort Worth's nineteenth-century vice district. The small, tablet-size markers are engraved with the emblem of the bartender's league, the initials LIB. Also buried here in "Soiled Doves Row" is Irish brothel owner **Mary Porter** (1844–1905), the queen of Hell's Half Acre. In one five-year period in the 1890s, she was arrested 130 times and never spent the night in jail. The twenty-five-foot multi-grave plot in which she is buried was owned by her competitor Pearl Beebe. Three prostitutes who worked for Beebe are also buried in the plot. In 2009, some local historians chipped in to purchase a marker for Mary's unmarked grave. Along with birth and death dates, the flat granite marker is inscribed: Mary Porter—"Call Me Madam."

Timothy Isaiah "Longhaired Jim" Courtright (1848–1887), first US marshal of Fort Worth, is buried in a plot with a simple grave marker erected by his descendants. Born in Illinois, he had a reputation for being fast with a gun and early in his career was also known for his chest long hair, which he wore loose. Elected marshal of Fort Worth in 1876 to clean up the unruly city, he served for three years. After his tenure, he left Fort Worth, returning twice following altercations with the law. By the mid-1880s, he was back in Fort Worth working at his own private detective firm, its primary activity a "protection racket" for the town's gambling joints, for which his firm received payment. Luke Short, part owner of the White Elephant Saloon, refused to pay and on the night of February 8, 1887, a shootout occurred. According to onlookers, Courtright's pistol got hung up on his watch chain and Short was able to gun him down. The former marshal was shot three times, once in the heart, and died within a few minutes. Short was exonerated on grounds of self-defense.

William Madison "Gooseneck Bill" McDonald (1866–1950) is buried in Trinity Cemetery. A thirty-eight-foot-tall obelisk monument that he commissioned and was erected before his death and a historical marker at his family plot give testament to his importance in Fort Worth history. A legend in his day, he is believed to be the first black millionaire in Texas.

Before he moved to Fort Worth, he lived in Kaufman County. His father, a freed slave, had once been owned by the Ku Klux Klan's first grand wizard. At just eight years old, William went to work for a white lawyer who helped him go to college. Before he was twenty-one, he operated a school and organized a state fair to show off the accomplishments of black farmers. He became active in politics in 1890 and his ability to unite black and white voters led to his prominence as a leader of the "Black and Tan" faction of the Republican Party. He served as a delegate to many state and national conventions and was active in the party for thirty years. Additionally, he was active in black Masonic societies, serving as state secretary for forty-seven years. In 1906, McDonald moved to Fort Worth, where he bought a few businesses, built several buildings, and opened the Fraternal Bank and Trust, which became a thriving financial institution. One of the few to survive the Great Depression, his bank helped many struggling white-owned banks. Fraternal Bank and Trust started as the repository for black Masons but expanded to serve other African Americans when white banks weren't open to them. McDonald helped a lot of young black entrepreneurs start businesses. While his business and political life thrived, McDonald's personal life was tumultuous. He was married five times and his only child, William Jr., passed away while studying law at Howard College in 1918. His plot contains the graves of his wife, **Mattie Helen Ezell** (1878–1926), whom he married in 1896 and was the mother of his only child, their son **William Jr.** (1898–1918), and **Harry Manack** (1903–1930), a cashier who worked at McDonald's bank and died of pulmonary tuberculosis. Although the surname McDonald also appears on Harry's headstone, he was the son of Harry Manack Sr. and wife Willie Taylor, according to his death certificate.

HONEY GROVE

Honey Grove (pop. 1,700) is fifteen miles south of the Oklahoma border and ninety miles northeast of Dallas. According to town legend, it was discovered by David Crockett and a company of his men from Tennessee as they traveled to Texas to join the revolutionary forces. When they reached the area, they camped in a grove, just north of the present town square, near a spring of water. Crockett found many trees in the grove hollowed inside with swarms of bees and an abundance of honey. In letters he wrote to Tennessee, he told of the ideal place where he had camped, calling it the "honey grove." He vowed to return and settle there, but fate got in the way. In 1842, several pioneers began to arrive, including Crockett's friend Samuel Erwin, who called the settlement Honey Grove. A post office was established in 1846 and the town was incorporated in 1873. When a branch of the Santa Fe Railroad from Paris to Dallas came through Honey Grove in 1885, the town began to prosper as a retail center and shipping hub for area farmers.

Oakwood Cemetery at 5th Street off Highway 82 in Honey Grove was established in 1846 with the burial of **James G. Gilmer** (1814–1846) on his land grant. A native of Kentucky, Gilmer had only lived in the area for a few months when he took ill and died, leaving behind his wife, **Elizabeth "Betsey" Parrish** (1815–1865) and four young sons, one an infant. Two years later, **Benjamin Stuart Walcott** (1809–1878) married Elizabeth. The couple had two sons. Elizabeth's three oldest sons joined the Confederate forces and were all killed in 1862. Her fourth son with Gilmer, his namesake, became a prominent citizen in Honey Grove, serving as mayor and postmaster. Walcott is credited with establishing the town with the first store, school, and church buildings on land he and Elizabeth donated. The couple also donated three acres that included Gilmer's grave as a public graveyard, which became known as Oakwood because of the large oak trees on the property. Elizabeth's grave is between those of her first and second husbands, marked by two obelisk monuments in the oldest part of the cemetery, which now encompasses more than forty-five acres and has more than 6,200 graves. Pioneers, Civil War veterans, members of the town's pre–Civil War slave community, and freed black citizens are buried here.

Born in Louisiana, **Thomas Bell Yarbrough Sr.** (1841–1897) settled in Honey Grove in 1865 and opened Yarbrough Dry Goods, developing a reputation for fair and upright dealings with his customers. In 1876, he established the first newspaper, *The Honey Grove Independent*, was superintendent of the Methodist Sunday school, and a cashier at the town bank. Attesting to his character, his epitaph reads: "Mark the perfect man and behold the upright for the end of that man is peace." Thomas is buried between his two wives. His first wife **Sallie F. Waggoner** (1845–1880), with whom he had four children, died in childbirth. Her marble pillar monument also memorializes their infant son who died at birth a few days before his mother. His second wife, **Sue Moody** (1849–1908), had three children, one who survived infancy. A flat granite marker indicates her grave.

Paris

Although the first recorded settlement of the area was in 1826, Paris (pop. 25,000) was founded by George W. Wright, who donated fifty acres in 1844. Incorporated the next year, the town, twenty-two miles east of Honey Grove, was named by one of Wright's employees. By the eve of the Civil War, 700 residents lived in Paris, a cattle and farming community. When the railroad arrived in 1876, it became a shipping

A statue of a young girl holding flowers is an unusual memorial for a man, but it marks the grave of Thomas Bell Yarbrough Sr., an early Honey Grove merchant and newspaperman.

center. In 1877 and again in 1916, major fires destroyed much of the town, including its 1897 Victorian county courthouse. Instead of rebuilding it in the historic town square, city leaders commissioned an Italian marble fountain to be placed in the square. In 1993, the city erected a replica of the Eiffel Tower, three miles from the town square. The Texas tower is sixty-five feet in height (the one in France is 1,063 feet high) and a shiny red cowboy hat sits at the top of the spindle. It also has twenty-seven LED lights programmed to the seasons. Besides the Eiffel Tower, another frequented tourist stop is the town cemetery known for its "Jesus in Cowboy Boots" monument.

Evergreen Cemetery, at the intersection of Business Highway 19/24 and Evergreen Street, has more than 40,000 graves, many moved from the old City Cemetery in the center of town when Evergreen was established in 1866. The cemetery's unique stonecutting art includes angelic figures and religious imagery, flowers, vines, cotton bales, broken trees, anchors and chains, sheep, a life-size buffalo, and a replica of the front page of *The Paris Morning News*.

Willet C. Babcock (1828–1881), born in New York, settled in the town in 1859, and became one of the town leaders as well as an undertaker and entrepreneur. Babcock's twenty-foot-tall granite monument includes a six-foot pedestal upon which stands a life-size statue of a robe clad figure with long hair leaning on a cross. The figure is depicted wearing cowboy boots and boot-cut pants underneath his robes, earning its nickname "Jesus in Cowboy Boots." The pedestal is inscribed "Willet Babcock, Oct. 6, 1828, died 1881, Love Never Dies." It features upside down torches, symbolizing the end of a life. In addition to being an undertaker, Babcock was also the owner of an opera house and a manufacturer of fine furniture, so it is unclear why German stone mason **Gustave Klein** (1850–1884)—who crafted many of the elaborate statues in the cemetery and who is also buried in Evergreen—decided to add cowboy boots to the figure. This mystery contributes to the intrigue of the statue.

The Adams family plot features another marble and granite monument made by Gustave Klein. At least as tall as Babcock's, it features an angel standing on an ornate pedestal, her arms crossed on her chest, a crown upon her head. The grave marker memorializes **Captain John Newton Adams** (1839–1881) and his wife **Florrie Reed Adams Bywaters** (1846–1903). A small urn on a pedestal nearby memorializes twelve children. On one side of the pedestal is inscribed: "In Memory of Our Darling Babies," on the other, "**Stella May**, born April 19, 1869, died June 16, 1869."

Captain Adams, born in North Carolina, served in the Confederate forces. At the time of his death, he was working as a banker and merchant in Paris. Born in Alabama, Florrie was sixteen when she married Adams in 1861. They came to Texas, living in Jefferson before settling in Paris. Their first infant was born and buried in Jefferson. After coming to Paris, they lost one baby after another until their family plot was populated with twelve little graves. A year after her husband's death, Florrie married Joseph K. Bywaters. No children were born to this union. Her obituary contained the following: "We never think of Mrs. Bywaters without grieving with her at the loss of her children, none of whom lived to bless their parents except one little Stella, who after a few months died with whooping cough. . . . How she deserved and received sympathy for the loss of her loved ones, for one by one they went before, and now she has joined her angel band in that land of the Leal (synonym for Heaven) where they in their baby robes of glittering white will receive their mother whom they never knew here, and whose heart has grieved for them all of these years."

The monument for **James Morgan Pride** (1848–1893) and his sister **Marzee Jo Pride** (1857–1895) resembles a rock ledge upon which three sheep are lying. Marzee's obituary references the death of her brother—a wealthy West Texas rancher who had been murdered two years before. Marzee was apparently so grief-stricken even after two years that on August 7, the anniversary of his death, she threw herself headlong into a well forty-five-feet deep filled with six feet of water. Marzee was spending the night with her sister at the time and barking dogs woke the family. According to the obituary, "her aged mother [was] not expected to survive the shock." She died almost a year later, on June 2, 1896, aged sixty-eight. Her name, **Mary Ann Bailey Pride** is inscribed on one of the stones of the memorial.

A tall pillar monument topped by an urn memorializes **Samuel Bell Maxey** (1825–1895) and his wife **Marilda Denton** (1833–1908). Born in Kentucky, Maxey was a West Point graduate who fought in the Mexican War. After moving to Paris in 1857, he became active in politics. During the Civil War, he raised a regiment, the Ninth Texas Infantry, and took his unit to fight in Mississippi. He was promoted to brigadier general and in 1863 received a promotion to commander of Indian Territory. He worked to recruit and train members of the Cherokee, Creek, and Choctaw tribes. After the war, Maxey continued to support the Native American tribes when he served in the US Senate and was an outspoken advocate of Indian rights. Maxey died

A cross of tree limbs with a Knights of Pythias shield, among other emblems, marks the grave of David Harrison Moore, a twenty-seven-year-old saloon owner and gunfight victim who died in 1886.

of a gastrointestinal disease in Arkansas, where he had gone for treatment. His body was shipped back to Paris for burial. He and his wife had no biological children. In 1863, they adopted six-year-old Dora Bell, whose mother had died in childbirth and whose father had died at Shiloh in 1862.

KNIGHTS OF PYTHIAS

The Knights of Pythias is a fraternal organization founded in Washington D.C. in 1864, the first to receive a charter under an Act of the US Congress. Founded by Justus H. Rathbone, the organization was inspired by the Greek legend of Damon and Pythias, which illustrates the ideals of friendship, including honor and loyalty. Membership has historically been open to men in good health, eighteen or older, who are not Communists or Fascists, who do not advocate the overthrow of the government in which they are citizens, who are not professional gamblers or involved with illegal drugs or alcohol, and who must have a belief in a Supreme Being. By the end of the "Golden Age of Fraternalism" in the early 1920s, the order had nearly a million members. Today, there are less than 50,000 worldwide. The emblem seen on the gravestones of members include a knight's helmet and a falcon (a symbol of vigilance) sitting atop a shield with the letters, F, C, and B, which stand for Friendship, Charity, and Benevolence. Swords, battle axes, and a spear, representing the weapons used against their enemies, adorn the emblem.

PLANO

Fifteen miles north of Dallas, Plano (pop. 286,000) developed in the early 1840s with the settlement of pioneers from the Peters Colony, named after William S. Peters who obtained a North Texas *empresario* grant made by the Republic of Texas. Most of the colonists were from Kentucky and Tennessee. Kentucky farmer William Foreman moved to the area with his family in 1846. He erected a sawmill and gristmill and built a general store, setting up a post office in his home. In 1852, postal authorities approved the name Plano, Spanish for "flat," as the name of the town suggested by local residents as a reference to the local terrain. Raising livestock and farming the rich, black land were the principal businesses.

Bacchus Cemetery, 7485 Bishop Road at the corner of Legacy Drive, was founded as a family cemetery in 1847 with the burial of **Daniel Cook** (1831–1847), son of **Henry Cook** (1775–1862) and **Sarah Kincaid Cook** (1793–1889), members of Peters Colony. Cook settled in Plano with his family in 1846 and built a log house nearby, a landmark on the Shawnee Trail. His sixteen-year-old son's burial site indicated by a simple tablet tombstone is the earliest marked grave in all of Plano. Cook's daughter, **Rachel Cook Baccus** (1830–1912), deeded the burial ground to his heirs in 1878. The cemetery was named in her honor. Today, the cemetery of about 285 marked graves with distinctive nineteenth-century tombstones is enclosed within a wrought-iron fence connected by rugged brick pillars and surrounded by shops, restaurants, homes, and businesses.

Henry Cook was born in Virginia but was raised in Green County, Illinois. He served as a lieutenant in the War of 1812. Widowered three times and married four, Henry had a forceful and magnetic personality. His third wife died, leaving him with five children. He married his fourth wife Sarah, eighteen years his junior, in 1825, and together they had six children. Twenty-one years later, at age seventy-one, Henry, Sarah, and his eleven children left in a caravan of seven wagons from Illinois. When they reached their destination near the present-day Bacchus Cemetery, Henry patented the land as a Peters Colonist.

Sarah "Sally," born in Kentucky, grew up in a large extended family (twenty plus children), which prepared her for life with a big family on the frontier. At the time of her arrival in Texas with her husband and children, North Central Texas was a vast wilderness. The Cooks built their log cabin on a hill crest overlooking extensive landscapes. It was a trail marker by day and a lighthouse by night, visible in all directions. Their house became known as the Lonesome House, because of its solitary location.

After her husband's death in 1862, Sally applied for a widow's pension based on his service in the War of 1812. When she finally collected the lump sum of eight dollars a month for seven years, she promptly purchased a zinc obelisk monument for her husband's grave, which looks as good today as when it was erected.

Collingsworth Cemetery, established in 1895 behind the home of Milt Collinsworth, is today surrounded by a black wrought-iron fence, tucked between two houses in a suburban neighborhood on 3108 Vermillion Drive. Its park-like setting beneath large trees and benches belies the sad and tragic story of its founding.

In May 1895, the family welcomed a traveling salesman into the home for the night. The next morning as he was leaving, he mentioned that he was feeling sick. The Collinsworth daughter who had helped change the man's bed linens became sick. She was diagnosed with smallpox. Despite the early diagnosis, the doctor was unfamiliar with proper treatment measures. The disease spread quickly through the family resulting in four deaths within thirty days. Many extended family members came together in the Collinsworth home for the funerals and the illness spread further. Eventually more than ten relatives succumbed to the illness. Plano officials quarantined the area extending to the north and south by present-day Spring Creek Parkway and Park Boulevard and to the east and west by what is now Coit and Preston Road to avoid a citywide epidemic. The city also passed a resolution to vaccinate everyone and prohibited passage on all through roads.

The following notice appeared in the *Dallas News* and was republished in the May 23, 1895 issue of the *McKinney Democrat*:

> The smallpox epidemic in the community west of Plano has proven to be fatal and very sad with the Collinsworth family. . . . Tobe Collinsworth, 23 years old, whose parents live in Livia, Kentucky, died with small-pox this evening at the home of Mrs. Levi Collinsworth, five miles west of Plano, who lost her husband with the dreaded disease ten days ago. This is the fourth death in the Collinsworth families in the past month from this disease. Mrs. F. M. Collinsworth now has the disease and Mrs. Levi Collinsworth and 9-year-old daughter are the only ones that have recovered after taking same.

The cemetery was in use until 1925. As many as thirty Collinsworth family members may be buried here, although only six stones remain.

SHERMAN

Seventy-five miles north of Dallas, Sherman (pop. 46,000) was founded in 1846 by Grayson County commissioners. Named after General Sidney Sherman, a hero of the Texas Revolution, the town was moved from its initial site at the center of the county in 1848 because of a lack of wood and water. The new site about three miles east of the original location was determined by a mammoth pecan tree that stood on the southeast section of what is now the public square. The town grew rapidly as a commercial center and was a stop on the Butterfield Overland Mail route through Texas. The railroad arrived in 1872. By the 1880s, it had five flour mills, an iron works, and three newspapers. The town's population had grown to 10,213 by 1900.

West Hill Cemetery at the intersection of Ricketts and Lamar Streets is operated by the City of Sherman on approximately 120 acres near the center of town. Founded in 1859 with the burial of the town's first mayor, Burrell P. Smith, the historic cemetery also includes Hebrew, black, and Confederate sections. On May 15, 1896, a tornado cut through the west side of town, killing about sixty-six people, many of whom are buried here. Among notable individuals buried in West Hill is **Thomas Jefferson Shannon** (1808–1861), born in Kentucky, who came to Texas in 1839. Shannon and Samuel Blagg, another early settler, donated land for the new town. Shannon became a cattle industry pioneer, bringing the first Durhams to the United States. Queen Victoria gave him three of the breed after he wrote her of his interest in them. Shannon paid the freight charges, and the animals were brought overland to North Texas.

The most renowned individual buried in this cemetery is **Olive Oatman Fairchild** (1837–1903), who was kidnapped as a child by Yavapai Indians and traded to a Mojave tribe that tattooed her chin with blue lines. Such tattoos were worn by both Mojave men and women to identify tribe members in the afterlife. "[They] pricked the skin in small regular rows on our chins with a very sharp stick, until they bled freely," Olive would later write.

Originally from Illinois, Olive, her parents, and six siblings were traveling to California in March 1851 when they were attacked by Yavapai Indians on the Gila River in Arizona. Olive watched in horror as her parents, brothers, and sisters were bludgeoned to death with war clubs. Only thirteen-year-old Olive and her seven-year-old sister Mary were spared. One of her brothers, fifteen-year-old Lorenzo, survived the attack and escaped. Olive and Mary were taken as slaves and later sold to a Mojave chief. Mary died of starvation in 1855 during a drought that struck the Mojave valley. In February 1856, due to the efforts of her brother, Olive was found and returned. She shared her story with a California clergyman, Reverend Royal B. Stratton, who chronicled her experience in a best-selling book called *Life among the Indians; Being an Interesting Narrative of the Captivity of the Oatman Girls* (1857), a tale so embellished that later Olive tried to locate copies of his book and destroy them. While on a lecture circuit in Michigan to talk about her captivity, she met **John B. Fairchild** (1830–1907), a wealthy rancher and banker whose brother had been killed in an Indian attack the same time Olive was in captivity. They married in 1865 and relocated to Sherman, Texas, in the mid-1870s. They adopted a daughter and lived a comfortable life in Sherman. But Olive rarely left home and when she did, she wore a veil to cover her face, becoming known as the "veiled lady." In 1881, she spent nearly three months at a medical spa in Canada, largely in bed. She suffered a chronic form of post-traumatic stress for most of her later life. She and her husband are buried in a family plot with a substantial granite marker upon which the name FAIRCHILD is inscribed. A Texas Historical Marker was placed there in 1969.

Olive Oatman. Photo by Benjamin F. Powelson, c. 1863, Albumen
silver print.

NATIONAL PORTRAIT GALLERY, SMITHSONIAN INSTITUTION.

WEATHERFORD

Thirty miles west of Fort Worth, Weatherford (pop. 37,000) was named after Jefferson Weatherford, a member of the Texas Senate. Incorporated in 1858, Weatherford was located on the crest of a divide between the Trinity and Brazos valleys and was midway on the stage run between Fort Worth and Fort Belknap. North Texas's principal frontier settlement for its first decade, Weatherford was also where county residents took shelter when Indians plundered the region. By the 1880s with railways reaching the town, it became a retail and shipping hub for farmers and ranchers, with the population reaching 5,000 in the 1890s. Watermelon became the main agricultural product in 1900. In the mid-1800s, local farmers, ranchers, and merchants bought, sold, or traded their livestock, handmade items, produce, and other supplies during the monthly legal trials at the courthouse. Initially known as a monthly "Stray Day" sale, it evolved to today's First Monday Trade Fair.

Old City Greenwood Cemetery at 400 Front Street was established in 1863. Remains of those buried in other areas were moved to this new cemetery. In 1925, the civic league and cemetery association was formed. They beautified the nicely shaded cemetery and widened and graveled the driveways. Among the estimated 4,000 graves are those of city and state leaders, veterans of several wars, and legendary Texas pioneers **Oliver Loving** and **Boze Ikard.**

Oliver Loving (1812–1867), cattle rancher and pioneer of the cattle drive who with Charles Goodnight (see Goodnight Cemetery) developed the Goodnight-Loving Trail, died on September 25, 1867.

Originally buried in Fort Sumter, New Mexico, he was reinterred at Greenwood Cemetery on March 4, 1868. Mortally wounded by Indians while on a cattle drive, he was the inspiration for the character of Captain Augustus "Gus" McCrae in the television miniseries based on Larry McMurtry's Pulitzer Prize–winning novel *Lonesome Dove*.

Born in Kentucky, Loving, his wife **Susan Doggett Morgan** (1809–1884), their five children (four more would be born in Texas), and several family members moved in 1845 to the Republic of Texas, where Loving received 640 acres spread through three counties—Collin, Dallas, and Parker. To market his large herd, Loving began to drive his cattle out of Texas. During the war, Confederate forces commissioned him to drive cattle along the Mississippi River for its troops. The Confederacy's loss was also Loving's, who was left unpaid several hundred thousand dollars. In 1866, having heard about the probable need for cattle at Fort Sumner, New Mexico, where several thousand Indians had been settled on a reservation, Loving gathered a herd, combined it with Charles Goodnight's, and began a long drive to the fort. Their route later became known as the Goodnight-Loving Trail. They later reunited in southern New Mexico, where they went into partnership with John Chisum at his ranch in the Bosque Grande, about forty miles south of Fort Sumner. In the spring of 1867, Loving and Goodnight returned to Texas, ready to start a new drive. This third drive was slowed by heavy rains and Indian threats. Loving went ahead of the herd for contract bidding, taking only his trusted scout Bill Wilson with him and intending to travel only at night because of the Indian threat. Loving became impatient and pushed ahead during

After Bose Ikard's death, Charles Goodnight erected this marker for him with the inscription: "Served with me four years on Goodnight-Loving trail. Never shirked a duty or disobeyed an order. Rode with me in many stampedes. Participated in three engagements with Comanches. Splendid behavior. -C Goodnight."

the day. His action provoked a Comanche attack in which he was seriously wounded. Despite his injury, Loving sent Wilson back to the herd, eluded the Indians, and, with the aid of Mexican traders, reached Fort Sumner. In bed, dying of gangrene, he asked Goodnight to bury him in Texas. Goodnight agreed. With the herd still needing to get to Colorado, Goodnight agreed to Loving's temporary burial at Fort Sumner. He drove the herd on to Colorado, and when he returned, he had Loving's body exhumed and carried home. He was reburied in Greenwood Cemetery on March 4, 1868. Loving has been inducted into the National Cowboy Hall of Fame in Oklahoma City. Loving County, Texas, and Loving, New Mexico, are named in his honor.

Bose Ikard (1843–1929), one of the most famous black frontiersmen and trail drivers in Texas, was born a slave in Mississippi. In 1852, he moved to Texas with the family of his owner, Dr. Milton L. Ikard. He continued to work for Dr. Ikard for a few years following emancipation, but in 1866 joined a cattle drive to Colorado led by Charles Goodnight and Oliver Loving. After Loving was killed by Comanches, Ikard continued to work for Goodnight for several more years and became a trusted friend. Ikard and his wife, **Angeline** (1862–1902), with whom he had ten children, settled in Weatherford, Texas, in 1869. He developed a reputation for being a man of honor and integrity; Goodnight once said that he trusted Ikard more than any living man. Ikard was the inspiration for the character of Joshua Deets in the *Lonesome Dove* miniseries. The Bose Ikard Elementary School in Weatherford, Texas, is named in his honor. In 1997, Ikard was inducted into the Texas Trail of Fame. A statue of him was erected at the Fort Worth Stockyards.

Terlingua Cemetery is one of the most emblematic of the harsh West Texas experience.

CHAPTER 7

MOUNTAIN TRAIL REGION

Continental shifting, volcanic action, wind, and rain shaped this region that stretches across two time zones. Rugged mountains and mesas, steep river canyons, and desert panoramas are bordered on the south by the Rio Grande. A century before the Pilgrims landed at Plymouth Rock, a Spanish expedition arrived here in the 1530s, encountering agricultural communities and nomadic tribes. In 1598, Juan de Oñate crossed the Rio Grande in present-day El Paso and set up a provincial capital connected to Mexico City by a 1,800-mile road. This trade route passed through El Paso, where a permanent mission was founded in 1659. In 1680, Pueblo tribes in the Santa Fe area revolted, prompting Spanish settlers and Tigua Indians to establish the El Paso settlements of Ysleta and Soccoro, Texas's oldest permanent settlements.

Throughout the seventeenth and into the mid-nineteenth centuries, Indian attacks and the area's isolation kept growth at bay. After the US Army established military outposts along the Texas frontier, far West Texas became a destination route, with stagecoaches bringing mail, new residents, and California gold prospectors on the San Antonio-El Paso and Butterfield Overland Mail routes. By the 1880s, with the arrival of four railroads, the region's future as a commercial hub was secured and economic opportunities opened for ranchers able to purchase vast rangelands by the Davis Mountains and Big Bend, many of which still operate today.

EL PASO

At the western tip of Texas, New Mexico on the west, and the country of Mexico on the south, El Paso (pop. 685,000) lies in a harsh desert environment between two mountain ranges. When Spanish explorers arrived, they called it El Paso del Norte (the Pass of the North). Its first settlements were populated by Spaniards and Indians from the Tigua tribe. By the middle of the eighteenth century about 5,000 people lived in the El Paso area—Spaniards, mestizos, and Indians—the largest complex of population on the Spanish northern frontier.

After the Mexican War in 1848, the boundary between Texas and Mexico was fixed at the Rio Grande. By late 1849, aided by the gold rush to California, five settlements and ranchos along the Texas side had been founded by Americans—T. Frank White, Simeon Hart, Benjamin Franklin Coons, James Magoffin, and Hugh Stephenson. Coons's rancho became the nucleus of El Paso, Texas.

The US military post Fort Bliss was established in 1854, and the Butterfield Overland mail arrived in 1858. A year later, pioneer Anson Mills completed his plat of the town of El Paso, Texas. Because of the confusion over the name of the new Texas city, the Mexican town across the river, El Paso del Norte, was changed to Ciudad Juárez in 1888.

The arrival of the railroads in 1881 and 1882 transformed a sleepy, dusty, adobe village of several hundred inhabitants into a flourishing frontier community that reached a population of more than 10,000 by 1890. A western boomtown, El Paso also became known as "Six Shooter Capital" and "Sin City," with scores of saloons, dance halls, gambling establishments, and brothels lining the main streets. In the 1890s, citizens petitioned town leaders to stop El Paso's most visible forms of vice and lawlessness, and in 1905 the city finally enacted ordinances closing houses of gambling and prostitution.

Concordia Cemetery at 3700 Yandell Drive is a Texas Historic Cemetery known as El Paso's Boot Hill, where over 65,000 have been buried since the 1850s. The cemetery was once part of the 900-acre Rancho Concordia established in the 1840s by entrepreneur and Missouri native **Hugh Stephenson** (1798–1870) and his wife **Juana Maria Azcarate** (1800–1857), an aristocratic daughter of a wealthy Mexican merchant, owner of land, cattle, and mines. Juana Maria died in 1856 of injuries sustained when a deer she had raised as a fawn gored her. She was buried near a chapel (no longer there) on the property. Later, her remains were moved to the French family plot at the cemetery. French was the surname of the Stephenson's son-in-law who purchased and then resold the land back to his in-laws after the Civil War. The graveyard, then outside the city limits of El Paso, gained widespread use in the 1880s after being opened to the public by another of Stephenson's daughters. By 1890, various sections had been purchased by different groups and were designated Catholic, Masonic, Jewish, black, Chinese, Military, Jesuit, city, and county. Buried here are gunfighters, lawmen, Buffalo Soldiers, Texas Rangers, Civil War Veterans, and early Mormon pioneers.

The Chinese burial ground at Concordia is partitioned from the rest of the cemetery by a rock wall and iron-gated entry. Although there are almost 300 graves, few have markers because many of the original tombstones were stolen or deteriorated over the years. Replacement markers consist of concrete slabs with the name and death date of the interred etched in Chinese characters. Most of the burials here are of single males, because the Exclusion Act of 1882 severely constricted the number of Chinese immigrants to the United States, especially women. Chinese immigrants first arrived in El Paso shortly before the Southern Union Pacific Railroad completed its line in 1881. In 1900, El Paso had some 400 Chinese inhabitants, with less than 1 percent female.

John Wesley Hardin (1853–1895) was born in Bonham, Texas. Named after the founder of Methodism, he soon displayed a quick and hot temper that would get him into trouble time and again. He was famous, or infamous, as the most profligate killer in the Old West. He claimed to have killed more than thirty men, all of them before he reached the age of twenty-three. Yet he considered himself a pillar of society maintaining that he never killed anyone "who did not need killing." His autobiography published a year after his death is one of the first recorded confessionals of a serial killer and is a classic in outlaw literature.

While serving a twenty-five-year term in state prison for murder, he studied law. He was pardoned after fifteen years in March of 1894. He moved to El Paso to establish a law practice and was soon in trouble again. On August 19, 1895, El Paso city constable **John Selman** (1839–1896) strode into the Acme Saloon where Hardin was standing at the bar playing dice and shot him in the head, killing Hardin instantly. According to a newspaper account published a few days later, the reason involved Selman's son, who was on the police force. Selman Junior had arrested a female friend of Hardin's a few nights before and Hardin had threatened to run him out of town. Constable Selman went into the Acme saloon the next night with a friend. When Hardin saw him through the mirror at the back of the bar, he began to reach for his gun, but Selman's gun was already out. He shot Hardin in the head and as he fell, Selman shot him two more times. Selman gave himself up immediately. He was tried for the murder, but his trial ended in a hung jury. Awaiting a retrial, Selman went about his business, which included drinking and playing cards in a local saloon. On April 6, 1896, less than a year after killing Hardin, Selman,

The grave of Western outlaw John Wesley Hardin, enclosed in a wrought-iron cage, is one of the most visited at Concordia Cemetery.

who'd been drinking, got in an argument in the alley of the Wigwam Saloon with a US deputy marshal. A shootout between them left Selman mortally wounded. His flat granite marker at Concordia, donated by the Western Outlaws and Lawmen's Association in 2003, is inscribed with his name, birth and death dates, his occupation, and the following: "Slayer of John Wesley Hardin, August 19, 1895."

On August 27, 1995, a graveside confrontation over the body of John Wesley Hardin took place between Hardin's descendants and Concordia Heritage Association members. His descendants wanted to reinter his body in Nixon, Texas, next to the grave of his first wife—also to be relocated from another cemetery. They presented a disinterment permit to remove the gunfighter's remains. Association members handed them a court order prohibiting the removal of the body. They accused each other of seeking tourist revenue generated by the location of the body. The court order stopped the disinterment, and the descendants appealed the order. In a final judgment a few years later, the court ruled that Hardin's remains would stay in El Paso.

Not far from Hardin's grave, a metal cross marks the burial place of Texas Ranger **Ernest St. Leon** (1859–1898), also known as "Diamond Dick," a nickname given by his fellow officers for his fondness for wearing a diamond stickpin on his lapel. St. Leon, a French-American law enforcement officer, was born in Canada and reared in San Antonio. He joined the Texas Rangers in 1890 and was considered one of their finest undercover officers. However, he was dismissed several months later due to his drinking. He continued his undercover work in an unofficial capacity and was brought back into service as a Ranger in 1893. He again left the service in 1894, returning in 1897. In August of 1898, St. Leon was involved in a gunfight with three horse thieves in Socorro, Texas, a small settlement southeast of El Paso on the north bank of the Rio Grande. He shot one of the bandits in the hip and then was himself shot in his left shoulder, the same bullet piercing his lung. He died after reaching El Paso and was survived by his Mexican wife.

Florida J. Wolfe (1867–1913), also known as "Lady Flo," was born in Illinois and arrived in El Paso around 1882. She was an attractive black woman who flaunted tradition but earned the respect of citizens on both sides of the border. While working as a nurse in the home of the American consul in Mexico, she met Lord Delaval James de la Poer Beresford (1862–1906), an Irish millionaire who had purchased two of the best cattle ranches in northern Mexico. She and Beresford fell in love and he persuaded her to give up her position and live with him. While this was not a problem in Mexico, it was illegal in the United States for an interracial couple to be married or live together. The couple resided in Ciudad Juarez, but frequently traveled between that town and El Paso in separate carriages. But once, Beresford was arrested for walking with his paramour on the street.

Lady Flo gave grand parties and made contributions to the El Paso Fire and Police Departments. After Lord Beresford's death in a train wreck in Minnesota in December 1906, Lady Flo claimed his property as his common-law wife. His family in Ireland contested her claim and after a protracted court battle she received $15,000 and a few hundred head of cattle. She spent the remaining years of her life in El Paso, regularly attending the Second Baptist Church and giving away what was left of her fortune to the poor and downtrodden. Lady Flo died of tuberculosis in May 1913 and was buried at Concordia. A semicircle of wooden benches marks her grave, which is shaded by four small desert willows, appearing like an oasis in the arid terrain of the cemetery.

FORT DAVIS

In the foothills of the Davis Mountains, Fort Davis (pop. 1,200) is an unincorporated community with the highest elevation of any town in Texas at 5,050 feet above sea level. About 200 miles southeast of El Paso via Van Horn, the garrison was founded in 1854 on the site of an earlier Indian village along the old San Antonio-El Paso Road. Occupied by Confederate forces during the Civil War for only a short time due to its isolated location, it was re-occupied by the Ninth US Cavalry in 1867. Located at the crossroads of two important trails, Fort Davis was a key town in the Trans-Pecos country. The army abandoned the fort in the early 1890s. After a population downswing, the town rebounded, becoming a ranching center, tourist, and hunting center. Many of the buildings at Fort Davis have been restored and the old fort is now operated by the National Park Service as a National Historic Site.

A Texas Historic Cemetery, **Fort Davis Pioneer Cemetery**, 202 Musquiz Drive/State Hwy 118, is at the base of the Dolores Mountain. The mountain was named after Dolores Gavino Duporto, a local woman who spent a lifetime lamenting the tragic loss of her lover. Dolores's fiancé José was a goatherd and she communicated with him while he was out tending his goats by building a fire every Thursday night on the low mountain south of town. Shortly before their wedding day, Mescaleros killed and scalped José while he was tending his goats. Overcome with grief, Dolores continued to climb the mountain every Thursday night and light a fire for her long-lost lover for the rest of her life. She died in 1893 and was buried near the path she took on her trips up the mountain. Her grave is unmarked and its whereabouts unknown. Today, the path she took is called Dolores Mountain Trail and is a short distance from the historic cemetery.

An elevated wrought-iron sign and Texas Historical Marker front a fenced path to the two-and-a-half-acre Fort Davis Pioneer Cemetery situated between a couple of farmhouses. When the Fort Davis Historical Society took ownership of the cemetery in 1966, there were no records of burials. A Boy Scout troop erected crosses on known graves and built a covered seated area. The cemetery, with an unknown number of graves, was in use from the 1870s to 1914. Many of the

Crosses mark the spot in the Fort Davis Pioneer Cemetery where an adobe tomb once stood as the burial location for seven children of the same family who died during a diphtheria epidemic in the fall of 1891.

tombstones are dilapidated, either illegible or with no inscription, but there are several intriguing markers and stories about those interred.

Anton Diedrick Dutchover (1820–1904) and his wife **Refugio "Cora" Salcido Dutchover** (1842–1908) are buried in a fenced plot here. Diedrick is one of the first European settlers of Fort Davis. In 1842, he was walking the streets of his native Antwerp when he witnessed a murder. The killers, fearing exposure, shipped him away on the first outgoing vessel. For several years, he was kept a virtual prisoner until he got his chance to go ashore in Galveston. Since he spoke only Flemish, he had a hard time communicating. When a pair of soldiers recruiting for the Mexican War asked his name, he didn't respond, not understanding the question. At last, one said in exasperation, "Aw, he's Dutch all over. We'll call him that." Thus, he was listed on the roll as Diedrick Dutchallover. The name was shortened to Dutchover.

After the Mexican War, Dutchover lived in San Antonio, gaining experience as a frontier scout. In 1850, Big Foot Wallace (see Austin, Texas State Cemetery) asked him to serve as shotgun guard on the first stage run from San Antonio to El Paso. He worked as a guard for several years for the stage line. One of the stops along the route was Limpia Canyon out of the Pecos River Valley into the Davis Mountains, then called the Limpia Mountains. Anton liked the area and decided to make it his home. During this time, Dutchover met Refugio "Cora" Salcido. Of Spanish heritage, she was born in Mexico and was living in El Paso when they met and fell in love. They married in 1861, moving to Fort Davis, where Dutchover owned a small sheep ranch in Limpia Canyon, five miles south of the fort. Indian attacks were a constant threat, especially after the Eighth Infantry left at the onset of the Civil War. The Mescalero Apaches stole so many of his sheep that Dutchover often lamented that he was "their private sheep provider." When federal troops returned in 1867, Dutchover was employed as an army contractor to haul timber from Sawmill Canyon for use in rebuilding the fort. Even with a heavy guard, he would frequently lose oxen at night to the Apaches. Dutchover spent the rest of his days near Fort Davis and was still there when the last soldiers left in 1891. Cora died in 1912, eight years after her husband, when the wagon coach in which she was riding turned over as she returned from Mass. The couple left ten children and many descendants. The Dutchover name remains prominent in far West Texas.

During a two-week period in 1891, the children of Buffalo soldier George Bentley (1845–1923) and his wife Concepción "Chana" Rodriguez (1855–1950), who ranged in age from two months to seventeen years, each died a terrible death. According to a newly arrived doctor at Fort Davis, he treated the children but had few options. Diphtheria is a highly contagious upper respiratory disease often caused by bacteria in unpasteurized milk. Victims experience sore throats, raging fevers, and increasingly impaired breathing as a membrane grows across the trachea. Eventually, death comes from suffocation. The doctor later told Barry Scobee, a journalist who became an authority on Trans-Pecos history, that he had never seen such a serious outbreak of the disease. "People died like flies," the doctor wrote in a 1936 letter to Scobee, "including the Bentley children." Soon a vicious rumor was circulating that the deaths had come as fulfillment of a curse placed on Bentley for bayoneting an Apache infant while in the military, an unsupported allegation. The couple went on to have three more children, two daughters and son, and were married almost fifty years at the time of George's death in 1923.

PRESIDIO

Farmers have lived at Presidio (pop. 3,700) since 1500 BC. By 1400 AD, local Indians lived in small, closely grouped settlements, which the Spaniards later called pueblos. Eighty-one miles southwest of Fort Davis, the town (incorporated in 1981) is on the border across the river from Ojiaga, Mexico. In the 1700s, the Spaniards built the Presidio del Norte on the southern bank of the river to protect area missions. Anglo settlers came to Presidio in 1848 after the Mexican War, opening a horse ranch on the US side of the Rio Grande and private forts, one of them called Fort Leaton, built by early settler Ben Leaton. In 1849, a Comanche raid almost destroyed Presidio, and in 1850, Indians drove off most of the cattle in town. A post office was established at Presidio in 1868, and the first public school was opened in 1887. Growth was slow into the twentieth century. When the railroad reached Presidio in 1930, the town had less than 100 inhabitants. Fort Leaton State Historic site is on a bluff in Presidio overlooking the Rio Grande.

El Cementario del Barrio de los Lipanes on the corner of Market Street and Barton Avenue lies in the heart of an old Lipan Apache settlement. The neighborhood later came to be known as Barrio de los Lipanes by the local community. In the 1790s, Spanish viceroy Bernardo Gálvez established the area as a peace settlement for the tribe as part of a policy to end the centuries-long war with the Apaches. The first Lipans to live here were members of the Tcha shka-ózhäyê (Little Breech Cloth) and Kó'l Kahn (Prairie Grass) Bands of the Lipan Apache Nation. The

Little Breech Cloth Band later relocated to South Texas, where they live today, and the Prairie Grass Band stayed in Presidio.

Long neglected, the cemetery was awarded status as a State Archaeological Landmark in 2014. Three years later, a Texas State Historical marker was placed in the cemetery. An archeological survey determined that the cemetery contains at least forty-five graves, with possibly twelve more. Two grave markers still standing are inscribed with the names **Felipe Aguilar** and **Manuel Aguilar**. Descendants of these men live nearby. The last burial took place in 1949. Most of the graves are indicated by scattered mounds of rocks, and there are four raised sarcophagi fashioned with rock and mortar.

TERLINGUA

Terlingua, sixty-three miles east of Presidio, is thirteen miles from the border of Mexico on the outskirts of Big Bend National Park. The name Terlingua is derived from the Spanish words *tres* and *lenguas*, meaning three tongues. Historians say that this refers to either the three languages spoken in the area—Spanish, English, and Native American—or the three forks of Terlingua Creek where three settlements were established. Terlingua was formerly an abandoned quicksilver mining camp. The discovery of cinnabar, from which mercury is extracted, brought in a few thousand miners. By 1900, there were four mining companies. According to Stuart T. Penick, a member of the US Geological Survey party, who wrote about the camp in 1902: "Terlingua was a sprawling camp of temporary sheds and shelters composed of various kinds of material, such as tin, canvas, old sacks, sticks, and adobe bricks. The only permanent buildings were the commissary and smelter. There were from 200–300 laborers of the lowest class of Mexicans there. They seemed to be temporary, for very few of them had families."

The Chisos Mining Company, owned by a Chicago industrialist, was organized in 1903 and began operation the same year. Chisos would become the largest producing mine in the area and for a time the largest mercury producer in the United States. The Chisos Mining Company also owned and operated the entire "new" town of Terlingua, including a general store, providing a company doctor, post office, hotel, telephone and water service, and a school. Growing to a population of more than 1,000, the town, except for the company school, was segregated—one side for Mexicans, the other for Anglos. Production continued for four decades. After the mine closed in the 1940s, most of the residents moved and Terlingua became a ghost town. It experienced a resurgence in the early 1970s due to its proximity to Big Bend National Park. Today the area supports a population of about 100 residents. Terlingua is also famous for its annual chili cook-off and in 1967 was deemed the "Chili Capital of the World."

One of Terlingua's biggest attractions is its cemetery located along the downhill slope of the town set against the rugged view of the Chisos Mountains and the Sierra del Carmens. One of the most photographed cemeteries in Texas, **Terlingua Cemetery** on FM 170 and Terlingua Ghost Road was established in 1902 and is listed on the National Register of Historic Sites. At one acre, this cemetery contains more than 300 marked graves. Fatal mining accidents often occurred due to inadequate ventilation and lack of modern mining equipment. Miners also suffered from a form of mercury poisoning

No large marble monuments or statuary adorn the gravesites in Terlingua; instead, stacked rock sarcophagi with grotto inserts, slate rock mounds, old wooden and filigree crosses, and folk art predominate in this historic burial ground dotted with creosote bushes.

in which inhaled fumes from the smelting process stimulated the secretion of saliva, causing the teeth to loosen and fall out. In addition to miners and their families, victims of the Spanish flu pandemic of 1918–1919 are buried here, along with the usual miscreants and regular Joes. **Felix Valenzuela** (1882–1938), whose grave is marked with a wooden cross encased in a block of cement, was a constable in Terlingua. He was shot and killed when he and the justice of the peace, also the manager of the Chisos Mining Company, stopped a car near the Mexican border that was suspected of transporting illegal liquor. One of the suspects grabbed the justice's pistol and shot Constable Valenzuela. The three Mexican suspects escaped across the river. A newspaper account reported that "Valenzuela had been employed at the mines for a number of years and bore a good reputation there." Survived by a large family, he was buried at the Terlingua Cemetery.

The cemetery is still in use by locals. Each year, during the Mexican celebration of the Day of the Dead on November 2, residents remember and honor the departed with traditional flower arrangements, candles, and paper streamers, adding splashes of color to this sunbaked desert cemetery, one of the most emblematic of the harsh West Texas experience.

VAN HORN

In the Chihuahuan Desert region of far West Texas, Van Horn (pop. 2,000), 120 miles southeast of El Paso on I-10 East, was established twelve miles north of springs at the foot of the Van Horn Mountains in the 1880s. The nearby "seep-water wells," named the Van Horn Wells, were already well known to resident Hispanics and nomadic Apaches in the area. These springs served the stagecoaches and mail coaches traveling the 1859 Butterfield Overland Stage, as well as military operations stationed at the spring. The town was named after Lieutenant James Judson Van Horn who commanded an army garrison at the Van Horn Wells from 1859 to 1861. After the outbreak of the Civil War, he was taken prisoner by Confederate forces. Later released in a prisoner exchange, he served honorably in the US Army until his death in 1898. When the Texas and Pacific Railway arrived in 1881, so did men whose preferred method of solving conflicts was the occasional gunfight, which occurred into the 1920s. In 1896, only seventy people populated the West Texas town.

Van Horn Cemetery at the corner of Bell Street and West 6th Street and next to the high school football field was established in 1888. **Baby Beach**, the child of **James Hannibal Beach** (1849–1921) and **Nancy Blundell Beach** (1858–1944), died on September 14, 1888, twenty days after birth. The infant's plot resembles a crib of decorative iron grillwork featuring a commemorative gate and plaque indicating that the Baby Beach burial was the first grave in the cemetery. Next to the baby's grave are those of her parents. The flat grave marker James shares with his wife is inscribed, "Father of Van Horn."

The story of the first adult burial in the Van Horn Cemetery is likely the most ironic of all those in this book, although some armchair historians dispute its veracity, for good reason. In 1884, **Augustus Sanders Goynes** (1840–1892), born in Mississippi, brought his family to Van Horn. Working as a rancher, he also purchased and sold ranchland in the Presidio area. In an effort to market the dry Van Horn climate, he reportedly suggested that the town adopt the motto, "This Town Is So Healthy We Had to Shoot a Man to Start a Cemetery," a refrain that gained enough popularity to hang in the lobby of the downtown Clark Hotel.

On June 30, 1892, Goynes rode his horse onto the property of his brother-in-law, Francis "Frank" McMurray, where a survey was taking place. Goynes accused McMurray of killing his and other ranchers' cattle and then the argument turned to the ownership of the land, which Goynes asserted was his by virtue of having sunk the well on it. The surveyor who witnessed the altercation said that Goynes called McMurray "a damned liar" when he replied he had paid for the well.

"Baby Beach" was the first to be buried in Van Horn Cemetery.

A few minutes later, the surveyor heard two shots and saw McMurray on his horse galloping off, followed by Goynes who had his pistol out and attempted to shoot but was unable to pull the trigger. In the meantime, McMurray turned around on his saddle and fired two or three times at Goynes, hitting him. Goynes fell off his saddle to the ground, clutching at his bleeding stomach. He died within a few minutes, his final words—"He has killed me."

Goynes became the first man to be buried in the Van Horn Cemetery. While he is credited with coining the town motto, it is more likely he inspired it.

Cementario Loma De La Cruz, Del Rio.

CHAPTER 8

PECOS TRAIL REGION

Tabletop mesas, rugged limestone canyons, ancient rivers snaking through valleys, wide-open prairies—the landscape of this region typifies the Wild West. Native Americans, leaving traces of their existence through rock art in the Lower Pecos canyons, hunted buffalo here. In the mid-1700s, the Comanches swept in displacing the early Indian tribes. Determined to defend their territory, they attacked the new settlers and cattle drovers going through the region. The beginning of the end of the Indian Wars occurred with the establishment of the frontier forts. The decade of the 1870s saw dwindling numbers of Native Americans being relocated to government reservations, just in time for the arrival of the railroad. This region of twenty-two West Texas counties is rich in history. Many of the modern highways follow the ancient trails of the prehistoric people, Spanish explorers, Plains Indians, ranchers, farmers, and oilmen.

BRACKETTVILLE

Twenty-two miles northeast of the Rio Grande and 125 miles west of San Antonio, Brackettville (pop. 2,000) was named after Oscar B. Brackett, who established the first general dry-goods store near the site of Fort Clark in 1852. A regular stop for the San Antonio-San Diego stage line, the settlement was six miles south of Las Moras

Mountain near the Las Moras Springs. Roving bands of Indians who had hunted and camped at Las Moras Springs harassed early settlers. After the Civil War, the settlement attracted cattle rustlers, buffalo hunters, gamblers, and businessmen. Known as Brackett or Brackett City when it applied for a post office in 1873, the postal service changed the community's name to Brackettville because another Texas community was named Brackett. By 1900, Brackettville had a population of around 1,000. John Wayne's 1960 film, *The Alamo*, was filmed on a set constructed six miles north of the town on the Shahan Angus Ranch. The replica of the old San Antonio mission and town was a tourist attraction for almost fifty years. The Alamo Village, as it was called, closed after the death of the ranch owners in 2010.

Seminole Indian Scouts Cemetery on FM 3348 off Fort Clark Rd, three miles south of Brackettville, was established in September 1872 on the Fort Clark Army Cavalry Post founded twenty years earlier. These scouts were part of the mixed-blood Seminole and African American population that had migrated to northeastern Mexico from 1849 to 1850 to escape slave hunters. In the early 1870s, in response to offers of scouting jobs in Texas, almost 200 Seminole Indian Scouts moved to Fort Duncan in Eagle Pass. Their successful operations along the Rio Grande attracted the attention of other officers, and in the summer of 1872, some of the scouts and their families were transferred north to Fort Clark. On April 14, 1881, the Scouts fought their last Indian battle following the final important raid on Texas soil near the Rio Grande. Fort Clark remained a horse-cavalry post for the US Army until 1946, when it was deactivated.

Approximately 100 or more Black Seminole Scouts, who played a major role in protecting the Texas Frontier from hostile Indians, are buried here with their descendants and families. In the early 1940s, the US War Department provided headstones that now mark their graves, through the efforts of members of the Seminole Negro Indian Scout Cemetery Association. Dusty and barren, with a few scattered trees and Spanish dagger cactus, this burial ground has more than 425 graves and many old tombstones.

Seminole Indian Scouts **Pompey Factor** (1849–1928), **Isaac Payne** (1854–1904), and **John Ward** were awarded the Congressional Medal of Honor for their bravery at Eagle's Nest Crossing near present-day Langtry, Texas. During the Red River War (1874–1875) between the Comanche and Kiowa and the United States, Private Pompey Factor, Private Isaac Payne, and Sergeant John Ward, along with their commander, Lieutenant John L. Bullis, were surrounded by Comanche warriors. Factor and Payne mounted their horses to make their escape. Sergeant Ward noticed that Lieutenant Bullis could not mount his frightened horse. While Ward helped the lieutenant, Factor and Payne held off the Comanche attack until all four could ride to safety. On May 28, 1875, the three troopers were given the Congressional Medal of Honor. They were three of only eighteen black soldiers during the Indian Wars who received such an honor. Factor and Ward are buried within their own plots, each surrounded by white metal fencing.

Isaac Payne is buried next to **Adam Paine** (1843–1877), another Congressional Medal Award recipient, in plots surrounded by white metal fencing. Paine was a big man, six feet tall, about 200 pounds.

Grave of Seminole Indian Scout Pompey Factor, Medal of Honor recipient.

He refused to wear a regulation uniform; he instead wore a leather headpiece with buffalo horns. At Canyon Blanco, near the Red River on September 26, 1874, Private Paine and four other scouts were sent out to search for hostile Indians. They were attacked by forty Kiowas and fled, fighting as they went. Private Paine stayed back to protect the others, allowing them to get away as he fired at their pursuers. His horse was shot out from under him. Using the downed animal as a shield, he killed one of the attackers and captured the dead man's horse to escape. For courage in the face of the enemy, he was awarded the Medal of Honor on October 13, 1875. After his discharge from the army in 1875, he killed another trooper and escaped to Mexico. The fugitive returned to the Seminole village near Brackettville and was shot and killed there at a New Year's celebration on January 1, 1877.

DEL RIO

Del Rio (pop. 36,000), thirty miles west of Brackettville, 154 miles west of San Antonio, and across the river from Ciudad Acuña, was established near San Felipe Springs and the creek of the same name. It has been described as Western in character, traditions, customs, and mores, a reflection of Hispanic Santa Fe rather than of the Old South culture of many Texas towns. Spanish missionaries arrived at this Rio Grande settlement on St. Phillip's Day in 1635 and called it San Felipe del Rio (St. Phillip of the River). Hostile Indians destroyed their mission, but the name survived until 1883. At that time, the Post Office Department suggested shortening the name to Del Rio to avoid confusion with another similarly named Texas town. Ranching and agriculture have always been integral to the economy of Del Rio. During the late nineteenth century, sheep and goat raisers found the scrub terrain to be an ideal place for their livestock, turning Del Rio into a focal point for the wool and mohair industry. The expansion of the railroad in the 1880s spurred the development of sheep and goat ranching and attracted German and Italian settlers; however, Mexican residents have always made up the majority, and today account for 80 percent of the population.

Cementario Loma De La Cruz (Hill of the Cross Cemetery) at the end of Noriega Street on the far south of Del Rio was established in 1884 on four acres donated by **Doña Paula Losoya Taylor Rivers** (1830–1902) who, along with her second husband **James H. Taylor** (1832–1876), helped found the town of Del Rio. On sparsely vegetated land with clusters of Spanish dagger and tumbleweeds, this cemetery, a burial ground as early as 1872, is named after a nearby hill used as a lookout for Indians. During one skirmish, three Indians and two Mexicans were killed and buried on the hillside. A cross was placed at the top of the hill, giving it its name.

Since early Del Rio settlers buried their dead on their own properties, neither Doña Paula nor her husband is buried at this cemetery. They are believed to be buried on the family homestead property with their two infant children and Paula's son from her first marriage, Felix Losoya, who died in a horseback riding accident in 1873. The site of the family cemetery is unknown.

The land upon which Cementario Loma De La Cruz rests was once under the sea and is prone to flooding. Fallen monuments, cracked and broken tombstones, uplifted vaults—some of them partially exposed—are scattered throughout the cemetery. Additional damage done to the historic cemetery is due to vandalism. Restoration projects over the years included enclosing the cemetery with a fence, adding a stone and metal entrance gate, and erecting a granite memorial marker dedicated to those buried there and "known only to God." A survey of the cemetery resulted in the mapping of some 450 actual gravesites, with indications of many more whose markers have been lost over time.

Former US Army Indian scouts **Victor Frausto** (1825–1905) and his son **Thomas Frausto** (1846–1902), both born in Mexico and recruits in the Seminole Negro Indian Scout Detachment stationed with the Fifth Cavalry at Fort Clark in Brackettville, are buried in Cementario Loma De La Cruz. Two other sons, Gregorio (1852–1948) and Quirino (died 1897), also enlisted. Gregorio is buried in San Felipe Cemetery in Del Rio. Quirino's burial site is unknown. They all enlisted in 1878. Victor, Thomas, and Quirino served one year and then returned to sheep herding in Del Rio. Gregorio served six years. There is a Frausto Street in Del Rio named after this family.

FORT STOCKTON

Fort Stockton (pop. 8,500) is 185 miles north of Del Rio and almost midway between El Paso and San Antonio on Interstate 10. Named after Lieutenant Edward Dorsey Stockton, an officer in the US First Infantry who died in San Antonio in 1857, the fort was established in 1859 at Comanche Springs, a major source of water in the arid countryside and stopover on many major western routes. Abandoned at the onset of the Civil War, the post was re-occupied in 1867 by the Ninth US Cavalry, a regiment of black troops. In 1868, San Antonian Peter Gallagher bought the land that included the military garrison and Comanche Springs, platted 160 acres for a town site named St. Gaul, and established two stores at Comanche Springs. By 1870, the town had a population of 420 civilians, predominantly Irish, German, and Mexican Catholics from San Antonio. When Pecos County was organized in 1875, St. Gaul became the county seat. The name, however, was never popular with the citizens, and on August 13, 1881, it was changed officially to Fort Stockton. In 1882, after the Apaches had been defeated, the army began withdrawing the troops, the last contingent leaving in the summer of 1886. By then, farmers had moved in to grow crops irrigated by the natural springs and the Pecos River. Sheep and cattle ranches sprang up, bringing merchants and other employment opportunities. A convenient stop on the road to El Paso, Fort Stockton grew into a thriving community catering to travelers.

The **Old Fort Stockton Cemetery** on the corner of Water Street and 8th Street is a small burial ground of about forty marked graves surrounded by a low limestone wall. Originally for fort soldiers, it became a civilian burial ground when remains of the fifty-six soldiers were moved to Fort Sam Houston in San Antonio in 1888. Testifying to the hardships of frontier life, few markers record anyone over the age of forty. Local residents continued to use this cemetery until 1912.

Two notorious "lawmen," **Andrew Jackson Royal** (1855–1894) and **Barney Kemp Riggs** (1856–1902), are buried here. Royal was a Pecos County sheriff who served only one term, from 1892 to 1894. During those two years, he became the most hated lawman in Fort Stockton history. Quarrelsome and intimidating, he killed an employee after the two got into a dispute. The longer he was in office, the more aggressive he became. He threatened several leading citizens for having supported his opponent in the 1892 election, and his intimidation got so bad that five Texas Rangers were sent to the town at the request of fearful citizens. Royal was arrested, along with his deputies, for schemes involving his re-election campaign. He ended up losing the election and his life at age thirty-nine, when a mysterious

The tombstone of notorious Fort Stockton "lawman" Andrew Jackson Royal has fallen off its pedestal. Behind his plot and to the right is the pillar monument marking the grave of Deputy Barney Riggs, also a dubious character.

assailant entered the soon-to-be ex-sheriff's office and shot him dead. Several buckshot holes dotted his shoulder and neck. No one was ever arrested for the crime, which continues to be one of the biggest historical mysteries of the city.

Buried in the old fort cemetery in a fenced family plot, his pillar tombstone bears the inscription "assassinated," along with the following: "Sleep Husband dear/and take thy rest./God called thee home he/ thought it best./It was hard indeed to/part with thee./But Christ's strong arm/supporteth me/Gone but not forgotten." In the same plot marked by a sleeping child on a tombstone is **Andrew Roy "Little Andy" Royal** (1893–1898), the ex-sheriff's five-year-old son. The inscription on his headstone reads: "A little flower of love/That blossomed just to die/ Transplanted now above/To bloom with God on high."

Barney Riggs, whose worn obelisk tombstone stands in the middle of the cemetery, was born in Arkansas and moved to Texas with his family as a child. His penchant for violence apparently started at home, as several of his brothers and descendants were also prone to aggression. By the time he reached Fort Stockton in the early 1890s, he'd killed several men; had been involved in myriad criminal activities, including horse stealing; and had been sentenced to life in prison for murder, serving at the Arizona Territorial Prison in Yuma. He was pardoned after a year, in 1887, for saving the warden's life in a riot. By the time he arrived in Fort Stockton, he fit right in as a deputy under the notorious Sheriff Royal. He was arrested along with the sheriff for tampering in the elections. After Royal was killed, Riggs continued his bad behavior, often fueled by liquor. Finally, in 1902, his son-in-law shot him in the chest, killing him instantly, the outcome of a family quarrel.

Herman Koehler (1849–1894), unlike Royal and Riggs, represents the good citizens of Fort Stockton. He is buried in a fenced plot near Royal's with a nicely etched, sand-colored obelisk tombstone next to a flowering verbena plant. In 1884, German-born Koehler opened a saloon, general store, and bank in a stone building in Fort Stockton. Koehler, who died at age forty-five, was known for his benevolence. In 1901, several city leaders financed the first hotel in the town and named it the Koehler Hotel in his memory. Today, the building houses the Annie Riggs Memorial Museum. Annie, Barney's ex-wife, purchased the hotel—a sprawling, single-story adobe brick building with wraparound verandas and gingerbread trim—with money she received from her ex-husband's estate. She renamed it the Riggs Hotel, running it as a boarding house until her death in 1931. In 1956, her heirs deeded the hotel to the Fort Stockton Historical Society for use as a museum.

JUNCTION

Junction (pop. 2,400) was founded in 1876 and named for its location at the confluence of the North and South Llano Rivers. About 200 miles east of Fort Stockton and 115 miles northwest of San Antonio along Interstate 10, the town grew slowly. Two courthouse fires in the 1880s destroyed all county records. By 1900, with a population of 536, the town's economy was based on livestock, wool, mohair, pecan, and grain production. With hundreds of natural springs, Junction calls itself the "Land of Living Waters" and is a popular hunting destination.

Junction Cemetery at 999 South Llano Street contains the graves of the town's pioneers, including at least two veterans of the Mexican War, twenty-eight veterans of the Confederate States Army, one veteran of the Texas Frontier Troops, several Texas Rangers, veterans of both World Wars, and victims of Indian depredations. On the left of the entry into the cemetery is the historic section founded

A tablet tombstone and a slab marker etched with the words "Indian Captive, Confederate Widow, Frontier Mother, Died Age 36" mark the grave of Alice Taylor Rayner at Junction Cemetery.

in 1880, which includes reburials from an older downtown cemetery. Several rock sarcophagi and obelisk, tablet, and pillar tombstones dot this pastoral cemetery featuring large shade trees and a backdrop of rolling hills.

As a young child, **Alice Taylor Rayner** (1855–1892) witnessed the killing of family members by Kiowas. She and other kin were taken into captivity by the same band of Indians. Those captured were held several months before being ransomed to freedom (see Fort Griffin Cemetery, Elizabeth Ann Carter Clifton). At age twenty-nine, Alice was widowed when her husband was killed by a neighbor.

Her obituary in the January 25, 1892, *Waco Evening News* reads:

One of the saddest burials witnessed here for some time took place last week. It was the burial of Mrs. Rayner, who died of pneumonia. Notwithstanding she had good attention by physicians and friends she had to succumb, leaving five children who have been fatherless for five or six years, two boys and three girls. The scene at the cemetery was almost heartrending to hear the cries, pleadings and prayers of the three little orphan girls. The eldest, aged twelve, who had been by her mother's bedside both day and night, soon fainted, and for some time seemed to be unconscious of her grief. The next older one, Bertie, about ten, pleaded with earnestness in about the following strain: 'O mamma, won't you please come back just a little while? O Jesus, please let mamma come back a little while so that I can kiss her sweet lips and tell her how much I love her. O mamma, won't you never, never come back? O please do!

The Kountz family plot contains the graves of **Harriet S. Kountz** (1830–1890), her husband **Ezekiel Kountz, M.D.** (1828–1881) and a memorial marker for their son **Isaac N. Kountz** (1860–1876), one of their seven children. Harriet and Ezekiel were married in Virginia in 1848. After the Civil War, the family settled in Junction. Dr. Kountz was elected the first county and district clerk of Kimble County, organized in Junction on January 3, 1876. Harriet became the first postmaster, working from their home, and later at a general store in downtown Junction, which also served as a drugstore and doctor's office.

While they lived in Junction, Indian attacks were common. Sixteen-year-old Isaac and his twelve-year-old brother, Sebastian, were herding a small flock of sheep on a hillside near their home on Christmas Eve 1876 when a band of Comanches rode up and shot Isaac. Sebastian escaped. Isaac's ledger marker is inscribed "Murdered by Savage Indians, December 24, 1876, Aged 16 years."

A few years later, Ezekiel learned that Fort Clark in Brackettville was looking for more doctors. He confided to Harriet his desire to move there and she agreed with the stipulation that it would be their last move. They sold their store and moved to Brackettville in 1880. They had been there only a year when Ezekiel died in December 1881. He was buried in Brackettville and later reinterred at the Junction Cemetery. Harriet returned to Junction, where she died in 1890.

Harriet's marble obelisk monument with a carved finger pointing to heaven stands between the flat markers of her husband and son. Ezekiel has two granite ledger markers in Junction Cemetery: one under the name of Captain E. K. Counts for his service in the Confederate States Army and one under Ezekiel K. Kountz, M.D. Sometime after the Civil War, Ezekiel changed the spelling of his last name to Kountz, the original German spelling.

A stalwart angel statue in Hedley's Rowe Cemetery marks the grave of a young woman who took her own life.

CHAPTER 9

PLAINS TRAIL REGION

This region of the Texas Panhandle includes the High Plains, the North Central Plains, and Llano Estacado. From vast plains to spectacular canyons, this trail region is where the cowboy culture and ranching heritage continues to thrive. It is a harsh land with extremes in temperature—chilling cold in the winter, Hades hot in the summer. Large herds of bison once ranged here and there are still remnant herds in this region cared for by private ranchers and Texas Parks & Wildlife. By the 1870s, tensions between the Indians and settlers reached a climax. Buffalo hunters were slaughtering huge numbers of buffalo for their hides, leaving the meat to rot, and the federal government had defaulted on obligations to the tribes. The Southern Plains Indians rebelled, starting the final war that lasted from 1874 to 1875. The Red River War ended the nomadic life of the Plains Indians and ushered in the era of the cattlemen.

BOY'S RANCH "OLD TASCOSA"

Once a raucous pioneer town forty-two miles northwest of Amarillo, Tascosa was known for gunfights and barroom brawls where local ranch hands and cowboys gathered after a hard day's work. Originally named after the Atascosa (boggy place) Creek, the settlement began with Hispanic sheepherders who grazed their flocks in the area and built huts along the creek. When cattle ranching became prominent, many of the herders returned with their sheep to New Mexico. After 1875, with large ranches dominating the area, Tascosa became a shipping hub for them and the seat for Oldham County in 1880. A blacksmith shop, general store, saloons, and dance halls opened up. The town became known as the Cowboy Capital of the Plains, attracting notorious outlaws such as Billy the Kid and famed lawmen Pat Garrett and Bat Masterson. Local cowboys staged an unsuccessful strike for higher wages at the town. In 1886, when the railroad bypassed Tascosa, businesses moved, and by 1915 only fifteen people remained.

In 1938, Panhandle rancher Julian Bivins donated 120 acres that included Old Tascosa to Cal Farley for the establishment of a residential community for at-risk children, ages five to eighteen. Tascosa became known as Boy's Ranch and today what remains of the town is the old stone courthouse that houses a museum and its famous cemetery.

Boot Hill Cemetery on US 385, just north of the Canadian River, sits on a hill at Boy's Ranch. The cemetery, with just thirty-two grave sites, was originally part of Tascosa. The name was borrowed from a cemetery in Dodge City, Kansas, the final resting place of buffalo hunters, cowboys and transients, most of whom died suddenly with their boots on, hence the name Boot Hill. Another famous Boot Hill Cemetery is in Tombstone, Arizona. Most of those buried in Tascosa were killed in gunfights. Small white crosses inscribed with names indicate burial sites.

The first burial was that of **Bob Russell** (1856–1880), a twenty-four-year-old saloonkeeper killed in March 1880 by Jules Howard in a showdown over Russell's flirtatious wife. Less than a year later, **Fred**

Leigh (1847–1881), a thirty-four-year-old Englishman, became the second burial. Leigh came up the trail in the early summer of 1881 in charge of bringing GMS cattle to the LS Ranch. He was described as a "young man of soft speech and mild temper, until he started drinking." After the cattle had been delivered, Leigh went to a Tascosa saloon where he had a run-in with the sheriff. The young man drank and brooded all night at camp and returned to town the next morning in a foul mood. Riding into Tascosa, he pulled out his gun and shot into a flock of ducks being fed in the yard of a townswoman, who promptly fainted. The sheriff ran to where the altercation was taking place and as he approached, Leigh went for his gun again, so the sheriff shot him right off his horse.

Three of the gunfight victims buried here—**Ed King**, age twenty-four; **Frank Valley**, age twenty-three; and **Fred Chilton**, age

The graves of the victims of the Great Tascosa Gunfight of 1866 and two of the earliest burials are in the front row at Boot Hill Cemetery.

twenty-one—were killed by Lamar "Lem" Albert Woodruff in what has become known as the Great Tascosa Gunfight of 1886. Lem was a bartender at the Jenkins Saloon. His saloon worker girlfriend, Sally Emory, dumped him for Ed King, a former Texas Ranger working at the LS Ranch, who was said to have been a loudmouth and troublemaker. He taunted his girl's former boyfriend, calling him "Pretty Lem," bullying the bartender with various insults, itching for a fight. In the early morning hours of Sunday, March 21, 1886, he got what he wanted. After a night of drinking and dancing, King met Sally just outside the Jenkins Saloon. Someone called his name and as he turned around, he was shot in the face. Lem Woodruff emerged, shooting him two more times. This started a chain reaction of blazing guns as King's friends and others rushed out of the various buildings. By the end of the gunfight, four men had been killed. Lem was not among them. He and a few others were tried for murder; the first trial ended in a hung jury and the second resulted in their acquittal.

The **Casimiro Romero Cemetery**, also called Old Tascosa Cemetery, at 1 Willis Loop just outside of Boy's Ranch and about one mile east of Boot Hill Cemetery, is a small burial ground named after an early pioneer. In 1876, Casimero Romero brought his family from New Mexico to settle on the Canadian River in what would become the town Tascosa. He brought 3,000 sheep with their herders and twelve freight wagons loaded with lumber, supplies, and household goods. Tascosa village grew around Romero's home. With the rise of cattle ranches and the railroad bypassing Tascosa, Romero's sheep and freighting business suffered. In 1896, he sold his ranch and moved back to New Mexico.

Elizabeth "Frenchy" McCormick (1852–1941) was born Elizabeth McGraw to Irish-Catholic parents in Louisiana. She ran away from a convent at age fourteen and went to St. Louis where she performed on the burlesque stage and in bars. She moved on to Dodge City dance halls and saloons. A cowboy gave her the nickname "Frenchy" because she could speak French. Around 1880, she met **Mickey McCormick** (1848–1912), an Irish gambler and livery stable operator from Tascosa, at the gaming tables in Mobeetie, Texas. He claimed he always won when Frenchy was beside him and she accompanied him back to Tascosa, becoming the "reining belle." She dealt monte in the gambling rooms that Mickey operated behind a saloon and entertained the cowboys and lawmen who passed through. She and Mickey were married in 1881.

Elizabeth "Frenchy" McCormick, the "Reining Belle of Tascosa," and husband Mickey McCormick, a gambler and livery stable operator, c. 1880s.
CAL FARLEY'S BOY'S RANCH.

After the railroad bypassed Tascosa in 1887, the town declined and the McCormicks lost their business. They continued to live in a small adobe house on Atascosa Creek. After Mickey died in 1912, Frenchy refused to move away from her husband's burial site, half a mile east of the cabin. She lived alone in the ghost town for twenty-seven years, without electricity or running water. With her health failing and her house crumbling into ruin, she allowed herself to be removed to Channing in 1939, on the condition that she be brought back to join her husband after death. She died of pneumonia on January 12, 1941, and was buried beside Mickey in the Casimiro Romero Cemetery. In 1965, "Ex-Boys Ranchers and Interested Friends" erected a headstone over her grave.

Charlotte "Lottie" Durkin Barker (1859–1887) was the granddaughter of Elizabeth Ann Carter Clifton (see Fort Griffin Cemetery). On October 13, 1864, at age five, she was captured along with her grandmother and two-year-old sister Milly during the Elm Creek Massacre. Her mother and baby brother were murdered during the raid. Lottie was released after nine months with tattoos on her arms and a dime-sized moon tattoo on her forehead. Her grandmother was released a while later. She was told that her little sister had died in captivity, which she never believed.

Lottie married Henry Barker (1852–1890) in 1874 when she was fifteen. He ran a meat market and served as a deputy sheriff at Fort Griffin. In 1883, they moved to Mobeetie and a couple of years later settled in Tascosa. The couple had five children. Her last child, Charles, was born in Tascosa on July 30, 1887. Lottie died eleven days after his birth, on August 10, 1887.

Indian captive Charlotte "Lottie" Durkin Barker is buried in an unmarked grave at Casimiro Romero Cemetery. Captured at age five in late 1864, she was released after nine months with tattoos on her arms and a dime-sized moon tattoo on her forehead.
COURTESY OF TANYA BUSTILLOS NAGARAJA.

Lottie, as it turned out, was right about Milly. She'd been adopted by a Kiowa warrior and his wife who had no children. They told the tribe to tell any inquirers that she had died. They raised her from the age of two as their daughter. Because she was so young, she had no memory of her earlier life. She married a Kiowa named Joe Goombi and they had several children. She did not know about her status as a white captive, a heavily guarded secret within the tribe, until 1930, four years before her death at age seventy-one.

GOODNIGHT

On the edge of the Llano Estacado—a 32,000-square-mile area referred to as the Staked Plains but called by settlers "the Great American Desert"— forty miles east of Amarillo, Goodnight is an unincorporated community with a population of about twenty-five. The settlement was named after **Charles Goodnight** (1836–1929), a pioneer Texas cattleman who settled on a nearby ranch in 1887. Soon afterward, it became a railway stop with a post office. The first building at the townsite was Goodnight's ranch house. A rural school district was organized in 1891, and Goodnight and his wife helped found a college, which operated from 1898 to 1917. Charles Goodnight remained the dominant force in the community until his death in December 1929. The emergence of the nearby town of Claude as the county's business center and improved transportation and communication facilities hastened Goodnight's demise. As of 1984 only one church and the community cemetery remained, along with the Goodnight Ranch facilities, now the Charles Goodnight Historical Center.

The **Goodnight Cemetery**, north of Highway 287, east to Ranch Road 294, on Country Road 26, is where Charles and his wife, **Mary Ann "Molly" Dyer Goodnight** (1839–1926), are buried in a large graveled family plot surrounded by a chain link fence. The cemetery is still active and has more than 280 graves.

Charles Goodnight (1836–1929), born in Illinois, was a pioneer in cattle ranching in New Mexico, Colorado, and Texas. He founded the Goodnight-Loving trail with Oliver Loving (see Weatherford—Old City Greenwood Cemetery). He came to Texas in late 1845 with his mother and stepfather. By 1857, after fighting against the Comanches, he joined the Texas Rangers. He was instrumental in the recapturing of the famed Indian captive Cynthia Ann Parker (see Groesbeck, Fort Parker Memorial Cemetery) in 1860. During the Civil War, he was in a Confederate frontier regiment guarding against Indian raids. In the spring of 1866, he and Oliver Loving drove their first herd of cattle northward along what would become known as the Goodnight-Loving Trail, joining up with John Chisum. It was during this trip that Goodnight invented the chuckwagon. As Loving was dying from injuries he incurred in a fight with Indians in 1867, Goodnight sat by his bedside for two weeks. He reportedly kept a photograph of Loving in his pocket long after his death, and later put a photograph of Loving on his desk. As requested by his dying friend, Goodnight carried his body from New Mexico to Weatherford for burial. The friendship between Goodnight and Loving was the inspiration for the Pulitzer Prize–winning novel *Lonesome Dove*, by Larry McMurtry.

In 1870, Goodnight married Weatherford schoolteacher Molly Dyer, his longtime sweetheart. Molly was born in Tennessee and her family settled in Texas in 1854 when she was fourteen. In 1860, the family of eleven, including Molly and her eight brothers, were living at Fort Belknap. Her mother died in 1864, one of her brothers was killed by Indians in 1865, and in 1866, her father died. With both parents deceased, she took over the care of her three younger brothers.

Goodnight took his new wife and brothers to a ranch he established in Pueblo, Colorado. With his brother-in-law Leigh, he established the Goodnight & Dyer Cattle Company. The family returned to Texas in May 1877 and settled in a dugout within the bounds of the present Palo Duro State Scenic Park. Goodnight established the JA Ranch with British rancher John Adair. By 1885, the ranch had grown to 1,325,000 acres. The couple had no children; they devoted their time to preserving a herd of native plains bison, establishing a school for the children of ranchers, and building a Methodist Church in the town of Goodnight.

Molly was a much beloved and revered figure in the Panhandle, often referred to as the "Queen of the Canyon." She died at age eighty-six after a week's illness following an attack of influenza. Her

A granite monument in the Goodnight plot extols Charles and Mary Ann Goodnight for their contributions to the Panhandle's cattle industry, higher education, and civic enterprises.

headstone reads: "One who spent her whole life in the service of others. For 56 years, the wife of Charles Goodnight."

A year after Molly's death, Goodnight, at age ninety-one, married a distant cousin, twenty-six-year-old Corinne Oletta Goodnight, a nurse and telephone operator from Butte, Montana, who nursed him during his illness. He died two years later and was buried next to Molly.

HEDLEY

Hedley was founded after the demise of a town called Rowe. Isaac Smith, a local farmer, donated land for the early town. Established in 1890, Rowe was thirty-three miles southeast of Goodnight, and named after Alfred Rowe, the British owner of the nearby RO Ranch. Initially, the town grew as it added a church, school, general store, bank, newspaper, railway depot, and cattle-loading pens. Problems arose over Smith's domination over the community. Since he donated the land, he believed he could tell residents what types of houses should be constructed. That didn't set well with his neighbors. Nevertheless, it was not until two years after his 1905 death that the townspeople began to leave, likely because of the high quantity of gypsum in the water and over-sandy soil. Starting in 1907, they moved to a new settlement half a mile to the southeast. They named the town Hedley and moved the post office over, as well as the shipping pens and depot. Rowe passed into oblivion. A school was built in Hedley in 1910 and the town became a cotton production center. Today, Hedley is a small community of about 300 residents.

Rowe Cemetery, a Texas Historic Cemetery, a mile northwest of Hedley on FM 1932, is significant for its associations with British rancher **Alfred Rowe** (1853–1912) and the now-extinct community of Rowe. The twelve-acre burial ground with more than 2,000 marked graves is a reflection of early area farming and ranching efforts and the harshness of pioneer life for permanent settlers in the Panhandle. With help from cattleman Charles Goodnight, Rowe established the RO ranch on Skillet Creek in 1880, and within ten years, he had amassed 100,000 acres of land and more than 10,000 head of cattle. His encouragement and support aided the development of Rowe as a commercial center on the Fort Worth and Denver City Railway line.

Kentucky native **Isaac Smith** (1822–1905) set aside two acres of his land for use as a community cemetery in 1898. The first burials were those of four infants from the Beedy family. Originally buried in the family garden, the four boys died in 1891 (Austin), 1892 (Daniel), 1893 (Edgar), and 1898 (Charley). Their graves were moved to the Rowe Cemetery upon its establishment and they share a granite tombstone with their names and the following engraved: "The fairest bud that flowers/nature knows oft ne'er/unfolds but withers e'er it blows."

After the community of Rowe became the town of Hedley, this cemetery continued to serve as the area's primary burial ground. Several Smith family members are buried here, including Isaac, his wife **Mary Dishman Smith** (1824–1910), his brother **Captain Nathaniel Smith** (1838–1911), and Nathaniel's wife **Isabella Langford Smith** (1840–1928). A bronze emblem with the inscription "Daughter of the Confederacy" is affixed to Isabella's flat granite marker.

The grave markers of **Lavenia "Ludie" Adamson** (1893–1911) and her brother **Wesley M. Adamson** (1899–1918), buried next to each other, bear mentioning. They were two of nine children born to local rancher **Silas Adamson** (1851–1927) and his wife **Josephine Howeth** (1859–1937), also buried in the cemetery. Ludie's grave is marked by an impressive marble statue of an angel standing in front of a cross. The angel is holding a Bible in one hand and her other fisted hand is raised to the sky. The inscription on the girl's monument is: "O' our precious Ludie left us so lonely here,/To Weep over our great loss for she was so dear."

Ludie, a month shy of her eighteenth birthday, was working at a telephone company in Altus, Oklahoma, when she "took her own life by taking a large dose of carbolic acid," according to a newspaper clipping.

The tombstone for Wesley, age nineteen, is a substantial tablet stone with his photo inserted. Wesley, a private in Company H, 142nd Infantry, 36th Division, died in France during World War I after only three months on the front. His inscription reads: "Nobly he fell while fighting for liberty."

Significantly, there are no Rowe family members buried in the Rowe Cemetery. Alfred Rowe moved his family to England when his children began their schooling. He traveled back and forth to the Panhandle twice yearly. After one visit, he secured passage on the *Titanic* for his return voyage. One of the few whose body was recovered after the ship sank, his remains were sent back to England for final burial.

MOBEETIE

Mobeetie (pop. 100), fifty-eight miles north of Hedley and twenty-seven miles west of the Oklahoma border, is one of the Panhandle's earliest settled towns, founded in 1874 as a buffalo hunters' camp.

Called Hidetown because its residents used buffalo hides to construct their dwellings, the settlement became a trading post when Fort Elliott, one of Texas's last frontier forts, was established nearby the next year. In 1878, the residents moved closer to the fort and called the new settlement Sweetwater City, named after a nearby creek. When the post office rejected their request for this name because of a duplication, they changed it to the Indian word for sweet water, *mobeetie*. Although a Comanche later told them that the word actually meant "buffalo dung," the commissioner's court county judge Immanuel Dubbs who took notes the day of the meeting when the name was discussed related that Commissioner Williams spoke the Cheyenne language and had said *mobeetie* was the Cheyenne word for sweet water.

The town became a commercial center for the Panhandle and was connected by a mail route with Tascosa, 123 miles to the west. According to Charles Goodnight, "Mobeetie was patronized by outlaws, thieves, cut-throats, and buffalo hunters, with a large percent of prostitutes. Taking it all, I think it was the hardest place I ever saw on the frontier except Cheyenne, Wyoming." Fort Elliott was abandoned in 1890 and when the railroad bypassed the town, its population declined. In 1893, the saloons closed after a revival meeting resulted in 300 conversions. On May 1, 1898, a tornado tore through the town taking seven lives and destroyed many of the buildings, which were not rebuilt. People began to move out. Today, Mobeetie is a small community in the heart of the ranching and agriculture areas of the Texas Panhandle.

Mobeetie Cemetery on County Road H just west of Dubbs Street was established in 1876. Some of the grave markers have been destroyed by tornadoes and natural decay. Burials include outlaws, accused horse thieves, those killed by an 1898 cyclone, ladies of the evening, and the infant granddaughter of General Sam Houston. In addition, it is the final resting place of the famed Texas Ranger, Captain G. W. Arrington.

The first person buried here was a saloon girl, **Molly Brennan,** the victim of a gunfight on January 24, 1876. Her granite grave marker, erected years after her death, describes her as a "blue-eyed, black-haired beauty," who was a "Lady Gay Saloon Girl," and describes the circumstances of her death. She jumped in front of Bat Masterson when Corporal Melvin King of Fort Elliott shot at Bat over a card game argument. Masterson killed King, but not before King got off the shot that killed Molly.

George "Cap" W. Arrington (1844–1923), called the "Iron-Handed Man of the Panhandle," shares a substantial granite monument with his wife **Sarah "Sallie" Burnett** (1862–1945), whom he married in 1882, and an infant son **Gilbert** (1884–1885). The monument is inscribed with his many achievements. He was a scout during the Civil War, captain of Company C of the Texas Rangers, Sheriff of Wheeler County and attached counties for eight years, and "a fearless officer to whom the frontier of Texas owes a debt of gratitude."

Arrington was born John Cromwell Orrick Jr. in Alabama. After a quarrel that led to a killing, he left his boyhood home and changed his name, fleeing to Texas in 1870. Always cautious because of enemies he had made as a peace officer, he was seldom seen in public without a gun. As he grew older, he suffered from arthritis and made frequent train trips to Mineral Wells for the hot baths. On one of these trips in 1923, he had a heart attack. He was taken to his home in Canadian, Texas, thirty-five miles north of Mobeetie, where he died on March 31.

Joseph "Joe" Allen (1866–1909) and **Jesse West** (1863–1909), along with Jim Miller and D. "Berry" Burrell, were lynched the morning of April 19, 1909 in Ada, Oklahoma, when a vigilante mob of about 100 men stormed the jail there. The four were hanged in an abandoned barn behind the jail. According to a newspaper report, they were all prominent cattlemen and had been implicated in the murder of US Marshal Allen A. "Gus" Bobbitt who had been shot in an ambush. He knew his killer, Jim Miller, and stayed alive long enough to tell the law. Miller, who had killed several men, was described as "a general all round bad man." Burrell, Miller's nephew, turned state's evidence at the examining trial, telling authorities that West and Allen had hired Miller to murder Bobbitt, their longtime enemy. Nevertheless, the grand jury refused to return an indictment, resulting in the mob lynching. By way of explanation for his father's crime, Jesse West's son told a reporter that Jesse had lived a tragic life. His older brother Van was murdered in 1893, his first wife perished in a house fire the next year, and in 1901 his thirteen-year-old son Martin was killed, which some believed instigated the murder of Gus Bobbitt.

Jesse, Joe, and Gus were prosperous ranchers who had once been in business together. All had been Masons, and Jesse and Joe were Woodmen of the World at the time of their deaths. Jesse and Joe operated the Corner Saloon selling whiskey in Pottawatomie County across the Canadian River from Ada. The saloon was notorious as a rowdy and dangerous spot in the Oklahoma Territory, where gunplay, violence, and vile behavior was the norm.

According to Gus, Jesse and Joe began conning area Indians by getting them drunk and buying their land for nearly nothing. When he tried to get them to stop these unethical practices, Jesse and Joe hired gunman Jim Miller to kill him. Other sources indicate that relations among the trio began to falter on the day of Martin's funeral. Jesse accused Gus in the theft of some of his cattle. Gus became incensed and "championed" the sixteen-year-old Seminole Indian boy who had killed Martin. A fight ensued and the resulting feud lasted for years during which Jesse was continually persecuted by Gus Bobbitt and his "gang."

To get away from the turmoil, Jesse and Joe Allen moved to the Texas Panhandle, settling near Canadian, Texas, sometime before 1906. They made frequent trips back to Oklahoma for business and during one of these trips they were arrested as accomplices in Gus Bobbitt's murder. The citizens of Ada believed the four jailed men were culpable in their friends' death and, fearful they would be released, took the matter into their own hands. No one was implicated or prosecuted for the lynchings. According to the county attorney, "No one in town appeared to know the participants and he didn't know them himself."

Joseph Allen and Jesse West are buried next to each other in Mobeetie Cemetery. Woodmen of the World tree stone monuments mark their graves.

WOODMEN OF THE WORLD

Tree stone monuments, often with axes crisscrossed on front and a medallion etched with the words "Woodmen of the World" populate many Texas cemeteries. Other symbols found on the tree stones include mauls, wedges, and tools used in woodworking. Interestingly, an occupation in the wood industry has never been required to be a member of Woodmen of the World, which was founded by Joseph Cullun Root in 1890 as a benevolent organization to benefit "Jews, Gentiles, Catholics, Protestants,

Agnostics and Atheists." The association of such diverse individuals was a sticking point with an earlier group he'd founded—Modern Woodmen of the World—and he was kicked out of that organization. When he started the new association, he removed Modern but kept the name "woodmen" because he was inspired by a sermon about "woodmen clearing the forest to provide for their families." Root saw Woodmen of the World as an organization that would "clear away problems of financial security for its members." Nevertheless, the Woodmen of the World organization is probably best known for its gravestones. From 1890 to 1900, its life insurance policies had a proviso that provided for the grave markers, free of charge for members. From 1900 to the mid-1920s, members purchased a $100 rider to cover the cost of the monument. After the mid-1920s, the grave markers were discontinued due to the increased cost of the stones.

One of four cherubs marking a family plot in Laredo's Calvary Catholic Cemetery.

CHAPTER 10

TROPICAL TRAIL REGION

The southern tip of Texas borders Mexico and the Gulf of Mexico. Spanish navigator Alonso Alvarez de Piñeda mapped the coastline in 1519 and throughout the subsequent years this region of twenty counties served as a buffer zone between Spanish provinces in Mexico in the south and French Louisiana in the east. Two distinct landscapes and climates comprise this region. Nearest the Rio Grande and the Gulf of Mexico, the Rio Grande Valley was formed from a river delta making it a rich agricultural area. Hot and humid in the summer, the weather turns balmy in the winter. Further inland is the Wild Horse Desert, hot and dry. In the early 1800s, large herds of mustangs ran wild in this desert region. Some had drifted up from Mexico; other were left behind from seventeenth-century Spanish expeditions. The herds were so vast, early explorers hired guards to watch their horses and mules to keep them from running away with the wild mustangs. Conflict for ownership over the region continued until the US-Mexico War of 1846–1848 established the Rio Grande as the international boundary. Many nineteenth-century entrepreneurs and ranchers in this region were Anglo; they married into prosperous Mexican families resulting in a distinctive bicultural heritage. Riverboats, agricultural pursuits, and ranching empires make up the story of the Tropical Trail Region.

Brownsville

At the southern tip of Texas and across the river from the Mexican town of Matamoros, Brownsville (pop. 184,000) has a strong bicultural heritage. In the eighteenth century under Spanish ownership, the area that would become Brownsville was used for ranching. When Texas declared independence from Mexico in 1836, only a few people lived in the region. A Mexican War military post initially called Fort Texas was established in the settlement near the river in 1846. The name was changed to Fort Brown after US Army major Jacob Brown was killed by cannon fire during a Mexican attack. After the war, in 1848, entrepreneur Charles Stillman started a riverboat company and founded Brownsville on land purchased from the heirs of Spanish grant owner José Narciso Cavazos, who'd been awarded fifty-nine leagues (261,276 acres) by the Spanish government in 1781. Stillman purchased the land from the children of Cavazos's first wife; however, legal ownership of the land belonged to the eldest son of Cavazos's second wife. As legal battles over ownership of the land ensued, Stillman established the town, incorporated in 1853. Brownsville was a prominent player in the Civil War, earning the title "back door to the Confederacy" because trade goods, especially cotton, could be taken to Mexico and shipped out, avoiding the Union blockade of Confederate ports. The Brownsville port continues to be an important economic hub for Texas, and Brownsville's Historic Townsite District, which includes the beautiful Old City Cemetery, brings thousands of visitors annually to this colorful South Texas town.

Brownsville's **Old City Cemetery** is recognized by the THC as an outstanding historical landmark and is listed in the National

WHAT LIES BENEATH: TEXAS

Register of Historic Places. Located at East Madison Street and East 5th Street, the cemetery was established in 1853 and deeded to the City of Brownsville in 1868. A brick walkway invites visitors into the fenced cemetery lush with palm trees. Throughout the cemetery in front of many gravesites are markers providing information on the interred individuals. Some of the most beautiful monuments and statuary in this cemetery are located near the back. Buried here are some of the earliest settlers to arrive in this part of the Rio Grande Valley. The number of above-ground crypts, ornate monuments, impressive statuary, and ironwork fences reflects the Spanish-French influence in the area. English, French, Spanish, and German tombstone inscriptions are indicative of the city's ethnic mixture. City leaders, victims of wars, gunfights, yellow fever, and cholera are buried here, and their graves are evidence of early conditions in the border town.

BROWNSVILLE'S OLD CITY CEMETERY CENTER

Across the street from the historic Brownsville burial ground is the Old City Cemetery Center, the first municipal cemetery center in Texas, established in 2007. Once a baggage room for the Old Southern Pacific Railroad Depot built in 1928, the center houses a permanent exhibit focused on the history of the cemetery and is open by appointment only and for various programs and tours throughout the year. A visitor's guide to the Old City Cemetery that includes burial information and a map is available at the center, sponsored by the Brownsville Historical Association.

A substantial, stylized cross on a large crypt marks the burial place that once held the remains of **John McAllen** (1826–1913), after whom the town of McAllen is named, and **Salomé Ballí Young McAllen** (1830–1898). In 1915, the couple was reinterred in Brownsville's Buena Vista Burial Park. Several of Salomé's Ballí relatives remain buried in the Old City Cemetery crypt.

Born in Ireland, John McAllen immigrated to Matamoros, Mexico in 1849. He met John Young, who employed him as a clerk in his store. He began to pursue his own business interests and in 1858, built the first sugar mill in the area. His boss died in 1859, and McAllen married his widow, Salomé Ballí Young, two years later. John was fortunate in his choice of a wife. In 1749, the first Ballís from northern Mexico arrived in the province of Nuevo Santander, what is now the Lower Rio Grande Valley. There they would become a powerful landed dynasty.

Salomé Ballí was a descendant of one of the early owners of the Santa Anita land grant of 95,000 acres. In 1848, she married her first husband and they expanded the ranch landholdings and had a son, John Joseph Young (1854–1921). Widowed at age twenty-nine, she owned $100,000 in real property and $25,000 in personal property. At that time, she was one of four individuals born in Mexico enumerated in a group of 263 "wealthy Texans." After her marriage to McAllen, they had a son, James (1862–1916), who was also buried in Buena Vista Burial Park in the McAllen family plot. Their marker is a simple but substantial granite tombstone engraved with their surname, bookended on either side with urns.

The mausoleum of the **Reverend Hiram Chamberlain** (1797–1866), father of Henrietta King (see Kingsville, Chamberlain Cemetery), behind a black wrought-iron fence along the brick pathway resembles a small house. A carved image of the book of Revelation is inscribed with the words, "Blessed are the dead which die in the Lord from henceforth: Yea, saith the Spirit, That they may rest from their labours; and their works do follow them. 14, Chap. 13, Verse." A large marble insert lists his contributions to Brownsville. Born in Vermont, he was ordained in 1823. He was pastor of the First Presbyterian Church in Brownsville in 1850, the first Protestant church organized on the Rio Grande.

Brownsville civic leader **Francisco Yturria** (1830–1912) is buried in a family plot along with his wife, **Felicitas Treviño** (1857–1920), adopted son **Santiago** (1857–1859), and **Yndalesio Treviño** (1832–1904), his brother-in-law and business partner. A Civil War profiteer and banker who was born in Matamoros, Mexico, Yturria began his business career working as a clerk for Charles Stillman, one of the founders of Brownsville, and by purchasing lands adjoining those of his wife's inheritance—land from a Spanish land grant in Cameron County. As a top aide to Stillman, Yturria was involved in the formation of Mifflin Kenedy and Company, the Rio Grande river boating monopoly that Stillman financed and that Mifflin Kenedy (see Brownsville, Buena Vista Cemetery) and Richard King (see Kingsville, Chamberlain Cemetery) operated. Yturria became the leading cotton broker of Matamoros during this time. He not only established and operated the Francisco Yturria Bank of Brownsville under a private charter, but he also owned and established a mercantile house in Matamoros. He was one of the wealthiest and most influential men of his time in southwest Texas, according to historian Dr. Gilberto M. Hinojosa.

Brownsville's Old City Cemetery has a number of impressive statues, such as this one in the Celaya family plot.

José Celaya (1856–1928) was secretary and treasurer of the Rio Grande Railroad of which his father, Simon Celaya, was a founding member. His marriage to Serafina Fernandez (1870–1920) daughter of José Fernandez (see below) solidified his fortune and they remained one of the most prominent families in Brownsville for decades.

The **Fernandez** family plot features a large monument adorned by a statue of Christ holding a large cross. Patriarch **José Fernandez** (1832–1911) was a pioneer in overland freight. He made a huge fortune in arms and supplies for Mexican and Civil War trade. He joined Porfirio Diaz's inner circle in 1876 and acquired a large coffee plantation in Veracruz. In Brownsville, he amassed sizeable property and bank holdings.

On an ornately carved pedestal that marks the grave of **Annie Dougherty Closner** (1861–1903) stands a statue of a young woman holding a small cross to her breast, symbolic of the virtue of faith. While not as large as the others mentioned, it is nonetheless similarly impressive. Born in Brownsville, Annie died at age forty-two of an "incurable malady," leaving three young children. Her husband John was sheriff of Hidalgo County at the time of her death. A year later, he married Annie's sister Alice.

CEMETERY ARCHITECTURE

The ethnic character of Brownsville is evident in the adornment of gravesites. Exquisite examples of marble cemetery art and architecture stand alongside crypts made of local brick and

---

humble markers expressing folk customs. During the nineteenth century, "garden" cemeteries were popular and included chapels and mausoleums. Turn-of-the-century cemeteries feature Greek Revival, Gothic Revival, Romanesque, Classic Revival, and Egyptian Revival.

Buena Vista Burial Park at 125 Mcdavitt Boulevard just east of US 77 Expressway is an active cemetery with more than 5,000 graves. Although the cemetery was not officially established until the early 1900s, there are several graves dating to the 1800s. The most prominent nineteenth-century burials are those of **Mifflin Kenedy** (1818–1895), partner with Richard King of the renowned King Ranch, and his wife **Petra Vela de Vidal Kenedy** (1825–1885). Eight family members are buried in a family plot marked by a twenty-foot-high marble monument in the Classical Revival style. On the base is a woman dressed in a Grecian robe carrying flower buds within her stole, symbolic of those buried here whose lives were cut short.

The Mifflin Kenedy family was one of the most influential in South Texas during the nineteenth century. Mifflin was born in 1818 in Pennsylvania to Quaker parents. At sixteen, he went on his first voyage, spurring his interest in navigation. From 1836 to 1846, he worked as a clerk and acting captain on several steamers on the Ohio, Missouri, Mississippi, and other rivers. Kenedy came to Texas in 1846 to serve as a steamboat captain with the US Army during the War with Mexico. He ferried troops and supplies up and down the Rio Grande.

Petra Vela de Vidal Kenedy.
[KENEDY COLLECTION] THE SOUTH TEXAS ARCHIVES & SPECIAL COLLECTIONS,
TEXAS A&M UNIVERSITY-KINGSVILLE, KINGSVILLE, TEXAS.

When hostilities ceased in 1848, he recognized the opportunity on the new frontier and decided to stay.

In 1850, he and Richard King formed a steamship partnership called M. Kenedy and Company. Two years later, Mifflin married

Petra Vela de Vidal, the wealthy widow of Colonel Luis Vidal of Mier, Mexico. Petra's father had been a provincial governor under Spain and her husband was an officer in the Mexican regular army before he died in 1849 of "vómito" during a cholera epidemic. Petra packed her bags and her children and moved to Brownsville, where she met Mifflin Kennedy. A devout Catholic, she married Mifflin in a Catholic ceremony. Petra had eight children from her marriage with Vidal and she and Mifflin had six children of their own. She dedicated much of her life to childbearing, childrearing, and the domestic support of the family and their ranch. Mifflin started ranching with a flock of Merino sheep that he brought to Texas from Pennsylvania.

In 1860, Mifflin and King purchased the Santa Gertrudis Ranch in South Texas as full partners, a partnership that was dissolved in 1868 so Mifflin could purchase his own ranchland. In 1869, he moved with his family from Brownsville to the 172,000-acre Laureles Ranch in Nueces County. About 161 workers, including vaqueros, shepherds, and laborers, worked at the ranch, one of the first in Texas to be fenced. During the Civil War, Mifflin's steamboat company had twenty-six boats shipping cotton along the Rio Grande. The steamboat company was dissolved in 1874. Having been successful in steamboating, trading, and ranching, Kenedy entered the field of railroad construction in 1876 to help build the Corpus Christi, San Diego, and Rio Grande line from Corpus Christi to Laredo. He supplied the money and credit to build 700 miles of the San Antonio and Aransas Pass Railway, and he and his wife settled in Corpus Christi.

The couple suffered several tragedies involving the deaths of their children, which may have contributed to the "unknown malady" that took Petra's life in March of 1885. Her three eldest children from her first marriage—two sons and a daughter—had died several years before in one of the epidemics that plagued the river town. A baby daughter, **Phebe**, passed away in 1861. In 1865, her twenty-year-old son, **Adrian Vidal**, was shot and killed by French royalists during their attempted takeover of Mexico. In 1876, her youngest son, **William,** died of consumption in New Orleans at age seventeen. Eight years later, in 1884, just two months before her own death, another son, **James "Spike" Kenedy**, died of typhoid fever at age twenty-nine. James, also called Santiago, had survived a near fatal gunshot wound in Dodge City in 1878 after a shootout with a posse that included Bat Masterson and Wyatt Earp. James accidentally killed Dora Hand, one of the city's most popular and beloved honky-tonk singers. Gravely ill with a "shoulder full of buckshot," James was released from jail after about three weeks. His case was dismissed for lack of evidence and because of the intervention of his father and several other wealthy ranchers. Nevertheless, James suffered for the rest of his short life from the injury. He left a wife, **Corina Balli Kenedy** (1857–1932), buried elsewhere, and four-month-old son **George** (1884–1920), who is also buried in this family plot.

Also buried here are Mifflin and Petra's eldest son, **Thomas Kenedy** (1853–1888) and his wife **Yrene Ysnaga Kenedy** (1862–1887). Yrene, pregnant with their first child, died after falling down a flight of unfinished stairs at a house she and Thomas were building. Their unborn child also died. Thomas died a year later when he was shot and killed by the estranged husband of a woman he was seeing.

The couple's much-beloved youngest son William has the distinction of having been buried and reburied three different times. First buried in New Orleans in a vault at the Metairie Cemetery, his remains were moved in 1890 to Brownsville's Old Cemetery to be buried in the family plot next to his baby sister Phebe and his half-brother Adrian. He was moved again to Buena Vista Burial Park after Mifflin passed away in 1895. Phebe's remains were also moved. Adrian's remains were left in Brownsville's Old City Cemetery.

Petra and Mifflin, who died ten years after his wife, were first buried in Corpus Christi. Sometime in the mid-1900s, their granddaughter Sarita transferred her grandparents' remains to Buena Vista Burial Park.

TAPHOPHOBIA

During the nineteenth century, many feared being buried alive. Although it would seem that declaring one dead should be a straightforward process, physicians and morticians alike in the eighteenth and nineteenth centuries were practicing with less certainty than their modern counterparts. They often relied on methods of observation such as smell and touch, and embalming was not practiced. In the nineteenth century, both Mary Shelley's 1818 Gothic novel, *Frankenstein*, and Edgar Allen Poe's 1844 short story "Premature Burial" exploited fears of being buried alive. In Shelly's case, the question concerned what constituted death. In Poe's work, the narrator describes his struggle from "attacks of the singular disorder which physicians have agreed to term catalepsy," an actual medical condition characterized by a death-like trance and rigidity to the body. The story focuses on the narrator's fear of being buried alive and doing what he can to prevent it. He asks his friends to make sure he is actually dead before burial. As a backup, he builds a tomb with equipment allowing him to signal for help. Despite his precautions, as is typical in a Poe story, his greatest fear is realized. Because of such literature and accounts of premature burial passed down through generations, the pandemic of doubt spread across the world, sparking a century's worth of ingenious devices intended to ease doubts associated with live burials. One such device was a "coffin alarm." A bell was attached to the headstone with a chain that led down into the coffin to a ring that went around the finger of the deceased. If that person were to awaken and find themselves accidentally buried, they would pull on the chain and the bell would ring in the cemetery yard. Some experts believe the idiom "saved by the bell" originated from the use of safety coffins.

PEÑITAS

The historic town of Peñitas (pop. 4,600) is seventy-five miles northwest of Brownsville and ten miles northwest of McAllen in southwestern Hidalgo County. Peñitas is the Spanish word for "little pebbles," named after nearby gravel pits. One of the earliest settlements in the United States, Peñitas was established in the late 1520s by Catholic priest Fray Zamora and five military officers who came with the unsuccessful Panfilo De Narvaez expedition. Calero Indians who lived along the Rio Grande in dugout houses and thatched huts befriended the settlers and an amicable relationship developed. In the mid-1700s, a small village and mission were founded south of the Rio Grande (in what is now Mexico), and the area north of the river became ranchland. In the mid-1800s, Peñitas became a refueling stop for steamboats and by the early twentieth century had residences, stores, a cemetery, a post office, a school, and a depot for the St. Louis, Brownsville, and Mexico Railroad. The 1880 census listed seventy-five families living on what was then called Peñitas Ranch. Today, Peñitas, incorporated in 1992, continues to thrive as a community rich in cultural heritage.

Peñitas Cemetery (St. Anthony Cemetery) is on a fenced, one-and-a-half-acre parcel dotted with drought-resistant trees such as mesquite and hackberry, and shrubs such as prickly pear nopal on the northside of Military Road (FM 1427), just east of Zamora Road. The cemetery was originally adjacent to St. Anthony Catholic Church. The church moved half a mile away on South Main Street. Maintained by the Peñitas Cemetery

Association, the cemetery was established in 1836. Of 636 graves, eighty-seven are of unknown individuals. Additionally, there are several old tombstones with undiscernible names and unmarked crypts. Those buried here include pioneer families who arrived in the 1800s and their descendants, as well as veterans of foreign and domestic wars.

Two Union Army soldiers buried here are **José Maria Loya** (1830–1900), who served as a private in the Texas Cavalry Independent Partisan Rangers from 1863 until 1865, and **Ignacio Zamora** (1835–1917), a *vaquero* who served as a sergeant in the Second Regiment Texas Cavalry Company from 1864 to 1865. About 2,550 Mexican-Texans fought for the Confederacy during the Civil War and about 950 fought in the Union Army, according to Jerry D. Thompson, author of *Vaqueros in Blue and Gray*. Loya and Zamora were descended from Spanish colonial families who founded the settlement of Peñitas. After the Mexican-American War, people of Mexican origin whose homes were north of the Rio Grande were often targets of land theft and violence. Loya and Zamora may have joined the Union Army to retaliate against their Confederate neighbors. Additionally, bounty money was offered to enlist in the Union Army, a powerful incentive for local Hispanics who not only opposed slavery, but who also were dealing with the loss of family land grant properties. They went to Brownsville to enlist into local regiments, such as the Second Regiment of the Texas Cavalry, in fear of being conscripted and sent far away.

Pharr

The city of Pharr (pop. 85,000), twenty miles west of Peñitas, is within a Spanish land grant made in 1767 to Juan José Hinojosa. In the late nineteenth century, Hinojosa's heirs sold portions of the land. In 1909, John C. Kelley Sr. and Henry N. Pharr, a Louisiana sugarcane grower, became co-owners of 16,000 acres with two miles of frontage on the river. Pharr founded the Louisiana and Rio Grande Canal Company and constructed an irrigation system for a sugar plantation. Kelley founded a company that platted the town he named Pharr in honor of his partner. The sugar plantation venture collapsed after a few years and the irrigation system instead supplied water to local vegetable and cotton farms. Today the town is a major commercial port of entry due to the Pharr-Reynosa International Bridge.

The **Eli Jackson Cemetery**, also known as the **Eli Jackson-Brewster Cemetery**, on US 281/Military Highway east of its intersection with South I Road/South Veterans Road just outside the Pharr city limits, is a Texas Historic Cemetery. The burial ground was founded with the death in 1865 of **Nathaniel Jackson** (1798–1865), an Alabama native who settled there in 1857 and established a 5,500-acre ranch. A former slave owner, Jackson, who was white, came with his wife **Matilda Hicks** (1800–1870), who was black, their children, and his freed slaves. Jackson raised livestock and grew vegetables, cotton, and sugarcane. He built a chapel for the community and was known for his generosity and hospitality. He and Matilda aided runaway slaves who came to the ranch in need of lodging and other resources, helping them escape into Mexico.

Upon Jackson's death in 1865, his heirs divided the ranch. The share to his son **Eli** (1832–1911) included the family cemetery. Eli and his wife, **Elizabeth Kerr** (1847–1900), and their children continued the family tradition of hospitality. Eli served as a county official, as did his son **Nathaniel "Polo" Jackson** (1875–1929). Polo's daughter **Adela** (1899–1992) operated the ranch and cared for the cemetery until her death in 1992.

There are many unmarked burials in this cemetery of less than 100 graves, including those of Nathaniel and his wife Matilda. Ancestors of the Carrizo-Comecrudo Indian tribes are also buried here. The Brewster surname came from **William Brewster** (1835–1882), a physician from Connecticut, according to the 1870 and 1880 censuses, who married Nathaniel's step-granddaughter, **Minerva Singleterry Brewster** (1847–1909) in 1866. They had ten children. William, who went by the name Guillermo, was buried in Matamoros, Mexico.

SANTA ANA WILDLIFE REFUGE

The 2,088-acre Santa Ana Wildlife Refuge, eleven miles southeast of Pharr and seven miles south of Alamo, is on FM 907, a quarter mile east on US Highway 281. Bordering the Rio Grande, the refuge is a remnant subtropical forest that protects the few ocelots and jaguarundis remaining wild in the United States. In addition to these rare cats, over thirty-three species of other mammals, 372 species of birds,

The Santa Ana Cemetery in the Santa Ana Wildlife Refuge is the only vestige of a once-thriving ranch. The tomb of Cristoval Leal, descendant of the original grantee, and his wife is on the right of the photo.
COURTESY OF JENNIFER SANCHEZ.

200 species of butterflies, and thirty-four species of reptiles have been recorded in Santa Ana. Established in 1943, Santa Ana National Wildlife Refuge is positioned along an east-west and north-south juncture of two major migratory routes for many species of birds. In 1967, the refuge was designated a Registered Natural Landmark "because of its exceptional value in illustrating the natural history of the United States of America." The refuge has more than fourteen miles of trails. The wildlife refuge is named after the Santa Ana land grant of two square leagues bestowed in 1834 to **Benigno Leal** (1800–?) who established his *Rancho del Adentro* (Inside Ranch). Benigno was married to **Victoria Ballí** (1802–1887).

The **Santa Ana Cemetery**, a little over a mile inside the refuge, is the only vestige of the once-thriving ranch that supported forty families. A partial fence of 150-year-old ebony logs and an arched wrought-iron entry that says *Cementario Viejo* (Old Cemetery) marks the burial ground of about thirty graves, most of unknown individuals, indicated by wooden crosses. An above-ground crypt of handmade bricks marks the burial spot of **Cristoval Leal** (1833–1876), adopted son of the original grantee, and his wife **María Rafaela Treviño** (1830–?), who was his first cousin and daughter of nearby El Gato land grantee José Maria Treviño. Rafaela erected the tomb for her husband with a Spanish inscription, here translated to English: "Here on August 5, 1876, were placed the remains of D. Cristoval Leal. He died at the age of 43, leaving grateful memories of a good husband and a loyal citizen. Maria Rafaela Trevino, his wife, consecrates this to his memory. RIP."

The couple had a son, also named Cristoval, born in 1855, who was considered mentally deficient. When his mother died, he placed a bundle of rags in her coffin while mourners looked on. Many believed his mother's jewelry was in the bundles and the tomb was vandalized. Their son traded the last of his lands for a fiddle and a new suit of clothes, according to descendants. During the border bandit raids of 1915–1916, the tomb was broken into and the remains of the couple were scattered about. After the federal government purchased the ranch, the tomb was repaired and what was left of the remains were reinterred.

A large wooden cross and historical marker in this cemetery marks the grave of **Thomas Walter Jones** (1827–1853), the earliest marked burial here. A surveyor from Washington D.C., Jones was on the border surveying team hired after the 1848 Treaty of Guadalupe Hidalgo ended the Mexican War. While working as assistant surveyor on the lower Rio Grande, Jones drowned on July 23, 1853. His historical marker indicates he was buried on the Dr. Eli T. Merriman Ranch. Dr. Merriman, a Yankee doctor and Mexican War veteran, purchased one league of the Santa Ana grant from Cristoval and his mother Victoria in 1852, and his portion was where the cemetery was located. Merriman sold the ranch in 1878 and the land changed hands many times until the federal government purchased it for the refuge.

COTULLA

The southwestern town of Cotulla (pop. 5,000), named after Polish immigrant Joseph Cotulla, is 200 miles from the Rio Grande Valley, ninety miles south of San Antonio and sixty-eight miles northeast of Laredo. The La Salle County town sits at the southern edge of the Nueces River, which until 1836 formed the undisputed western boundary of Texas. That changed in 1848 when the Treaty of Guadalupe Hidalgo fixed the boundary between the United States and Mexico at the Rio Grande. A small garrison, Fort Ewell, was established in what would become Cotulla in 1852, but it was abandoned two years later due to flooding. In 1865, Joseph Cotulla obtained cattle leases in this Nueces Strip area and began purchasing large parcels. He then offered the International and Great Northern Railroad company 120 acres out of his ranch for a townsite in exchange for building the track through his property. The company agreed and a depot and town were founded in 1882. By 1890, the town, with a population of 1,000, was known for being wild and rowdy. Railroad conductors were said to have announced their arrival by calling out, "Cotulla! Everybody get your guns ready." Three sheriffs and nineteen residents are said to have lost their lives in gunfights in the town. The town's economy has been primarily based on sheep and cattle ranching, and in the 1950s, the discovery of oil in the area helped to bolster the economy.

The **Cotulla Cemetery** on FM 468, a half mile southeast of the I-35 intersection, was established in 1891, although the earliest marked grave is dated 1882, and numerous graves bear the date 1886, when smallpox struck the region. The cemetery, the chief burial site for LaSalle County, is on a small hill dotted with juniper and palm trees. Originally divided into Mexican and Anglo sections, the Mexican section in the back now comprises the largest burial area. Cotulla's Hispanic population today is almost 85 percent. President Lyndon Baines Johnson started his teaching career in Cotulla in 1928 and his experience teaching Mexican-American children in the segregated school system there is said to have motivated his support of the Higher Education Act of 1965.

The family plot of town founder **Joseph Cotulla** (1844–1923) is one of the first fenced burial plots at the entrance into this Texas Historic Cemetery. Seventeen of Cotulla's family members are buried here, along with his father-in-law **Simon Rieder** (1821–1898).

In 1857, at age twelve, Joseph arrived in Texas with his widowed mother and a group of other Polish Silesians. In 1863, he enlisted in the Union Army, First Texas Cavalry. His decision to join the Union Army was likely due to his abhorrence of slavery, something shared with his fellow Poles. The next year, he migrated to the Nueces Strip—Apache land that also attracted outlaws who frequently raided ranch settlements. In 1871, he married **Mary Reider** (1854–1908), daughter of Atascosa rancher Simon Reider, for whom Joseph had worked for several years. He divided his time between his father-in-law's ranch and his La Salle County property. In 1882, his wife and four children arrived on the first train into town. The Cotullas had five sons and four daughters, all of whom lived into adulthood. The family ranching empire once covered more than 25,000 acres and supported more than 5,000 heads of cattle in La Salle County.

Among the distinctive tombstones in the Cotulla Cemetery are two that stand out for their mystery. Who were the **Five Summerton Brothers** whose marble tombstone in the shape of a small cube marks a curbed burial plot in the Mexican part of the cemetery? No one seems to know who they were, when they died, or cause of death. Another fascinating grave marker is that of **J. Perez** (unknown dates of birth and death). One side of his grave has a concrete cross embossed with his last name and initial. On the other is a concrete niche upon which his face is carved. Who he was, who carved the effigy, and who commissioned it is unknown.

KINGSVILLE

Named after legendary nineteenth-century cattle baron Captain Richard King, Kingsville (pop. 25,000) was established by his wife Henrietta Chamberlain King and son-in-law Robert J. Kleberg on part of the 825,000-acre King Ranch to entice the St. Louis, Brownsville, and Mexico Railway through the area. In 1904, the first passenger train came through town and railway headquarters were established in Kingsville, incorporated in 1911. The railroad was the main source of income, and farms and ranches dotted the area located forty-two miles from the Gulf Coast town of Corpus Christi. Many of the first businesses were established by the King Ranch, which built a bank, hotel, ice plant, waterworks, cotton gin, and started a weekly newspaper. Kingsville became a trade center for local families. Kingsville remains a vital part of the Texas ranching industry. The King Ranch raises approximately 30,000 Santa Gertrudis and Santa Cruz cattle and maintains a small herd of Longhorn for the breed's history.

In April 1909, **Chamberlain Cemetery**, a Texas Historic Cemetery on 735 West Caesar Avenue, was opened and named after Henrietta King's father, Hiram Chamberlain (see Brownsville, Old City Cemetery). The forty-acre tract included a portion with many earlier burials. Henrietta was buried in the cemetery upon her death in 1925. Captain King, originally buried in San Antonio's City Cemetery, and son **Robert E. Lee** (1864–1883), originally buried in St. Louis before being interred in San Antonio, and daughter **Ella** (1858–1900), buried in St. Louis, were moved later that year to the King family plot in Kingsville. Also buried in Chamberlain Cemetery are many of Kingsville's founding citizens, including **Uriah Lott** (1842–1915), a visionary builder of railroads throughout Central and South Texas.

Richard King (1825–1885), a steamboat captain born in New York City, arrived in Texas in 1847 joining Mifflin Kenedy (see Brownsville, Buena Vista Cemetery) for service during the

Mexican War transporting troops and supplies on the Rio Grande. A principal partner in two steamboat companies, his firms dominated the Rio Grande trade from the mid-1850s to the early 1870s. In several partnerships, King first bought land in the Wild Horse Desert in 1853 when he purchased the 15,500-acre Rincón

Captain Richard King, c. 1880.
KING RANCH, INC., KINGSVILLE, TEXAS.

de Santa Gertrudis grant. In 1854, he purchased the 53,000-acre Santa Gertrudis de la Garza grant. These two irregularly shaped pieces of wilderness became the nucleus around which the King Ranch grew. He ran his ranch as an *hacendado*, bringing almost the entire population of the Mexican town of Cruillas to work for him. The townspeople had sold all their cattle to him during a drought. Realizing they had no income, King told them he'd provide food, shelter, and a steady paycheck if they would move with him to work on his South Texas ranch. Many of them agreed. Among his new employees were expert stockmen and horsemen who became known as Los Kineños—King's people. They and many generations of their descendants still live and work on the ranch today. A small cemetery underneath a copse of large trees within the ranch is the final resting place of many of the early Kineños, although others are also buried in Chamberlain Cemetery.

Several famous King Ranch horses, including the thoroughbred **Assault** (1943–1971), the seventh horse to win American horseracing's Triple Crown—the 1946 Kentucky Derby, the Preakness Stakes, and the Belmont with jockey Warren Mehrtens—are buried at the ranch. When Assault was twenty-eight, he broke a bone in his left foreleg and was euthanized.

When King died on April 14, 1885, from stomach cancer at age sixty, he was staying at the Menger Hotel in San Antonio. He'd been there for several weeks in what is now the King Ranch Suite on the second floor of the hotel, and at the end, he was surrounded by family and friends, including Captain Mifflin Kenedy. His funeral was

Henrietta M. Chamberlain King, c. 1885.
KING RANCH, INC., KINGSVILLE, TEXAS.

held in the hotel's parlor. By the time of his death, he had made over sixty major purchases of land, amassed some 614,000 acres, and was $500,000 in debt.

His wife **Henrietta M. Chamberlain** (1832–1925), whom he married in 1854, assumed ownership of her husband's estate. Henrietta was an unlikely marriage candidate for the rough and tumble yet handsome Richard King. She was the oldest child of a Presbyterian minister, didn't drink, and was simple in her tastes. But theirs was a love match and after her husband's death, according to Tom Lea in his book *The King Ranch*, "when she sometimes allowed herself gray or white, her dress and bonnet were severely black." Under her supervision, the King Ranch was freed of debt and increased to 825,000 acres spread over six counties in South Texas, larger than the state of Rhode Island.

The couple had five children. Their youngest daughter **Alice** (1862–1944) married **Robert Kleberg** (1853–1932), who helped Henrietta run the ranch. When Henrietta died in 1925 at age ninety-two, her body lay in state in a bronze casket in the grand salon of the twenty-seven-room, 37,000-square-foot main house at the ranch. Hundreds arrived to pay their respects. The Kineños led the funeral procession to the cemetery where they circled the open grave on horseback, holding their hats at their sides.

A substantial pillar monument topped with a large urn, sculpted by Frank Teich, marks the King family plot in the Chamberlain Cemetery, where Richard, Henrietta, and several descendants are buried.

FUNERAL CUSTOMS

During the nineteenth century, premature death was so prevalent that social etiquette grew around how to properly conduct mourning. Strict rules developed, especially for widows who were required to wear black, and not just any black—it had to be a "dead hue and not a lively black." Mourning lasted for a year and involved "severe plainness" and withdrawal from society. Widows often continued to wear black for the rest of their lives. The most famous widow during this era was Queen Victoria who mourned in black for the remaining forty years of her life after her husband, Prince Albert, died in 1861.

Many funeral customs were based on superstitions. For example, when the body was taken from the house, it was carried out feet first because if carried out headfirst, it could look back and beckon others to follow into death. When someone died in the house and there was a clock in the room, it was stopped at the time of death or the family would have bad luck. Covering mirrors after death became a cornerstone of Jewish tradition but was also common in many religions and cultures. According to the Talmud, the soul can enter through reflective surfaces. Even the custom of the wake, in which someone stayed up to sit with the "dead," was a way to make sure the person was really deceased.

LAREDO

Laredo (pop. 266,000) borders Mexico on the Rio Grande in southwest Texas about 200 miles northwest of Brownsville, 118 miles due west of Kingsville, and sixty-eight miles south of Cotulla. A major port of entry into the United States from Mexico, the town was established in 1755 and called Villa de San Agustín de Laredo. It was named after the city of Laredo on the Bay of Biscay in the Spanish Province of Santander, home of Colonel José de Escandón who was in charge of colonizing the Mexican provinces in northeastern Mexico and parts of what is now Texas. Spanish officer Tomás Sánchez de la Barrera y Gallardo was with the Escandón expedition. He requested and received permission to establish the new settlement on the banks of the river.

Sánchez brought three families to the site and they built simple adobe homes and thatched-roofed *jacales*, raising goats, sheep, and cattle. The townsite became a villa in 1767. San Agustín Plaza, where a small church had already been built, was laid out as a common area for residents. Indian bands of Carrizo, Borrado, and Lipans traded with the Spanish villagers and the town grew steadily. As surrounding ranchos became prosperous, Comanche and Apache raids increased and a military garrison was established in 1775. Laredo became a staging point for General Antonio López de Santa Anna during the 1836 Texas Revolution. After the boundary between the United States and Mexico was established at the Rio Grande, Laredo was cut in half. A number of families who did not wish to live under the American flag moved across the river to live in what is now Nuevo Laredo. The arrival of the railroad in 1881 brought economic growth, as well as Anglo residents. By 1900, the population had grown to 13,500, and a separate society of Anglos developed alongside the original Mexican community.

During the Spanish period, Laredo's first *camposanto* was at San Agustín Church, and burials took place in front of the church. A second stone church was built in 1778. According to church records, citizens paid to be buried within the sanctuary. At least ninety burials were found inside the church foundation perimeter during an archeological excavation in the late 1990s. It is believed that Laredo's founder Don Tomás Sánchez is one of the burials. Two burials in the altar area were possibly the two original parish priests.

In 1849, a new cemetery north of the town square was laid out and surrounded by a stone fence. By 1876, another cemetery was established, known as the "Mexican Catholic Cemetery." As Laredo grew in the late 1880s, the city's need for yet another cemetery increased. In 1892, a large plot of land three-and-a-half miles northwest of the plaza was designated for a new cemetery complex, half of which would be a new Catholic cemetery and the other half a City Cemetery for other religious faiths, fraternal organizations, and public burials.

LAREDO SMALLPOX RIOT

Before the new Catholic cemetery opened, a smallpox epidemic ravaged Laredo's Mexican barrio, taking the lives of many of the town's children from October 1898 to April 1899. By the end of January 1899, 100 cases had been reported and Dr. W. T. Blunt, a State of Texas health officer, instructed the city to

---

conduct house-to-house vaccinations, fumigations, burning of clothing and effects, and remove infected individuals to field hospitals, a quarantined area called the "pesthouse." A number of Laredo residents balked at these edicts and Texas Rangers were called in to help medical teams conduct the house-to-house treatments. Friction between Mexican-Americans and the Rangers was long-standing and protests broke out resulting in what became known as the "Laredo Smallpox Riot." Several residents were killed; a few Rangers were wounded. The Tenth US Cavalry was brought in to maintain peace and continue the treatments. Children continued to die, but by April deaths had decreased dramatically and Blunt lifted the quarantine in early May. Funeral processions with tiny wooden coffins throughout the winter and spring of 1899 were a constant reminder of the toll from this epidemic and many of those burials took place in the City Cemetery.

Calvary Catholic Cemetery, a Texas Historic Cemetery at 3600 McPherson Road, opened in 1901. The burial ground is large and nicely landscaped with gardens and tall palm trees, and includes sections for babies, religious, laity, soldiers, and other notable individuals. The earliest burials are noted by impressive monuments, statues, and tombstones on the northeast part of the cemetery, many of them reinterments from the original Catholic cemeteries. Centered within a roundabout is a unique domed mausoleum erected for **Bishop Peter Verdaguer** (1835–1911), who was born in Barcelona, Spain. He served as bishop in South Texas from 1890 until his death. A historical marker in front of the mausoleum details his seminal achievements for the Catholic community.

Captain Cristóbal Benavides (1839–1904) was a descendant of the town founder Tómas Sánchez. At the onset of the Civil War, he enlisted as a sergeant in a Confederate company of local Tejanos raised by his older half-brother **Santos Benavides** (1823–1891). He achieved the rank of captain defending the Rio Grande Valley against Union forces. After the war, he married **Lamar Bee** (1851–1921), daughter of Confederate General Hamilton P. Bee (see San Antonio, City Cemetery Historic District). The couple had six daughters and four sons. By 1890, Benavides was one of the wealthiest men in Webb County based on his sheep and cattle ranch and a Laredo mercantile business. In the late 1930s, his remains were removed from the old Catholic cemetery and reinterred in the Calvary Catholic Cemetery, where descendants erected the impressive memorial monument in his honor.

Santos Benavides (1823–1891), Cristóbal's half-brother—also a descendant of the town founder—is buried behind the Cristóbal Benavides family plot, along with his wife **Agustina Villarreal Benavides** (1822–1908). Full-length marble slabs featuring beautifully carved crosses cover the couple's graves and a historical marker stands at the gravesite of Santos, a prominent Laredo leader. Santos was the highest-ranking Tejano in the Confederacy and never lost any battles as an officer. The Battle of Carrizo, where he defeated the insurrectionist Juan Cortina, and the Battle of Laredo, in which he stopped a Union force of 550 soldiers, cemented his fame. Before the war, he was mayor of Laredo from 1856 to 1859, after which he served as chief justice of Webb County. After the war, he continued his mercantile and ranching activities, along with his brother Cristóbal, and remained active in politics. He believed in regional independence from national authority. He was elected to the Texas House of Representatives serving three terms, from 1879 to 1884.

Refugio Benavides (1821–1899), a rancher and Civil War officer who fought with his brothers and who was elected as one of the first city alderman under American rule, was reinterred in this cemetery in the 1940s. After the war, he was elected mayor of Laredo. Married twice, he had six children. A historical marker was erected at his simple gravesite in the Herrera family plot.

Many other notable individuals are buried at Calvary Catholic Cemetery, and its impressive monuments and lovely landscaping make this a must-see stop on any trip to this Wild Horse Desert town.

The Benavides family plot is a fitting memorial to a family with roots that go back to the founding of Laredo.

AUTHOR'S NOTE

The last few months of my work on this book were during the COVID-19 pandemic. I became very cognizant of how history repeats itself. A few hundred years before Christ was born, in the Book of Ecclesiastes, King Solomon observed, "What has been will be again, what has been done will be done again, there is nothing new under the sun." All the talk of "unprecedented times" solidified my belief in the importance of the knowledge of history. Steeped in the nineteenth century, writing about cemeteries, memorials, and the people interred—basically writing about death—I knew that the pandemic we were facing was not unprecedented. In fact, epidemics, pandemics, and plagues have occurred with deadly frequency over the centuries and so have various forms of "shutdowns," and resistance to such measures. In the nineteenth century, long-standing diseases such as smallpox (see what instigated the Laredo Smallpox Riot mentioned in this book), typhus, and yellow fever turned into epidemics several times over the course of the century. Cholera spread worldwide in six pandemics in the nineteenth century. There was even a bubonic plague pandemic, originating in China, that spread worldwide in the 1890s. Scientific advances in the medical field and the recognition of the importance of sanitation made such pandemics rarer and less lethal in subsequent centuries.

Many of the cemeteries included tell the stories of individuals, some known and many unknown, who succumbed to epidemics (diseases that affect a large number of people within a region) and pandemics (diseases that spread over multiple countries or continents). In fact, the mortality rate was so high during the nineteenth century that there was an entire industry of funerary rites and customs developed to help the bereaved. The sentiments engraved on many tombstones give expression to the anguish suffered when a loved one died.

And yet, looking further into the story of survivors, one learns about the resilience of humanity. The incidence of remarriage was high for practical reasons—children needed care and often a widow or widower was left with several. Nineteenth-century Texas was primarily rural, with agriculture, farming, and ranching the leading occupations. The nuclear family—father, mother, and children—each had vital roles in maintaining a way of life that would benefit the whole. When a mother or father died, farming and ranching, already difficult, became exponentially harder. Hence, the frequent incidence of remarriage.

I was born and raised in Texas, and so was steeped in Texas history from an early age. Nonetheless, many of the individuals covered in this book were new to me. Even those I knew of were illuminated in ways that made them more real and impressive. How they were memorialized in death also tells a story. An example is General Sam Houston, the first president of the Republic of Texas, who today is iconic in Texas history. Years after he died, a magnificent memorial by renowned Italian-American sculptor Pompeo Coppini was commissioned for his gravesite, but at the time of his death, he was vilified because he refused to support the Confederacy. Few people, except close family members and friends, attended his funeral in Huntsville.

While the gravesites of children, many marked by intricately carved babies and toddlers reclining on small pillow beds, were poignant, the graves with markers for "Unknown" or "Known Only to God" were also moving. Several sections at the Fort Parker Memorial Park Cemetery have rows of such markers—small square concrete tombstones inscribed with the word, UNKNOWN—a sobering reminder of our fate in years to come.

Another thing that struck me as I toured cemeteries around Texas was the myriad Confederate monuments and flags adorning the graves of the state's Confederate dead. With all the controversy today about removing such monuments from public places throughout the United States, it became clear that such an effort would prove difficult, if not impossible, in our state's cemeteries. Confederate memorials and monuments were commissioned to commemorate the memory of dead soldiers—sons, husbands, and fathers. Many soldiers never returned home. The Confederate memorials were erected for bereaved families to have a place to pay their respects and to keep their loved one's memory alive. The Texas State Cemetery in Austin is the final resting for more than 2,000 Confederate dead and also features a magnificent memorial tomb upon which a life-size recumbent figure of Confederate General Albert Sidney Johnston is rendered in marble. The statue by German-American sculptor Elisabet Ney is stunning in its craftsmanship.

Cemeteries are important repositories of our history and humanity. While the memorials, statues, and monuments to the luminaries of Texas history are breathtaking, the graves, both marked and unmarked, of ordinary individuals are also worthy of reverence and remembrance.

Cynthia Leal Massey
Helotes, Texas

ACKNOWLEDGMENTS

First, I must thank author Gail Jenner for suggesting this project as we drove from her family ranch in northern California to Walla Walla, Washington, to attend the Women Writing the West conference in October 2018. The idea was to propose a pioneer cemetery book for each western state. She'd do California, I'd do Texas, and we'd help find authors for each of the other states if these first two books turned out to be popular. It didn't take me long to give her a resounding, "Yes, let's do it!" At that conference, we pitched the idea to Erin Turner, editorial director for TwoDot Books, and within a few months, we got our contracts.

As I mentioned in the Introduction, the THC has done an exemplary job in its stewardship of the history of the state of Texas. Its THTR program enabled me to organize this book as a useful tool for those who wish to add cemetery visits on their Texas travels. Thank you, Teresa Caldwell, state coordinator of the Texas Heritage Trails Program, for your assistance in this matter.

The THC also publishes the *Handbook of Texas* online and it was an invaluable resource, which I used extensively.

Starting in February 2019, I began my travels throughout Texas and could not have done it without the assistance of my friends, several of whom opened their homes to me. I owe them a debt of gratitude: Cyndi Chavez, my daughter Meghan, Gail Jenner, Donna Navarro, Loralyn Smith, Cindy Sandell, and Pat Wilson. One of the perks of this trip was being able to travel with these women who provided much diversion and, dare I say it? Gallows humor. Loralyn and Pat, in particular, accompanied me on several excursions and helped saved me from potential calamity.

I was with Loralyn, an emergency room nurse, when my SUV got stuck between two sandbars on a dark, one-way country road in the piney woods of East Texas on a search for a cemetery. After about an hour of spinning wheels and various maneuvers that didn't work, we'd pretty much given up. We gathered our things to walk to a nearby farmhouse when we found some bricks in a gully about forty feet from the car. We wedged them underneath the tires and we were able to dislodge the wheels and back up, emerging from the woods just as the sun went down. How a bunch of bricks happened to be in a gully in a piney wood forest is a mystery, but I attribute it to God's intervention. We never located the cemetery, which I scratched off the list as too remote.

Pat, who once volunteered as a zoo docent, rescued me from a potential medical emergency during a visit to the Fort Griffin State Historic Site when we encountered a rattlesnake coiled on the hot gravel path outside the fort's old bakery building. The rattler was about thirty feet away from the building when I saw it. You know those people who say no question is stupid? They are wrong. My question, "Do you think it's dead?" was the epitome of stupid. Pat assured me that the snake was not dead, but very much alive and was simply warming up in the sun. The fact that it was coiled was also problematic. This is how snakes launch a strike. We turned around and rushed back to the main park building, where we were informed there was a rattlesnake den in that area. A sign would've been nice. The rattlesnake encounter brought to stark relief one of the many hazards fort soldiers had to contend with in the Texas wilderness.

On that same trip, we ran into J. T. Bowman, ranch hand at the Collins Creek Ranch, who helped us locate the Fort Griffin Cemetery, a civilian graveyard on a hill near the old pioneer town of Fort Griffin. The cemetery was overgrown with weeds and just the tops of some tombstones were visible. After the rattlesnake episode at the fort, I was hesitant to venture into the cemetery and shared my trepidation with J. T. He nodded and said, "Don't blame you." He then went to his truck, pulled out some leather chaps and put them on. "I don't want to get bit either," he said, "I'll go in and take your pictures." I handed him my camera and the pictures of tombstones I was looking for and off he went. "The best time to visit this cemetery is in the winter when everything is dead," he added, with not a trace of irony, as he stepped over the barbed wire fence. What a guy!

I stayed at the Plano home of award-winning author Irene "Cindy" Sandell and her husband Sandy for several nights. Not only did Cindy accompany me on the cemetery tours in North Texas, but she also made sure that I had coffee every morning, even though she and Sandy are not coffee drinkers and did not own a coffee pot. Knowing coffee aficionados can quickly go to the dark side without their morning brew, she got up early every morning to go to the local coffee shop before I was out of bed. What a friend! And Sandy grilled the most wonderful steaks the last night I was there. What an amiable and remarkable couple, and both history lovers to boot.

Lori Bihl Cox and her husband William "Wayne" Cox took us to the Opp-Bihl family cemetery out in the country near Menard. As I was taking pictures, I pricked my finger on a Spanish dagger plant and began to bleed profusely. Wayne applied an old folk remedy—wet chewing tobacco. It took away the sting almost immediately, and I kept it on my finger wrapped with a Band-Aid for the next hour. Lori has done a lot of research on the Bihl family and provided valuable information.

Writers Michelle Ferrer and Candace Fountoulakis joined Cindy and me for lunch and the Plano cemetery tours and provided source materials and enthusiastic support.

My cousin Jennifer Sanchez, with her husband Cesar, took pictures of several of the Rio Grande Valley cemeteries and provided news clippings and other information.

Others who offered assistance: Malinda Allison & Barbara Caffee, Honey Grove Preservation League; Mitch Baird, Fort Griffin State Historic Park; Lindsay Barras, Elisabet Ney Museum; Bob Bluthardt, Fort Concho; Mary Dearing, City of Bastrop; Ricky Garza & David Parsons, Brownsville Historical Association; Melissa Hagins, Texas Pecos Trail Executive Director; Beth Hollowell, Professional Tour Guide Association of San Antonio; Teddy Jones, Panhandle author; Sam Kotara, Polish Heritage Center, Panna Maria; Patsy Leigh, Cotulla Main Street; Madeline Moya, Austin History Center; Lisa A. Neely, archivist, King Ranch, Inc.; Mike Pacino, Carl Farley's Boys Ranch;

William Reagan, Limestone County Historical Commission; Oscar Rodriguez, Lipan Apache Tribe; Sylvia Reyna, San Antonio Public Library; Laura Whitehurst, Fort Phantom Foundation; and Mitchel Whitington, East Texas author.

My critique group: Irma Ned Bailey, Esther Drown, Len McClure, Jim Peyton, and Florence Weinberg read the original drafts of the manuscript and, as always, provided valuable insight. Florence, who holds a doctorate in French, a master's in Spanish, and is also fluent in German, translated several tombstone inscriptions.

Thanks to my husband, Dave, for being so supportive of my writing projects, especially this one that took me away from home so often in the past year. To the rest of my family and friends—thank you for your forbearance in listening to the tales about my trips, probably reiterated more than once. To my agent Sandra Bond, thank you for your assistance and continued support. Special thanks to Erin Turner for your editorial guidance and your willingness to take on this project and to Sarah Parke for taking the book to the finish line.

BIBLIOGRAPHY

Abilene Daily Reporter. "Cattlemen Hung to Rafters by Angry Oklahoma Mob Today," April 19, 1909, p. 1. Accessed from Newspaperarchive.com.

Abilene Morning News. "Millie Durgan [*sic*], Indian Raid Victim, Visits in Young Co," July 23, 1932, p. 3. Accessed from Newspaperarchive.com.

Adams, Rusty. "Whistling Past the Graveyard, Cemeteries in Texas," Real Estate Center, Texas A&M University, College Station, Publication 2167, June 2, 2017.

Allen, Paula. "Milam Park Markers Honor Early San Antonio Burials," *San Antonio Express-News*, January 16, 2016. www.expressnews.com/life/life_ columnists/paula_allen/article/Milam-Park- markers-honor-early-San-Antonio-burials-6764298.php.

Alpine Avalanche. "Terlingua Officer Is Fatally Shot," Alpine Texas, June 24, 1938, p. 1. https://newspaperarchive.com/alpine-avalanche-jun-24-1938-p-1/.

Ancestry.com. www.ancestry.com/.

Annual Report of the Quartermaster General of the Operations of the Quartermaster's Department for Fiscal Year Ending on June 30, 1874. United States, Quartermaster General's Office, C. Alexander, Publisher, 1874. Digitized by Princeton University, February 27, 2009. Accessed from GoogleBooks.com.

Arnold, Robert. "The Grave History of Galveston's Cemeteries," November 25, 2015. www.click2houston.com/news/2015/10/23/the-grave-history-of-galvestons-cemeteries.

Arriola, Jackie. "Diedrick Dutchover, A Unique Individual," *Texas Historian*, Vol. L., No. 2, November 1989, pp. 11–14. The Portal to Texas History. https:// texashistory.unt.edu/ark:/67531/metapth391250/m1/2.

Atlas Preservation. American Gravestone Evolution, Parts I & II. Accessed November 27, 2019. https://atlaspreservation.com/pages/historical1.

Austin Genealogical Society, "Hornsby Mexican Cemetery," Transcriptions by Lena Ybarra, 2008. www.austintxgensoc.org/cemeteries/hornsby-mexican-cemetery/.

Ayala, Elaine. "Descendants Set to Meet with Hospital Regarding 70 Human Remains Found during Construction," *San Antonio Express-News*, May 30, 2017. https://blog.mysanantonio.com/latinlife/2017/05/descendants-set-to-meet-with-hospital- regarding-70-human-remains-found-during-construction/.

———. "Descendants upset by San Antonio hospital's handling of recently discovered human remains," *San Antonio Express-News*, May 29, 2017. www.expressnews.com/news/local/amp/Descendants-upset-by-San-Antonio-hospital-s-11179799.php.

———. "Native Americans Want to Reimagine Alamo as a Cemetery," *San Antonio Express-News*, February 12, 2019. www.expressnews.com/news/news_columnists/elaine_ayala/article/Native- Americans-want-to-reimagine-Alamo-as-a-13608527.php#.

———. "Remains Found at Mission San Juan," *San Antonio Express-News*, November 18, 2012. www.mysanantonio.com/news/local_news/article/Remains-found-at-Mission-San- Juan-4048761.php#item-85307-tbla-10.

Back, Noah. "What Are Freemasons?" *Ezine Articles*, February 10, 2009. https://ezinearticles.com/?What-Are-Freemasons?&id=1978448.

Baird, Mitchell. Site Manager, Fort Griffin State Historic Site, Email correspondence, June 3, 2019.

Ballí, Cecilia. "Return to Padre," *Texas Monthly*, January 2001. www.texasmonthly.com/the-culture/return-to-padre/.

Barr, Michael. "A German Love Story, the Story of Friedrich and Emma Schnerr," *Texas Escapes Online Magazine*, November 15, 2018. www.texasescapes.com/MichaelBarr/German-Love-Story.htm.

Bell, Kathie. "Boot Hill Cemetery," *Dodge City Daily Globe*, September 8, 2015. www.dodgeglobe.com/article/20150908/NEWS/150909583.

Billings v. Concordia Heritage Association, Inc., Court of Appeals, El Paso, No. 08–96–00256- CV, Decided April 25, 1997. https://caselaw.findlaw.com/tx-court-of- appeals/1216054.html.

Biographies from Caddo Parrish LA, "Peter Youree," extracted from [p 178, *The National Cyclopedia of American Biography*, Vol. 10, by James T. White 1900]. http://genealogytrails.com/lou/caddo/bios.html.

Boardman, Mark. "On the Trail of Bigfoot," *True West Magazine*, July 15, 2014. https://truewestmagazine.com/on-the-trail-of-bigfoot/.

Bolton, Herbert E. "Spanish Mission Records at San Antonio." *The Quarterly of the Texas State Historical Association* 10, no. 4 (1907): 297–307. www.jstor.org/stable/30242814.

Bosque County History Book Committee. *Bosque County: Land and People (A History of Bosque County, Texas)*, Dallas, Texas, 1985. https://texashistory.unt. edu/ark:/67531/metapth91038/; University of North Texas Libraries, The Portal to Texas History, https://texashistory.unt.edu; crediting Denton Public Library.

Bowman, Bob. "Country Graveyards Here and There," *Texas Escapes Online Magazine*, March 18, 2012. www.texasescapes.com/BobBowman/Country-Graveyards-Here-and-There.htm.

———. "Three Tragedies," *Texas Escapes Online Magazine*. August 19, 2012. www. texasescapes.com/AllThingsHistorical/Three-Tragedies-BB306.htm.

Brado, Edward. *Cattle Kingdom: Early Ranching in Alberta*, Heritage House Publishing Company, Victoria, British Columbia, 2004, p. 266.

Breal, Jordan. "Trip Guide: Paris, Texas," *Texas Monthly*, January 16, 2014. www. texasmonthly.com/texas-trip-guides/trip-guide-paris-texas/.

Brooks, John. "Plano, 1891 (Then and Now)," *Plano Magazine*, December 29, 2015. http://planomagazine.com/plano-1891-then-and-now/.

Brownsville Historical Association. "Old City Cemetery Center." Accessed March 3, 2020. www.brownsvillehistory.org/old-city-cemetery-center.html.

Bryan Daily Eagle. "Shooting at El Paso," April 7, 1896, p. 4. Accessed from Newspaperarchive.com.

Bryan Eagle. "John Wesley Hardin Dead," August 22, 1895, p. 2. Accessed from Newspaperarchive.com.

Burkhardt, Gail. "Soldier Gets Military Honors 95 Years after His Death," *Lubbock Avalanche-Journal*, January 14, 2013. www.lubbockonline.com/ article/20130114/NEWS/301149844.

Caddo Lake Institute. "Great Raft History." Accessed January 11, 2020. https:// invasiveswatch.org/site/GreatRaft/History.aspx.

Caldwell, Clifford R. *Fort McKavett and Tales of Menard County*, C. R. Caldwell Publisher, Kerrville, TX, 2012.

Campbell, Heather G. "The Yellow Pestilence: A Comparative Study of the 1853 Yellow Fever Epidemic in New Orleans and the Galveston, Texas Scourge of 1867," *East Texas Historical Journal*: Vol. 37, no. 1, Article 8. https:// scholarworks.sfasu.edu/ethj/vol37/iss1/8.

Cartwright, Gary. "Sarita's Secret," *Texas Monthly*, September 2004. www. texasmonthly.com/articles/saritas-secret/.

Carvajal, Dr. Tony. *The Roads We Travelled*. "Prologue," by Dave Gutierrez. Xlibris Corporation, Bloomington, IN, May 8, 2015.

Carver, Charles. *Brann and the Inconoclast.* University of Texas Press, Austin, TX, 1957.

Catholic Encyclopedia. "Christian Burial." Accessed February 21, 2020. www.newadvent.org/cathen/03071a.htm.

Cedar Park Tourism Services. Cedar Park. "History." Accessed November 22, 2019. www.cedarparkfun.com/cedar-park-history/.

Centers for Disease Control and Prevention. "Achievements in Public Health, 1900–1999: Healthier Mothers and Babies," *Morbidity and Mortality Weekly Report,* Atlanta, GA, 48, no. 38 (October 1, 1999): 849–858. www.cdc.gov/mmwr/preview/mmwrhtml/mm4838a2.htm.

Center for Regional Heritage Research, Stephen F. Austin State University. "W. T. Scott Home," Accessed January 4, 2020. www.sfasu.edu/heritagecenter/5033.asp.

City of Brownsville. "A Brief History." Accessed May 4, 2020. www.cob.us/822/About-Brownsville.

City of Clifton. "History." Accessed October 20, 2019. www.liveinclifton.org/page/history.aspx.

———. Norse Historic District in Bosque County, Texas. Accessed November 19, 2019. www.visitclifton.org/page/norse-historic-district.aspx.

City of Fredericksburg. "History." Accessed February 15, 2020. www.fbgtx.org/208/History.

City of Hamilton. "History of Hamilton." Accessed October 22, 2019. http://hamiltontexas.com/181/History-of-Hamilton.

City of Kingsville. "About Kingsville." Accessed May 15, 2020. www.cityofkingsville.com/visit/about-kingsville/.

City of Richmond. "About Richmond—History." Accessed March 12, 2020. www.richmondtx.gov/about-richmond/history.

City of Round Rock. Historic Round Rock Collection: An Ongoing History. "The Story of Sam Bass," Accessed November 23, 2019. www.roundrocktexas.gov/departments/planning-and-development- services/historic-preservation/historic-round-rock-collection/sam-bass/.

City of San Angelo. "About San Angelo." Accessed January 20, 2020. www.cosatx.us/residents/about-san-angelo.

City of Sherman. "History of Sherman." Accessed April 13, 2020. www.ci.sherman.tx.us/314/History-of-Sherman.

City of Waco. "History, Waco Mammoth National Monument." Accessed November 26, 2019. www.waco-texas.com/cms-waco-mammoth/page.aspx?id=174.

Clark, Adelle Rogers. *Lebanon on the Preston: A Casual Biography of a Blackland Village*, Henington Publishing Company, Wolfe City, Texas, 1959.

Clayton, Lawrence and Farmer Joan Halford. (Editors). *Tracks along the Clear Fork, Stories from Shackelford and Throckmorton Counties*, Texas A&M University Press, College Station, TX, 2012.

Coe, Alexis. "The Killing of Neighbors," *The Awl*, September 16, 2013. www.theawl.com/2013/09/the-killing-of-neighbors/.

Colfax Chronicle, "Death of Mrs. E. H. Randolph," Colfax, Louisiana, April 26, 1919.

Colorado Citizen. Phillip Kretschmer Obituary, August 21, 1897. www.coloradocountyhistory.org/obits/k/kr-ky.htm.

Connelly, Christopher. "Meet the Man Believed to Be the first Black Millionaire in Texas," *KERA News*, December 19, 2016. www.keranews.org/post/meet-man-believed-be-first-black-millionaire-texas.

Coppini, Pompeo. *From Dawn to Sunset*. Naylor Press, San Antonio, Texas, 1949, p. 396.

Correa, Thomas. *The American Cowboy Chronicles Old West Myths & Legends: The Honest Truth*, Page Publishing, Inc., Conneaut Lake, PA, December 14, 2019.

Courtney, David. "The Texanist: What Do I Have to Do to Get Buried in the Texas State Cemetery?" *Texas Monthly*, August 11, 2018. www.texasmonthly.com/being- texan/how-get-buried-texas-state-cemetery.

Cox, Mike. "Flora's Tree," *Texas Tales Column*, September 29, 2011. Texas Escapes.com. www.texasescapes.com/MikeCoxTexasTales/Floras-Tree.htm.

———. "Ranger Cemeteries," *Texas Tales Column*, October 30, 2008. Texas Escapes.com. www.texasescapes.com/MikeCoxTexasTales/Ranger-Cemeteries.htm.

———. "Tascosa and Boothill, the Duck Fight," *Texas Escapes*, May 20, 2010. www.texasescapes.com/MikeCoxTexasTales/159-Tascosa-and-Boothill-Texas.htm

———. "Texas Rangers Have Their Own Arlington," *Texas Tales Column*, January 24, 2018. Texas Escapes.com www.texasescapes.com/MikeCoxTexasTales/Texas-Rangers- Have-Their-Own-Arlington.htm.

Culberson County Historical Museum blogspot. "This Town Is So Healthy (1883–92)," December 2007. https://culbersoncomuseum.blogspot.com/2007/12/this-town-is-so-

Cutrer, Emily Fourmy. *The Art of the Woman, the Life and Work of Elisabet Ney*. University of Nebraska Press, Lincoln and London, 1988.

Cyclopedia of American Medical Biography, from 1610–1910, Vol. II. "Dr. Warren Stone," Edited by Howard A. Kelly, M.D., W. B. Saunders Company, Philadelphia & London, 1912, p. 420. Accessed from Googlebooks.com.

Daily Ardmoreite. "Four Men Pay Price of Bobbitt's Death," Armore, Oklahoma, April 19, 1909. www.oklahomahistory.net/adalynch.html.

Dallas Landmark Commission. Landmark Nomination Form. "Freedman's Cemetery." Submitted by Mamie McKnight and Beth Hennessy, September 6, 1991.

Dallas Morning News. "Forgotten Graves Excavated, Archaeologists Work in Ex-Slaves' Cemetery," November 11, 1990. www.orlandosentinel.com/news/os-xpm-1990-11-11-9011110334-story.html.

———. "Parker Kellum, 85, Of Valley Mills, Dies," December 20, 1936, p. 16.

Dallas Ordinance Number 21203, "Establishing Historic Overlay District No. 54 (Freedman's Cemetery), February 6, 1992.

Daughters of the American Revolution. "Founders Memorial Park Cemetery (Old City Cemetery). Accessed March 8, 2020. www.dar.org/national-society/historic-sites- and-\properties/founders-memorial-park-cemetery-old-city-cemetery.

De Leon III, José. "Peñitas Unveils Historical Marker," *Progress Times*, Mission, Texas, March 2, 2019, p. 12. www.progresstimes.net/2019/03/02/penitas-unveils-historical- marker/.

Del Rio News Herald. "Grande Loma Cemetery," November 28, 2016. http://delrionewsherald.com/del_rio_grande/article_997838c2-b5aa-11e6-bdee-67649b01468a.html.

———. "Memorial Day Service Set at Indian Gravesites," May 27, 1984, p. 1. Accessed from Ancestry.com.

———. "Town's Dead Outnumber the Living," [Scottsville Cemetery] November 3, 1982, p. 19. Accessed from Newspapers.com.

Dexeus, Ana. "The Bones of Our Ancestors. The End of Burials in Churches in the Late 18th Century," *Contributions to Science*, Institut d'Estudis Catalans, Barcelona, June 2015, pp. 85–94. https://issuu.com/institut-destudis-catalans/docs/cs_11_1_issuu.

Dooley, Sheila. "*Recuerdo*, Cemetery Inscriptions and Memorial Language in Brownsville, Texas," *Still More Studies in Rio Grande Valley History*, Editors: Milo Kearney, Anthony Knopp and Antonio Zavaleta, The University of Texas at Brownsville, 2014, pp. 333–367.

Dunn, Jeff. "The Mexican Soldier Skulls of San Jacinto Battleground," San Jacinto Battleground Conservancy, April 1, 2010. Accessed from FriendsofSanJacinto.com.

Dunn, Lori Bihl. Email Correspondence and Information Regarding Frank Bihl, January 22, 2020.

EC-47 History Site, "Fort Concho-Medal of Honor-Served Here," Commemorative Partner Program Committee, 2017. www.vietnam50thcpp.com/ft-concho-medal-of-honor-served-here.

El Paso County Court Records. Testimony of A. N. Parker, Surveyor, at Inquest Before J. J. McCullough, J.P. Pct. No. 7, El Paso County, Texas, July 7, 1892. RE: Killing of A. S. Goynes.

El Paso Daily Herald. "The City Council," [Del Buono] January 28, 1892, p. 2. Accessed from Newspaperarchive.com.

Ely, Glen Sample. *The Texas Frontier and the Butterfield Overland Mail, 1858–1861*, University of Oklahoma Press, Norman, 2016.

Encyclopaedia Britannica. "Waco." Encyclopaedia Britannica, Inc., December 11, 2018. www.britannica.com/place/Waco.

Ennis, Michael. "Ich Bin ein Texas," *Texas Monthly*, June 2015.

Estill, Harry F. "The Old Town of Huntsville," *The Quarterly of the Texas State Historical Association* 3, no. 4 (April 1900), pp. 265–278, Texas State Historical Association. www.jstor.org/stable/30242743.

Estlack, Roger. "Marker Secures History of Rowe Cemetery," *The Clarendon Enterprise*, September 13, 2001. www.clarendonlive.com/?p=3798.

Evans and Worley. *Evan's and Worley's Directory of the City of El Paso, Texas 1896–97*, Dallas, Texas, 1896. Frank Del Buono. University of North Texas Libraries, The Portal to Texas History. https://texashistory.unt.edu/ark:/67531/metapth213971/; https://texashistory.unt.edu; crediting El Paso County Historical Society.

Fannin County Genealogical Society. Oakwood Cemetery—Honey Grove. Accessed April 8, 2020. www.txfannin.org/cemetery/092/oakwood-cemetery.

Faulkner, Frank and Linda. *San Antonio Cemeteries Historic District, Images of America*. Arcadia Publishing, Charleston, South Carolina, 2014.

Feldman, Lauren. "Cattle Queen, The First Woman to Ride Up the Chisholm Trail with Her Own Brand," *American Cowboy*, June 1, 2017. www.americancowboy.com/people/lizzie-johnson-texas-cattle-queen.

"50 Years of Traveling Texas" Texas Forest Trail Region, *Texas Town & City*, Texas Municipal League, April 2019, pp. 34–36.

Find a Grave, database and images (www.findagrave.com).

Fisher, Lewis F. *Saving San Antonio*. Maverick Books, Trinity University Press, San Antonio, Texas, 2016.

Floyd, William E. "The History of Honey Grove, Texas," July 1923, as reprinted in the April 6, 1973 *Honey Grove Signal-Citizen*. Accessed online from www.honeygrovepreservation.org/floyd-history.html.

Fort Concho Guidon. "Fort Concho Remembers Forgotten Soldiers," Fort Concho National Historic Landmark, 1, no. 4 (1992): 1 and 4.

———. "Unknown Fort Concho Soldiers Identified!" Fort Concho National Historic Landmark, 1, no. 3 (1992): 1 and 6.

Fort Davis Chamber of Commerce. "Fort Davis History." Accessed April 16, 2020. https://fortdavis.com/fort-davis-history/.

"Fort McKavett Cemetery, Menard County," compiled by Frederica Burt Wyatt, Gloria B. Mayfield and Dolores I. Bishop, July 6, 2000. www.cemeteries-of-tx.com/Wtx/Menard/FortMcKavett.html.

FortPhantom.org. "History Overview: The Rugged Beauty of Fort Phantom Is Rich in History." Accessed January 14, 2020. http://fortphantom.org/history/.

Fort Worth Chamber of Commerce and Dr. Richard Selcer. "Fort Worth History," City of Fort Worth. Accessed April 6, 2020. http://fortworthtexas.gov/about/history/.

Fort Worth Record. "Pioneer Called Home," *Ophelia Crutchfield Eakins*, October 27, 1905. www.wikitree.com/wiki/Crutchfield-215.

Foster-Frau, Silvia. "Choking off Valley's 'String of Pearls—Natural Areas and Historic Sites Threatened by Border Wall," *San Antonio Express-News*, February 17, 2019, pp. A1, A18–A19.

Fountoulakis, Candace. "Baccus Cemetery," *Plano Magazine*, May 18, 2016. http://planomagazine.com/baccus-cemetery/.

Fox, Anne A. "Archaeological Investigations at Fort Griffin State Historic Park, Shackelford County, Texas," Center for Archaeological Research, The University of Texas at San Antonio Archaeological Survey Report, No. 23, 1976.

Fredericksburg Standard, "Heinrich Arhelger Slain by Indians in February 1863," May 1, 1946, pp. 1 and 6. Accessed from NewspaperArchive.com.

Freeman, Martha Doty. *History of Fort Phantom Hill, the Post on the Clear Fork of the Brazos River, Jones County, Texas*, Fort Phantom Foundation, Abilene, Texas, 1999.

Friebele, Michael. "The Vanishing Sanger-Harris Mosaics," *Texas Architect Magazine*, Sept/Oct 2016. https://txamagazine.org/2016/09/07/vanishing-sanger-harris-mosaics/.

Galveston Daily News. "Four Tiny Coffins." December 7, 1894, p. 16. Accessed from Newspaperarchive.com.

———. "His Turn Comes," April 6, 1896, p. 1. Accessed from Newspaperarchive.com.

———. Mortuary Interments. Edith A. Neumann. April 9, 1871. Accessed from Newspaperarchive.com.

———. "A Mother's Deed." December 6, 1894, p. 16. Accessed from Newspaperarchive.com.

———. "Texas Briefs-Bastrop, Texas," January 8, 1913, p. 9. Accessed from Newspaperarchive.com.

Gately, Paul J. "State's Oldest Confederate Memorial Stands in Waco Cemetery," August 15, 2017. www.kwtx.com/content/news/States-oldest-Confederate-memorial-stands- in-Waco-cemetery-440603653.html.

Gillespie County History Society, Der Stadt Friedhof Cemetery, Audio Transcript. Accessed April 15, 2020. https://texastimetravel.oncell.com/en/fredericksburg-der-stadt-friedhof- cemetery-155468.html.

Greenfield, Rebecca. "Our First Public Parks: The Forgotten History of Cemeteries," *The Atlantic Monthly*, March 16, 2011. www.theatlantic.com/national/archive/2011/03/our-first-public-parks-the- forgotten-history-of-cemeteries/71818/.

Grissom, Carol A. "Cemetery Monuments Made of Zinc," Smithsonian Museum Conservation Institute. Accessed January 3, 2020. www.si.edu/mci/english/research/conservation/zinc_cemetery_monuments.html.

Gwynne, S. C. *Empire of the Summer Moon*. Scribner, New York, 2010.

Haile, Bartee. "Cholera, The Unstoppable Scourge in Texas," *Hays Free Press*, July 16, 2017, https://haysfreepress.com/2017/07/26/cholera-the-unstoppable-scourge-in-early-texas/.

Handbook of North Louisiana Online. "Youree, Henry Hudson." Published by LSU-Shreveport. Accessed January 4, 2020. http://nwla-archives.org/handbook/youreeHenryHudson.htm.

Handbook of Texas online. Published by the Texas State Historical Association. https://tshaonline.org/handbook/about-handbook.

Hard, Robert J., Fox, Anne A., Cox, I. Waynne, Gross, Kevin J., Meissner, Barbara A., Mendez, Guillermo I., Tennis, Cynthia L., and Zapata, Jose E. "Excavations at Mission San Jose Y San Miguel de Aguayo, San Antonio, Texas," Index of Texas Archaeology: Open Access Gray Literature from the Lone Star State: Vol. 1995, Article 1. https://doi.org/10.21112/ita.1995.1.1 ISSN: 2475–9333. https://scholarworks.sfasu.edu/ita/vol1995/iss1/1.

Harrigan, Stephen. "Coppini the Great," *Texas Monthly*, October 1984. www.texasmonthly.com/articles/coppini-the-great/.

Harvey, Bill. *Texas Cemeteries: The Resting Places of Famous, Infamous, and Just Plain Interesting Texans.* University of Texas Press, Austin, 2003.

HeraldDemocrat.com. "History 'lives' at West Hill Cemetery," September 22, 2014. www.heralddemocrat.com/living/lifestyle/history-lives-west-hill-cemetery.

Hinojosa, Dr. Gilberto M. "Francisco Yturria (1830–1912)," Special Collections & University Archives: Yturria Family. Accessed May 2, 2020. https://utrgv.libguides.com/SCA/yturria-family.

Historic Houston. Bastrop, Texas. "Fairview Cemetery." http://historichouston1836.com/fairview-cemetery-bastrop-texas/.

———. "Broadway Cemetery Historic District, Galveston, Texas, Parts 1, 2, and 3." http://historichouston1836.com/galveston-cemetery-historic-district-galveston-tx/.

———. De Zavala Cemetery. http://historichouston1836.com/de-zavala-cemetery/; 2012.

Historic Texas. "Penitas, Texas," May 2020. https://historictexas.net/hidalgo-county/penitas- texas/.

———. "Pharr, Texas," May 2019. https://historictexas.net/hidalgo-county/pharr-texas/.

Historical Marker Database. "United States Scouts Seminole-Negro Indian Scout Detachment, Muster Roll 1870–1914," Historical Marker. www.hmdb.org/m.asp?m=55412.

History Collection. "Being Buried Alive Was So Common in the Victorian Era That Doctors Used These 10 Methods to Prevent It." Acccssed May 4, 2020. https://historycollection.co/buried-alive-common-victorian-era-doctors-used-10-methods- prevent/.

History.com Editors. "Albert Sidney Johnston," A&E Television Networks, Publisher. August 21, 2018; www.history.com/topics/american-civil-war/albert-sidney-johnston.

"History to Die For. Concordia Cemetery." Brochure. Not dated. Concordia Heritage Association, El Paso, Texas.

Holden, Frances Mayhugh. "Death of a Martyr," *Lambshead before Interwoven: A Texas Ranger Chronicle, 1848–1878*, Texas A&M University Press, College Station, 1982, pp. 80–87.

Hollandsworth, Skip. "The Kings Palace," *Texas Monthly*, February 2016. www.texasmonthly.com/issue/february-2016/#features.

Honey Grove Preservation League. "Saving and Documenting the History of Honey Grove, Texas—Early History & Cemeteries." Accessed April 8, 2020. www.honeygrovepreservation.org/.

Huddleston, Scott. "Alamo Battle Looming over Status as Cemetery," *San Antonio Express-News*, April 11, 2019, A1, A16–17.

———. "Alamo Grounds Get Cemetery Status," *San Antonio Express-News*, May 11, 2019, pp. 1 and 11. www.pressreader.com/usa/san-antonio-express-news/20190511/281500752694296.

———. "Mystery Surrounds Remains of Alamo Fallen," *San Antonio Express-News*, September 14, 2017. www.expressnews.com/sa300/article/Mystery-surrounds-remains-of-Alamo-fallen-12199351.php.

———. "State Commission Recognizes Alamo Church in Downtown San Antonio as a Cemetery," *San Antonio Express-News*, June 17, 2020. www.expressnews.com/news/local/article/Texas-Historical-Commission-to-take- up-Alamo-15345348.php.

Hunter, John Warren. "Killing of John Vaden at Fort McKavitt," *Frontier Times Magazine*, November 1924.

Independent Order of Odd Fellows. The Sovereign Grand Lodge. "History." Accessed December 19, 2019. https://odd-fellows.org/history/.

Institute of Medicine (US) Committee on Palliative and End-of-Life Care for Children and Their Families; Field MJ, Behrman RE, editors. *When Children Die: Improving Palliative and End-of-Life Care for Children and Their Families.* Washington (DC): National Academies Press (US); 2003. Chapter 2, "Patterns of Childhood Death in America." www.ncbi.nlm.nih.gov/books/NBK220806/.

Isbell, Frances and Hidalgo County Historical Commission. "Santa Ana Wildlife Refuge Cemetery," 2005. www.cemeteries-of-tx.com/Etx/Hidalgo/Cemetery/santaana.htm.

Jordon, Terry G. *Texas Graveyards, a Cultural Legacy*. University of Texas Press, Austin, 1982.

Joyce, Matt. "Chasing Quicksilver History in Beautiful Big Bend," *Texas Highways*, November 2017 issue. https://texashighways.com/culture/history/chasing-quicksilver-mercury- mining-history-in-beautiful-big-bend/.

Juliette Fowler Communities. "Juliette Peak Fowler." Accessed April 4, 2020. https://fowlercommunities.org/about- us/history/juliette-peak-fowler/.

Keister, Douglas. *Stories in Stone, a Field Guide to Cemetery Symbolism and Iconography*. MJF Books, New York, 2004.

Kelly, Catherine E. "Mourning Becomes Them: The Death of Children in Nineteenth-Century American Art," *The Magazine Antiques*, July 26, 2016. www.themagazineantiques.com/article/mourning-becomes-them-the-death-of-children-in-nineteenth-century-american-art/.

Kennedy Memorial Foundation. "The Kenedy Family." Accessed May 5, 2020. https://kenedy.org/museum/the-kenedy-ranch/the-kenedy-family/.

Knights of Pythias. "History." Accessed January 21, 2020. www.pythias.org/.

Kolodziej, Elaine. "Young People Must Know That History Is Worth Preserving," *Wilson County News* online, February 25, 2020.

Kyle Cemetery. Accessed February 10, 2020. www.kylecemetery.org/.

Landry, Alysa. "Saving a Neglected Lipan Apache Cemetery," *Indian Country Today*, March 13, 2017. https://indiancountrytoday.com/archive/saving-a-neglected-lipan-apache- cemetery-xQeEkcG8m0qsox0kf4GrkA.

Laredo Chamber of Commerce. "A Brief History of Laredo, Texas." Accessed May 16, 2020. www.cityoflaredo.com/Sanchez/TSanchez.html.

Lawrence, Katie. "The Story Behind This Ghost Town Will Chill You to the Bone," *Only In Your State*, January 30, 2018. www.onlyinyourstate.com/texas/ghost-town- cemetery-tx/?fbc.

Ledbetter, Barbara A. Neal. *Fort Belknap, Frontier Saga*. Eakin Press, Burnet, Texas, 1982.

Limestone County Historical Commission. "Fort Parker Memorial Park." Accessed November 20, 2019. www.limestonehc.com/cemetery-preservation/fort-parker-m.

Little, Carol Morris. *A Comprehensive Guide to Outdoor Sculpture in Texas*. The University of Texas Press, Austin, 1996.

Littlejohn, Jeffrey L. and Victoria Bowman. "Joshua Houston," *East Texas History*. Sam Houston State University. Accessed December 12, 2019. https://easttexashistory.org/items/show/10?tour=5&index=1.

Lyle, Anthony (1999) "Exhumation and Analysis of Two Historic Burials from the Camposanto at Santa Rosa Hospital, San Antonio, Texas," Index of Texas Archaeology: Open Access Gray Literature from the Lone Star State: Vol. 1999, Article 2. https://doi.org/10.21112/ita.1999.1.2. ISSN: 2475–9333; Available at: https://scholarworks.sfasu.edu/ita/vol1999/iss1/2.

Maca, Kathleen Shanahan. "Angels of Grief," Tales from Texas, August 26, 2015. http://kathleenmaca.com/index.php/2015/08/26/angels-of-grief/.

———. Galveston Cemetery Tour Guide, October 7, 2019.

———. Galveston's Broadway Cemeteries, Images of America, Arcadia Publishing, Charleston, South Carolina, 2015.

———. "Uncovering History, Treasures Hidden for over 100 Years," Galveston Monthly, May 2014, pp. 20–24.

Maddox, Will. "A Home of Their Own: Juliette Fowler Communities' Care Spans 155 Years," Advocate Magazine-Lakewood/East Dallas, October 30, 2017. https://lakewood.advocatemag.com/2017/10/30/juliette-fowler-communities-125-years/.

Maltby, William J. Captain Jeff, Or, Frontier Life in Texas with the Texas Rangers, Whipkey Printing Company, Colorado, Texas, 1906.

Mancini, Skip. "Naming Mobeetie," High Plains History, July 8, 2012. www.hppr.org/post/naming-mobeetie.

Marian, Jakub. "Difference between Cemetery and Graveyard in English." Accessed November 19, 2019. https://jakubmarian.com/difference-between-cemetery-and- graveyard-in-english/.

Marion County Chamber of Commerce. "Jefferson Texas History." Accessed January 3, 2020. www.jefferson-texas.com/history/.

Marlowe, Jennifer. "Facts on the Brazos River in Wallis, Texas," USA Today Travel Tips. Accessed November 19, 2019. https://traveltips.usatoday.com/brazos-river-wallis-texas-64084.html.

Massey, Cynthia Leal. Helotes, Where the Texas Hill Country Begins, Old American Publishing, Houston, Texas, 2008.

Massey, Sara R. (Ed.) Texas Women on the Cattle Trail, Texas A&M University Press, College Station, 2006.

Maverick, James S. "Mr. Polly," Foreword to and a slightly condensed reprint of "Jose Policarpo Rodriguez, The Old Guide," Old West Magazine, Winter 1968.

McAuley, Bryan. "Angelina (Peyton) Eberly—a Pioneering Spirit," Texas Historical Commission, March 29, 2013. www.thc.texas.gov/blog/angelina-peyton-eberly%E2%80%94-pioneering-spirit.

McClennan County Texas—Cemeteries. Some Notable Persons in First Street Cemetery of Waco, Texas. Compiled by T. Bradford Willis, DDS, MSD. Accessed November 27, 2019. http://files.usgwarchives.net/tx/mclennan/cemeteries/notables.txt.

McKinney Democrat, "Deaths," May 23, 1895, p. 3. Accessed from Newspaper archive.com.

Menard County History: An Anthology, "Ft. McKavett," by Francis Fish, p. 37; "Pioneer Rest Cemetery," pp. 45–46; "Frank and Annie Katherine Bihl," by Francis Bihl Stockton, pp. 176–178; "John D. Sheen," p. 575. "Menard County Historical Society, Anchor Publishing Company, San Angelo, Texas, 1982.

Merrifield, Kelly. "From Necessity to Honor: The Evolution of National Cemeteries in the United States," National Park Service. Accessed March 20, 2020. www.nps.gov/nr/travel/national_cemeteries/Development.html.

Metz, Leon Clair. "St. Leon, Ernest (a.k.a Diamond Dick)" *The Encyclopedia of Lawmen, Outlaws, and Gunfighters*, Infobase Publishing, New York, 2002, pp. 233–234.

Michno, Gregory. "The Search for the Captives of Elm Creek," *Wild West*, April 2009. www.historynet.com/search-captives-elm-creek.htm.

Michno, Gregory F. and Susan J. Michno. *Circle the Wagons!* McFarland & Company, Inc., Jefferson, North Carolina, 2008, p. 178.

Military Medicine, "Introduction: Yellow Fever before 1900," Vol. 166, no. suppl_1, September 2001, pp. 3 and 4. https://doi.org/10.1093/milmed/166.suppl_1.3.

Millweard, Christy. "The Untold Story of a Slain Williamson County Deputy and the Outlaw Who Killed Him," KVUE News, July 19, 2017. www.kvue.com/article/news/local/the-untold- story-of-a-slain-williamson-county-deputy-and-the-outlaw-who-killed-him/269- 45801823.

Monday, Jane Clements and Frances Brannen Vick. *Petra's Legacy, The South Texas Ranching Empire of Petra Vela and Mifflin Kenedy*, Texas A&M University Press, College Station, 2007.

Morthland, John. "Cemeteries," *Texas Monthly*, March 3, 1999. www.texasmonthly.com/travel/cemeteries/.

Morton Cemetery Association. "History and Research." Accessed March 12, 2020. www.mortoncemetery.com/history-research.html.

Murderpedia, the encyclopedia of murderers, "John Wesley Hardin." Accessed April 15, 2020. https://murderpedia.org/male.H/h/hardin-john-wesley.htm.

Nacogdoches Convention and Visitors Bureau. "Caddo Indians of Texas." Accessed December 4, 2019. www.visitnacogdoches.org/about/history/caddo-indians/.

BIBLIOGRAPHY

National Museum of Funeral History. Houston, Texas. "19th Century Mourning." Accessed May 4, 2020. www.nmfh.org/exhibits/permanent-exhibits/19th-century-mourning.

National Park Service. "San Antonio National Cemetery, San Antonio, Texas." Accessed May 20, 2020. www.nps.gov/nr/travel/national_cemeteries/Texas/San_Antonio_National_Cem etery.html.

Neighbors, Joy. "A Grave Interest: Women's History in the Cemetery," March 22, 2011. http://agraveinterest.blogspot.com/2011/03/womens-history-in-cemetery.html.

———. "Woodmen of the World and the Tree Stone Grave Markers," June 21, 2011. http://agraveinterest.blogspot.com/2011/06/woodmen-of-world-and-tree-stone-grave.html.

Nesbitt Memorial Library. Colorado County Cemetery Records. About the Cemeteries. Columbus City Cemetery. www.columbustexaslibrary.net/local-history-and- genealogy-material/colorado-county-cemetery-records-about-the-cemeteries.html.

Neucere, Elizabeth. "Captain Joe Byrd Prison Cemetery," *East Texas History*. Sam Houston State University. Accessed December 11, 2019. https://easttexashistory.org/items/show/44.

New York Times, "Steamboat Disaster," January 29, 1871. Accessed from Newspaperarchive.com.

Nichols, Mike. "Common Ground: Sisters and Soldiers, Eagles and Soiled Doves," April 3, 2012. HometownbyHandlebar.com.

———. "Of Maps and Mysteries (Part 4): The Man Called 'Gooseneck Bill'," Part I, June 22, 2019. HometownbyHandlebar.com.

———. "Sodom on the Trinity (Part 1): A Cold Day in Hell," June 10, 2019. HometownbyHandlbar.com.

———. "Sodom on the Trinity (Part 2): Gilded Palaces of Sin," June 10, 2018, HometownbyHandlbar.com.

Nolan, Frederick W. *Tascosa, Its Life and Gaudy Times*, Texas Tech University Press, Lubbock, 2007, p. 308.

Oakwood Cemetery—Fort Worth. Accessed April 6, 2020. http://oakwood cemetery.net/index_files/History.htm.

O'Connor, Kathryn Stoner. *Presidio La Bahía, 1721–1846*. Eakin Press, Austin, Texas, 1966, pp. 213–215.

Order of Saint Benedict, The. "The Medal of Saint Benedict." Accessed February 3, 2020. www.osb.org/gen/medal.html.

Pack, William. "Seguin: The Painful Tale of a Texas patriot," *San Antonio Express-News*, January 23, 2015. www.expressnews.com/150years/leaders/article/Segun-The- painful-tale-of-a-Texas-patriot-6035629.php.

Panna Maria Historical Society. "Panna Maria, Texas: History Highlights." Accessed March 12, 2020. www.pannamariatexas.com/history-highlights.

Parker, Mary O. "Tale of Two Cotullas," *Texas Parks & Wildlife*, December 2010. https://tpwmagazine.com/archive/2010/dec/legend/.

Pate, Ann. Email correspondence regarding Fort Chadbourne Burials, June 7, 2019.

———.*Fort Chadbourne, a Military Post, a Family Heritage*. H. V. Chapman & Sons, Abilene, Texas, 2010.

Penitas Historical Society. "Penitas Cemetery." Accessed May 9, 2020. www.gluseum.com/US/Penitas/390591290991903/Pe%C3%B1itas-Historical-Committee#contact.

Polly Texas Pioneer Association. "Polly's Cemetery." Accessed February 19, 2020. www.pollytexaspioneerassociation.org/pollys-cemetery.

Pyle, G. F. "The Diffusion of Cholera in the United States in the Nineteenth Century," 1969. https://onlinelibrary.wiley.com/doi/pdf/10.1111/j.1538-4632.1969.tb00605.x.

Quincy Daily/Quincy Whig. "Great Loss of Life," June 15, 1857, p. 2. Accessed from Newspaperarchive.com.

Ragland, James. "If Texas' Prison Population Were a City, It Would Be the State's Largest," *Dallas Morning News*, September 16, 2016. www.dallasnews.com/opinion/commentary/2016/09/16/if-tex/.

Ragsdale, Kenneth Baxter. *Quicksilver: Terlingua and the Chisos Mining Company*. Texas A&M University Press, College Station, TX, 1976, p. 18.

Reagan, William. Chair, Limestone County Historical Society. Email correspondence, November 20, 2019.

Robinson, Bryan. "Chacalaca Trail Reveals Valley Nature at Its Very Best," *Valley Morning Star*, Harlingen, Texas, October 25, 1972.

Roesch, Karen A. "Texas Alsatians," Indiana University/Purdue University, Indianapolis, 2017. https://scholarworks.iupui.edu/.

Romer, Paul A. "The Death of William Minear," *Temple Daily Telegram*, July 27, 2009. www.tdtnews.com/archive/article_007bb24b-50b8-505a-8f2b-a4555f7c28c9.html.

Ross, Robyn. "Laid to Rest in Huntsville," *The Texas Observer*, March 11, 2014. www.texasobserver.org/prison-inmates-laid-rest-huntsville/.

Ross, Theo A. *Odd Fellowship: Its History and Manual*, M. W. Hazen Company, New York, 1888. https://archive.org/details/oddfellowshipit01rossgoog/page/n25.

Rosypal, Kathryn G. "The Story of Panna Maria, TX. Part 1, the First Polish Americans Find Hope in Texas," Polish Academic Information Center, University of Buffalo, 2000. http://info-poland.icm.edu.pl/classroom/PM/PM.html.

Ruan, Maxie Elizabeth. "Lipan Cemetery in Danger of Disappearing," *The Lipan Post*, Lipan Apache Tribe of Texas, August 19, /2015. www.lipanapache.org/TheLipanPost/CementerioLipanes.html.

Ruiz, Francisco Antonio. "The Story of the Fall of the Alamo, as Told in *The San Antonio Light* on March 6, 1886," reprinted March 6, 1907. www.sonsofdewittcolony.org/adp/archives/newsarch/ruizart.html.

Ryan, Terri Jo. "Brazos Past: Waco Author with Shady Tales to Tell Set for Book-Signing," *Tribune-Herald*, September 25, 2010. www.wacotrib.com/news/brazos-past-waco- author- with-shady-tales-to-tell- set/article_3044a933-d5b0–58de-a472- e67c4c525d8c.html.

Saint's Roost Museum. Clarendon, Texas. Donley County History, "RO Ranch." Accessed April 28, 2020.http://saintsroostmuseum.com/about/ro-ranch-2/.

San Antonio Daily News. "Personal Mention." [Frank Del Buono]. April 14, 1891, p. 8. Accessed from Newspaperarchive.com.

San Antonio Express. "Boy Accidentally Killed," August 23, 1914, p. 14B. Accessed from Newspaperarchive.com.

San Antonio Light. "The Cattle King—Captain Richard King, the Largest Stockman in the World, Dead." April 15, 1885, p. 4. Accessed from Newspaperarchive.com.

———. "Smallpox—Laredo Patients Are Being Removed to the Pest House." March 20, 1899, p. 1. Accessed from Newspaperarchive.com.

San Jacinto Battleground Conservancy. "Battleground History." Accessed February 29, 2020. www.friendsofsanjacinto.com/pages/history-san-jacinto-battleground.

Santos, John Phill. "Return to Cotulla," *Texas Monthly*, August 2015. www.texasmonthly.com/politics/return-to-cotulla/.

Scarborough, W. Frances. "Old Spanish Missions in Texas: III. San José de San Miguel de Aguayo de Buena Vista." *Southwest Review* 13, no. 4 (1927): 491–504. www.jstor.org/stable/43465870.

Schutze, Jim. "Old Times Not Forgotten," *Dallas Observer*, February 25, 1999. www.dallasobserver.com/content/printView/6401256.

Scott, Thomas Fletcher. "Phantom Hill Scott's Account of Life at Phantom Hill," Southwest Collection/Special Collections Library at Texas Tech University, Lubbock, Texas. Accessed from Ancestry.com, January 14, 2020.

Seraphic Franciscan Sisters, OLS. "History." Accessed March 12, 2020. www. seraphicsisters.org/index.php?page=pages/history.html&menu_id=4.

Shackelford County. Shackelford County Historical Commission, Arcadia Publishing, 2014, p. 13.

Simek, Peter. "Memorial Isn't Going Anywhere (For Now)," *D Magazine*, July 3, 2019. www.dmagazine.com/frontburner/2019/07/dallas-confederate-war-memorial-isnt- going-anywhere-for-now/.

Smith, J. B. "Reburial Slates 10 Years after First Street Cemetery Excavation," *Waco Tribune*, November 5, 2016. www.wacotrib.com/news/government/reburial-slated-years- after-first-street-cemetery-excavation/article_ae7c07aa-8c84-5998-8a6b- bdf45c5e1b46.html.

Snider, Tui. *Understanding Cemetery Symbols, a Field Guide for Historic Graveyards*. Castle Azle Press, Fort Worth, TX, 2017.

Southern Plains Tribal Health Board, Oklahoma City. "Caddo Nation, History." Accessed December 4, 2019. www.spthb.org/about-us/who-we-serve/caddo-nation/#1491134905128-b2e7d99c-28a3d752-8948.

Sowell, Capt. A. J. "Murder of Ann Whitney and Amanda Howard's Bravery," *Pioneer Sketches, Nebraska, and Texas 1915*. Reprinted in the *El Paso Morning Times*. February 29, 1912.

SporacleBlog.com. "Why Is Austin the Capital of Texas and NotHouston?" July 18, 2018. www.sporcle.com/blog/2018/07/why-is-austin-the-capital-of-texas-and-not-houston/.

Stephen F. Austin State University. Center for Regional Heritage Research. "Thomas Jefferson Rusk." Accessed December 30, 2019. www.sfasu.edu/heritagecenter/7036.asp.

Stockes, Robert J. *Communities and Households in the Greater American Southwest: New Perspectives and Case Studies*, University Press of Colorado, July 1, 2019.

Stutzman, Brad. "Local Officers to Honor A. W. Grimes," *Austin-American Statesman*, September 24, 2016, updated September 26, 2018. www.statesman.com/news/20160924/local-officers-to-honor-aw-grimes.

Sullivan, Dulcie. *The LS Brand: The Story of a Texas Panhandle Ranch*, University of Texas Press, Austin, 1968.

Sun, The, "Killing of Ben Thompson and King Fisher," Official Journal of Williamson County and City of Georgetown, March 20, 1884, p. 1. Accessed from Newspaperarchive.com.

Talbott, Tim. "Great River Tragedy," *ExploreKYHistory*. Accessed December 31, 2019. https://explorekyhistory.ky.gov/items/show/457.

Tarin, Randell. "The Disposition of the Alamo Defenders' Ashes," 2005. www.sonsofdewittcolony.org/adp/history/1836/the_compound/ashes.html.

Tanksley, P. A. "A History of the Desegregation of the Del Rio Public Schools, Del Rio, Texas," Conference before the U.S. Commission on Civil Rights-Education, Gatlinburg, TN, 1960, p. 30.

Taylor County News, "Col. T. L. Odom Dead," Abilene, Texas, April 1, 1897, p. 1. Accessed from Newspaperarchive.com.

Tennis, Cynthia L. (1995) "Excavation in a Historic Cemetery Milam Park Renovation Phase II," Index of Texas Archaeology: Open Access Gray Literature from the Lone Star State: Vol. 1995, Article 9. https://doi.org/10.21112/ita.1995.1.9. ISSN: 2475–9333. Available at: https://scholarworks.sfasu.edu/ita/vol1995/iss1/9.

Texas Archival Resources Online. "Sanger-Harris Collection." Dallas Public Library. Accessed April 4, 2020. https://legacy.lib.utexas.edu/taro/dalpub/08318/dpub-08318p1.html.

Texas Beyond History. "World of the Caddo, Mounds of Mystery," Accessed December 1, 2019. www.texasbeyondhistory.net/kids/caddo/mounds.html.

Texas Department of Criminal Justice. "History of the Texas Department of Criminal Justice—Satanta." Turner Publishing Company, Paducah, Kentucky, 2004, p. 17. Accessed from books.google.com.

Texas General Land Office. "Honoring a Widow of the Alamo—Elizabeth Crockett's Land Legacy," March 14, 2019. https://medium.com/save-texas-history/honoring-a-widow-of-the-alamo-elizabeth-crocketts-land-legacy-d364da8f8f0b.

Texas Historical Commission. "Caddo Mounds History." Accessed December 4, 2019. www.thc.texas.gov/historic-sites/caddo-mounds/caddo-mounds-history.

———. *Texas Heritage Travel Guide*. Austin, Texas, 2014.

———. Texas Historical Sites Atlas. https://atlas.thc.state.tx.us.

———. Texas Time Travel. "Historic Cemeteries." Accessed June 5, 2019. https://texastimetravel.com/node/28682.

———. Texas Time Travel. Texas Pecos Trail Region. "Annie Riggs Memorial Museum." Accessed April 14, 2020. https://texaspecostrail.com/plan-your-adventure/historic-sites-and-cities/sites/annie-riggs-memorial-museum.

Texas Military Forces Museum. "Memorial Day Reflections: Capt. José Rafael de la Garza." Accessed June 15, 2020. https://tmd.texas.gov/memorial-day-reflections-capt-jose-rafael- de-la-garza.

Texas Municipal League. "City of Menard." Accessed September 12, 2019. https://directory.tml.org/profile/city/882.

Texas Parks and Wildlife Department. "Edwards Plateau Ecological Region." Accessed January 22, 2020. https://tpwd.texas.gov/landwater/land/habitats/cross_timbers/ecoregions/edwards_plateau. phtml.

Texas State Cemetery. "Adam Paine [11271]." Accessed April 20, 2020. https://cemetery.tspb.texas.gov/pub/user_form822.asp.

Thomas Studio & Foundry. Chisholm Trail Commemorative Park, Round Rock, Texas. "Pioneer Woman." Accessed November 22, 2019. www.jimthomasbronzestudio.com/roundrock.php.

Troesser, John. "The Elisabet Ney Museum," Texas Escapes Online Magazine. May 2002. www.texasescapes.com/AustinTexas/ElizabetNeyMuseum/ElizabetNeyMuseumAustin.htm.

———. "Five Weeping Angels," Texas Escapes Online Magazine. May 18, 2019. www.texasescapes.com/Cemeteries/Three-Weeping-Angels.htm.

Troesser, John and Troesser, Kate Wong. "Texas Cemeteries," Texas Escapes Online Magazine. Accessed April 4, 2019. www.texasescapes.com/Texas-Cemeteries. htm#cemetery.

Ura, Alexa. "Texas Cemetery Sued over 'Whites Only' Policy," The Texas Tribune, May 5, 2016.

United States Department of the Interior. National Park Service. National Register of Historic Places Register Form for "Cotulla Ranch." April 24, 2014. www.nps.gov/nr/feature/places/pdfs/14000342.pdf.

United States Investor. Vol. 18, no. 2, "Probate Matters: George M. D. Grisby, August 18, 1906, p. 1275," Investor Publishing Company, Boston, New York, and Washington, January 12, 1907. Accessed from books.google.com.

University of Texas Rio Grande Valley. Special Collections and University Archives. "Yturria Family." Accessed May 4, 2020. https://utrgv.libguides.com/SCA/yturria-family.

Waco Examiner. "Our Dead, Timely Suggestions over Their Neglected Graves," December 10, 1881, p. 4. Accessed through Newspapers.com.

Walker County Historical Society. "Walker County History—Oakwood Cemetery." Accessed December 12, 2019. www.walkercountyhistory.org/oakwood_cemetery.php.

Walker County, Texas Cemeteries: Vol. 3, book, 2007; Huntsville, Texas. https://texashistory.unt.edu/ark:/67531/metapth662108/m1/1/; University of North Texas Libraries, The Portal to Texas History, https://texashistory.unt.edu; crediting Walker County Genealogical Society.

Walker, Jeremy. "This Cemetery Is San Angelo's Sacred Ground," *San Angelo Live,* March 5, 2018. https://sanangelolive.com/print/25562.

Walton, Geri. "Mourning Etiquette and Mourning Rules," October 24, 2014. www.geriwalton.com/mourning-etiquette-and-mourning-rules/.

Warm, Luke. "Love in the Time of Diphtheria, or Art & Science on the Brazos—'Miss' Elisabet Ney, Dr. Edmund Montgomery and the Haunting of Liendo Plantation," *Texas Escapes Online Magazine,* November 2008. www.texasescapes.com/Ghosts/Love-in-the-Time-of-Diphtheria.htm.

Warner, Phebe K. "Mrs. Charles Goodnight Was Panhandle's First White Woman," *Amarillo Daily News,* April 16, 1926, pp. 9 and 10. Accessed from Newspaperarchive.com.

Waymarking.com. "Catharina Garteiser, St. Dominic Cemetery, D'Hanis, TX, Relief Art Sculptures," posted August 31, 2015. www.waymarking.com/waymarks/wmPH73_Catharina_Garteiser_St_Dominic_C emetery_DHanis_TX.

———. "Leon A Harris Tombstone Mosaic," posted August 15, 2017. www.waymarking.com/waymarks/wmWCVA_Leon_A_Harr.

Weiser, Kathy. "Barney Riggs, Infamous Texas Gunfighter," *Legends of America,* December 2018. www.legendsofamerica.com/tx-barneyriggs/.

———. "Del Rio, Texas—Rio Grande City," *Legends of America,* December 2019. www.legendsofamerica.com/tx-delrio/.

———. "D'Hanis, French Colony of the Republic," *Legends of America,* November 2019, www.legendsofamerica.com/tx-dhanis/.

———. "Gus Bobbitt—Oklahoma Deputy Marshal," *Legends of America,* January 2020. www.legendsofamerica.com/gus-bobbitt/.

———. "One Bad Pecos County Sheriff," *Legends of America,* August 2017. www.legendsofamerica.com/tx-ajroyal/.

———. "Terlingua—Best Ghost Town in Texas," *Legends of America,* October 2019, www.legendsofamerica.com/tx-terlingua/.

Weisert, Anita Bass and Carl E. Kramer. "German Protestants on the Urban Frontier: The Early History of Louisville's St. John's Evangelical Church." *The Filson Club History Quarterly* 72 (, April 1998): 378–418.

White, Carl. "San Angelo's Fairmount Cemetery Marks 125 Years," Special to *San Angelo Standard-Times*, March 3, 2018. www.gosanangelo.com/story/news/local/2018/03/03/san-angelos-fairmount- cemetery-marks-125th-anniversary/360636002/.

Whitehurst, Laura. Fort Phantom Foundation. Email correspondence, January 17 and 20, 2020.

Willet, Jim. "Captain Joe Byrd Cemetery," Texas Prison Museum. Accessed December 18, 2019. www.txprisonmuseum.org/articles/cemetery.html.

Williams Sr. H. C. "Horrific Indian Raid in Young County," *Frontier Times Magazine*, February 1947.

Williamson County Texas History. "Slave Burial Ground in Old Round Rock Cemetery." Accessed June 20, 2019. https://williamson-county-texas-history.org/Round_rock/Round_Rock-Old_Slave- Cemetery_williamson_county_texas.html.

Woolley, Bryan, et al. *Final Destinations, a Travel Guide for Remarkable Cemeteries in Texas, New Mexico, Oklahoma, Arkansas, and Louisiana*. University of North Texas Press, Denton, 2000.

Wooster, Ralph A. "Wealthy Texans, 1860," *Southwestern Historical Quarterly* 71, no. 2 (October 1967) 163–180. Texas State Historical Association. www.jstor.org/stable/30240963.

World Population Review, 2020. https://worldpopulationreview.com/us-cities.

Zion Lutheran Church. "Cemeteries." Accessed February 11, 2020. www.zionheloteshistory.org/cemeteries.html.

INDEX

Italicized page numbers indicate illustrations.

INDEX

INDEX

INDEX

INDEX

ABOUT THE AUTHOR

Cynthia Leal Massey combines her background in journalism and love of history to write award-winning fiction and nonfiction. A former corporate editor, college instructor, and magazine editor, she has published hundreds of magazine and newspaper articles and several books. She is the author of *Death of a Texas Ranger, a True Story of Murder and Vengeance on the Texas Frontier*, winner of a Will Rogers Silver Medallion Award for Western Nonfiction, and recipient of the San Antonio Conservation Society Publication Award. She was the first-place winner of the Lone Star Award for Magazine Journalism and a finalist for the Texas Institute of Letters O. Henry Award for Best Work of Magazine Journalism for her article "Is UT Holding Our History Hostage," published in *Scene in SA* magazine. Pulitzer Prize–winning author Larry McMurtry called her novel *The Caballeros of Ruby, Texas* "a vivid picture of the Rio Grande Valley as it was fifty years ago [and] a very good read." Born and raised on the south side of San Antonio, Texas, Massey has resided in Helotes, twenty miles northwest of the Alamo City, since 1994. A full-time writer, she is a past president of Women Writing the West.